The Chiricahua Apache Prisoners of War

▼   ▼   ▼

FORT SILL 1894–1914

JOHN ANTHONY TURCHENESKE, JR.

D1521807

UNIVERSITY PRESS OF COLORADO

© 1997 by the University Press of Colorado

Published by the University Press of Colorado
P. O. Box 849
Niwot, Colorado 80544
Tel. (303) 530-5337

The University Press of Colorado is a cooperative publishing enterprise supported, in part, by Adams State College, Colorado State University, Fort Lewis College, Mesa State College, Metropolitan State College of Denver, University of Colorado, University of Northern Colorado, University of Southern Colorado, and Western State College of Colorado.

Library of Congress Cataloging-in-Publication Data

Turcheneske, John Anthony, 1943–
    The Chiricahua Apache prisoners of war: Fort Sill, 1894–1914 / John Anthony Turcheneske, Jr.
        p. cm.
    Includes bibliographical references and index.
    ISBN 0-87081-465-6 (casebound: alk. paper).
    1. Chiricahua Indians—Relocation—Oklahoma—Fort Sill.
2. Chiricahua Indians—Cultural assimilation.   3. Chiricahua
Indians—Government policy.   4. Indian prisoners—Oklahoma—Fort
Sill.   5. Indians, Treatment of—Oklahoma—Fort Sill.   6. United
States politics and government.   I. Title.
E99.C68T87   1997
976.6'004972—dc20   97-16012
                                                           CIP

This book was set in ITC Slimbach and Broadband ICG by
Stephen Adams.

The paper used in this publication meets the minimum requirements of the American National Standard for Information Sciences—Permanence of Paper for Printed Library Materials. ANSI Z39.48–1948
∞

10   9   8   7   6   5   4   3   2   1

Dedicated to my mother and father,
Mary Elizabeth Driscoll-Turcheneske and
John Anthony Turcheneske, Sr.

CONTENTS

▼   ▼   ▼

FIGURES

▼ ▼ ▼

PREFACE

▼   ▼   ▼

*T*he Chiricahua Apache prisoner-of-war saga, a little-known episode of which much was played out at Fort Sill, Oklahoma, occupies a unique niche in Native American history. In the first place, during the final Apache hostilities that occurred in the Southwest in 1886, none of the nearly 400 Chiricahuas so callously and cynically uprooted and exiled from their San Carlos, Arizona, home aided Geronimo and his small band of fellow belligerents. Yet, for a twenty-seven-year period, from September 1886 through early March 1914, these Chiricahuas were collectively punished for both his and his confederates' crimes. Equally egregious, they were held hostage to the whims of economic, political, and military expediency pursued by both War Department officials and Southwestern politicos, who were held in thrall by the presidential administrations of Grover Cleveland through William Howard Taft. Even more reprehensible, prisoner-of-war status was visited upon numerous innocent Chiricahua children born into captivity.

Despite these ignominies, the real tragedy that befell the Fort Sill Chiricahua prisoners of war was that a positive effectuation of the federal government's assimilationist goals—on one of the few occasions that this might have been possible—was ultimately denied them. Although army personnel promised the Chiricahuas, upon their arrival at this post, that Fort Sill would become their permanent home (indeed, President Grover Cleveland signed an 1897 executive order to this effect), War Department officials repudiated this commitment more than a decade later and instead transformed this military reserve into its field artillery training installation.

During the Chiricahuas' captivity, concerned officers-in-charge decided that the best route to their assimilation with white society might be cattle raising. The soundness of this proposal and the success of the endeavor were soon demonstrated. By 1897, the Chiricahuas had more than 1,000 head of cattle. By 1913, just prior to the removal from Fort Sill of those Chiricahuas slated for relocation to the Mescalero Indian Reservation in New Mexico, these Indians were made to sell their 10,000 head of cattle at a loss, which effectively pulled the economic rug out from under them.

This forced sale, which derailed their assimilation and future prosperity, wreaked economic havoc upon the Chiricahuas. As Raymond Loco so eloquently, albeit bitterly, explained, had the government permitted them to retain Fort Sill and the cattle herd, they might well have become the most prosperous tribal entity in Oklahoma. Instead, the Chiricahuas were evicted from Fort Sill. Each was given— elsewhere—an allotment smaller than the 160 acres originally intended. Consequently, according to Mildred Imach Cleghorn, her people found themselves "land poor." Even had each of these Indians obtained a 160-acre allotment, a tract this size would still not have been sufficient to provide the Chiricahuas with a viable economic base for self-sufficiency, either as individuals or as a whole. Ironically, even the most belligerent Native American groups did not suffer quite the same privations as the Fort Sill Chiricahua Apache prisoners of war. Hence, within the overall framework of U.S. government–Native American relations, the twenty-seven-year Chiricahua captivity—the last twenty years of which were spent confined as prisoners of war at Fort Sill, Oklahoma—represents an unprecedented—and unconscionable—case of injustice.

John Anthony Turcheneske, Jr.
River Falls, Wisconsin

ACKNOWLEDGMENTS

▼   ▼   ▼

*I*n chronicling the Chiricahuas' quest for freedom, I have incurred numerous debts of a scholarly nature. Words are inadequate to express the deep appreciation I owe Mildred Imach Cleghorn for her gracious assistance in arranging interviews at her home in Apache, Oklahoma, with herself, with Raymond Loco—grandson of Chief Loco of the Ojo Caliente band of Chiricahuas—and with Blossom Haozous, all of whom were born into captivity. The Reverend Doctor Robert Paul Chaat, of Medicine Park, Oklahoma, also kindly provided important background information. Interestingly enough, Reverend Chaat was the first Comanche Indian ordained by the Reformed Church in America, the denomination that ministered to the Chiricahua Apache prisoners of war during their confinement at Fort Sill. Without the profound insights provided by these four individuals, this work would have lacked an essential dimension that only the Indian voice can impart.

Profuse thanks go to the staffs of both the National Archives in Washington, D.C., and its regional branch in Denver, Colorado, for their expert guidance as I examined the relevant Indian and military records. I am also most grateful to the staffs of the Library of Congress Manuscripts Division, the Reformed Church in America's Gardner Sage Library (New Brunswick Theological Seminary, New Brunswick, New Jersey), Yale University's Beinecke and Sterling Memorial Libraries' Manuscripts Divisions, and Haverford College Library's Manuscripts Division.

This work would have been woefully incomplete had I not undertaken the requisite research in relevant Oklahoma archival and manuscript repositories. I therefore extend my deepest appreciation to the staffs of both the Morris Swett Technical Library and the U.S. Army Field Artillery and Fort Sill Museum, Fort Sill, Oklahoma. Also invaluable was the assistance proffered by the staff of the Oklahoma Historical Society's Indian Archives and Newspaper departments.

My heartfelt thanks go out to Professor Richard N. Ellis, who directed the dissertation upon which this work is based, for his unstinting encouragement and support. Profuse thanks are also due the University of New Mexico's Office of Research Grants and Fellowships for the financial support it extended, which permitted me to complete my remaining research.

Finally, I would like to note that some of the information contained in this work first appeared in article form. In 1977, the Oklahoma Historical Society conferred its 1976 Muriel H. Wright Heritage Endowment Award—a singular honor—upon "The United States Congress and the Release of the Apache Prisoners of War at Fort Sill" for being the best article published that year by *The Chronicles of Oklahoma.* In 1979, the *Red River Valley Historical Review* published "'It Is Right That They Should Set Us Free': The Role of the War and Interior Departments in the Release of the Apache Prisoners of War, 1909–1913."

PROLOGUE

▼   ▼   ▼

*G*ripped by anxiety over their imminent release from military custody, an innocent and displaced people quietly stirred throughout
Fort Sill's Chiricahua Apache prisoner-of-war encampments during the
cool early hours of Wednesday, April 2, 1913.[1] As the sun rose above
the Wichita Mountains, a small range rimming the post's northern perimeter, 163 of these Apaches, despite their misgivings, resolutely prepared for removal from what had become their deeply cherished
southwestern Oklahoma home of nineteen years. Completing their
chores by midafternoon, they clustered in small groups beside the train
that all too soon would transport them to New Mexico for resettlement
on the Mescalero Indian Reservation. As they gathered for the last time
with those Chiricahuas who would remain behind, a poignant scene, replete with emotional farewells, ensued. At 4 p.m., the locomotive's
whistle pierced the stillness of the late afternoon.[2] Amid belching
smoke and billowing steam, relatives and friends looked on sorrowfully
as those bound for New Mexico slowly pulled out of Fort Sill. For those
on board, nearly twenty-seven years of captivity would end two days
later when the train reached its final destination.

Yet, liberation from military custody engendered no sense of ju-
bilation among those Chiricahuas hurtling westward toward Mescalero. Rather, these prisoners of war found themselves seized with
apprehension, a sensation strongly reminiscent of the fear felt by those
Chiricahuas who had the tragic misfortune of being dispersed eastward
in 1886. As the train thundered across the high plains toward New
Mexico, these Chiricahua survivors of an ordeal of imprisonment that
during their pre-Oklahoma period of confinement recalls the death
camps, doubtless reflected on the unalleviated terror that began at the
Fort Apache Indian Reservation on a hot September day in 1886, when
an entire people were callously uprooted from an Arizona home they
would never see again.[3]

CHAPTER

1

Uprooted: An Innocent People Are Taken Captive

▼   ▼   ▼

*T*he noncombatant Chiricahuas' long odyssey of incarceration and despair began on September 7, 1886, when troops stationed at Fort Apache rounded up 382 unsuspecting Apaches under the pretext of sending them to see President Grover Cleveland, a ruse that allowed the post's officers to assemble them peacefully at this installation. Instead of going to Washington, these Chiricahua Apaches, innocent of any participation in the recently concluded hostilities perpetrated by Geronimo and his followers (Chiricahuas disaffected by conditions of reservation life at San Carlos), were held as prisoners of war and exiled.[1] Such perfidy brought down the curtain on an era of Anglo-Chiricahua conflict extending back to the 1860s that affected not only southeastern Arizona and southwestern New Mexico, but also the northeastern and northwestern reaches, respectively, of the Mexican states of Sonora and Chihuahua. Generally, confrontations arose over maladministration of Chiricahua affairs. However, Arizonans and their allies refused to distinguish between innocent and guilty Indians, insisting that the former were as culpable as the latter. Arizonans and their supporters maintained that Chiricahua removal was essential both to the prevention of future hostilities and to the territory's future prosperity.

Subsequently marched north to Holbrook, Arizona, over ninety miles of rugged desert and mountainous terrain, the guiltless Chiricahuas encountered searing heat, blowing dust, the unceasing turbulent din of torrential thunderstorms, and the ever present mud attendant upon such downpours, a sloppy mess that oozed and caked with every step.[2] Arriving at the Holbrook station of the Atlantic and Pacific Railway on September 12, the Chiricahuas commenced their eastward exodus in earnest, presenting a sad and bedraggled spectacle as soldiers forced this once proud people onto the train that finally wrested them from their homeland.[3] Such degradation, however, was merely preliminary to the prisoners' real privations, for worse was yet to come.

Once the Chiricahuas were aboard, their captors completed the grisly chore of sealing the train, a task that set the stage for ensuing illness and its ultimate consequences.[4] Buckets serving as latrines were rarely emptied. Sanitary facilities for washing were nonexistent.[5] Once opened, ration tins were partially consumed, then set aside to be used again. Severe and sometimes fatal cases of food poisoning developed, for no one thought to tell the Chiricahuas that food from these containers had to be consumed immediately or else discarded.[6] Under these inhumane conditions, women gave birth to babies, and children and old ones sick beyond redemption died.[7] Indeed, the Chiricahuas who managed to survive this ordeal were described by fellow prisoner of war Eugene Chihuahua as "almost dead."[8]

Psychological torments were also inflicted. Maintaining constant vigilance over their Chiricahua charges, troopers stationed on the outside platforms, rifles in hand, frequently made menacing gestures, as if to foretell their captives' fate.[9] Mercifully unnoticed by an already devastated Chiricahua nation, one more nefarious act remained in a drama already surfeited with the basest of cruelties. While that rolling hell swiftly rumbled toward the Rio Grande during the early morning hours of September 14, General Nelson Appleton Miles, the epitome of pompous martial mendacity, took his position near the Albuquerque depot of the Santa Fe Railway. Miles, who had engineered this removal as Department of Arizona commandant, gloated as these victims of a ruse traveled toward Fort Marion, Florida, their final destination. He expressed no little pleasure at "seeing the long train loaded with the worst element that ever infested" the Southwest "glide slowly past on its way to the East."[10] On September 22, when this journey of ignominy concluded, there descended the long dark night of the Chiricahua soul, the sting and bitterness of which are still felt today.

During their confinement at Fort Marion, the unfortunate Chiricahuas were plagued anew by a deceptive misnomer that would haunt and stigmatize them throughout the remainder of their captivity. Here at Fort Marion, the Chiricahuas became known as the "Geronimo Apaches." This appellation, which was later utilized by the Indian rights activists—the very people who attempted to ameliorate the Chiricahuas' situation—engendered and perpetuated a myth believed even today: that the innocent Chiricahuas were in cahoots with Geronimo. This is exactly what Arizonans and General Miles wanted the military establishment, the administration, and the nation to believe. Southwesterners employed this fiction to especially good effect in 1890, when they vigorously protested any removal of the Chiricahuas west of the Mississippi River, even to Fort Sill.[11]

That those innocent Chiricahuas who were forcibly exiled to Fort Marion, Florida, from their Arizona homes came to highly resent such a description is evidenced by the heated debate over whether to accept into their midst Geronimo and his fellow belligerents, who were being held at Florida's Fort Pickens. This argument ensued during the course of a council held shortly after the noncombatants' April 28, 1887, arrival at Mount Vernon Barracks, Alabama, to which they were transferred from Fort Marion. "What do we want to bring him among us for? He's a warrior man," was the initial remonstration. "We never did kill nobody, never caused trouble to anyone. He's going to give us a name."[12] Indeed, the nonbelligerent Chiricahuas, who would have Geronimo and his followers among them on May 13, 1888, already had a name—and it endured. As Mildred Imach Cleghorn, who was born into captivity at Fort Sill and would ultimately serve as Fort Sill Apache tribal chairperson, later observed, "they were judged guilty, collectively of war crimes, without the benefit of any court of justice." Simply, "women, children and babes in arms—who were the overwhelming majority—were exiled to a hostile and cruel land."[13]

After 1894, when these Indians finally relocated to Fort Sill, the persistence of this stigma ultimately prevented their release and subsequent land allotment, as a tribal entity, at this installation. Repeatedly ignoring the War Department's entreaties to retake custody of the Chiricahuas (ironically enough, the War Department neither intended to retain jurisdiction over nor anticipated holding the nonbelligerent

Chiricahuas for twenty-seven years), the Department of the Interior consequently failed to seize the opportunity to place them on a sound economic footing. In turn, capitalizing on this dereliction of duty, upper echelons within the military later determined another use for this post. Caught up in a vortex of events over which they had no control, the Chiricahua captives eventually became pawns of both the War and Interior Departments in determining whose vested interests would be best protected.

There are other reasons why the Chiricahua saga of imprisonment is unprecedented in the history of American Indian–federal government relations. Indeed, not even the most belligerent of tribes endured a twenty-seven-year period of captivity as did the Chiricahua prisoners of war. Those Chiricahuas taken from their San Carlos and Fort Apache reservation homes were completely innocent of any crimes against Arizona's people because none bore arms during the late Geronimo hostilities. Indeed, arguing in 1890 on behalf of the Chiricahuas, Lieutenant Lyman Walter Vere Kennon, a partisan of General George Crook, went further when he commented that "thus, for the sake of less than twenty" male combatants, "a whole tribe of nearly four hundred innocent people have been condemned to exile and imprisonment, which to many of them have [*sic*] meant death."[14]

Furthermore, those Chiricahua scouts who fought with the U.S. Army against their own people when the military waged its final campaign against Geronimo found themselves incarcerated alongside their blameless confreres by an unappreciative government. Even more tragic, such confinement created a situation in which guiltless children were born into captivity. Finally, their tribal identity obliterated, these displaced Chiricahuas would never again have a homeland of their own, let alone be returned to Arizona. To mask this long-standing mistake, these hapless Indians, while under military control in Oklahoma, were deceitfully referred to as the Fort Sill Apaches, not the Chiricahuas. In time, they would be removed even from this post, which was promised them as both their permanent home and the site of their release from military custody. As the Women's National Indian Association, severely criticizing government officials for their mishandling of the Chiricahua situation, presciently noted in 1890, "It seems impossible that this generation should have allowed such a stigma to be cast on its history."[15] Of no mean significance, therefore, what follows is the tragic saga of justice denied an innocent people held prisoner of war at Fort Sill.

How, then—to paraphrase the observations of Lieutenant Britton Davis—did such an unmitigated outrage come to pass?[16] In ascertaining the origins of the Chiricahua's plight, the bureaucratic bungling and bickering between the War and Interior Departments that preceded and accompanied the last of the Geronimo campaigns must be considered. In 1883, after the successful conclusion of the Sierra Madre campaign, the Interior Department relinquished police control over the San Carlos and Fort Apache Reservations to the military.[17] Unfortunately, certain officers directly in charge of the Chiricahuas interpreted this as being vested with complete administrative control over the full spectrum of reservation affairs. Consequently, a succession of disgruntled Indian Agents incessantly plied their Interior Department superiors in Washington with complaints that the military's usurpation of their authority placed them in an untenable position. By the spring of 1885, the divisiveness and discord between field representatives of the War and Interior Departments became so deep that those Apaches, such as Geronimo, disaffected by reservation conditions did not fail to notice.

While the military continued to request complete control over reservation policy, to which entreaties, initially at least, Interior adamantly refused its consent, those Indians constantly dissatisfied with reservation life at San Carlos and Fort Apache precipitated a confrontation over the army's ban against the manufacture and use of spiritous liquors.[18] This confrontation, which occurred during General Crook's tenure as Department of Arizona commandant, resulted in the final large-scale Apache belligerencies ever to afflict Arizona. After Geronimo bolted the San Carlos Reservation in May, Interior quickly abandoned its previous position and gave military officials the absolute control over reservation affairs they had so ardently sought. In doing so, Interior completely abrogated its trust responsibilities toward the Chiricahuas.[19] As subsequent events all too vividly illustrated, by rigidly refusing to resume custody over the Chiricahua nation as a unified people with lands of their own, Interior abetted the eventual displacement and dispersal of innocent human beings who became the victims of the cupidity for glory of Crook's successor, General Miles. Thus, although the vast majority of Chiricahuas, refusing to participate in the flight from the San Carlos and Fort Apache Reservations, tended their farms and looked to the military for protection from reprisals by those Apaches turned fugitive, Miles, upon whose shoulders responsibility for the infamous fate that awaited these Indians would later lie, immediately took advantage of Interior's abdication of jurisdiction over the Chiricahuas and lied to the nation during the summer of 1886, when he advised the army's commander, Philip S. Sheridan, that those who remained behind gave aid and comfort to the enemy.[20]

Miles replaced Crook as Arizona's departmental commanding officer due to a dispute between Crook and his War Department superiors regarding both the efficacy of employing Chiricahua scouts to locate Geronimo and his fellow belligerents and the nature of the surrender terms to be offered once they were found. According to Crook, the Chiricahua scouts were indispensable. Without their assistance, he believed, the belligerents would not have been located. Of course, finding them and procuring their capitulation were not the same thing. They would only submit if "granted satisfactory terms." Therefore, Crook decided to treat them as prisoners of war and send them to Fort Marion, where they would be "safe from Southwestern authorities who wished to hang them."[21] On Saturday, March 27, 1886, at Cañon de los Embudos in northeastern Sonora, Mexico, Geronimo, Chihuahua, Naiche, and 100 followers discussed surrender with General Crook. They insisted that either they should be permitted to return to their reservation without punishment, or, if they were to be held as prisoners of war, they should be removed to Florida for only two years and then returned to Arizona. Crook opted for Florida, believing the Chiricahuas would not accept other terms, and immediately so notified his superiors in Washington. Placing Lieutenant Marion Maus in charge of escorting the belligerents, Crook then departed for Fort Bowie in southeastern Arizona.[22]

Trouble quickly ensued. On March 30, Crook learned that Geronimo, Naiche, and thirty followers had returned to Sonora's mountain fastnesses on the night of March 29. On April 2, Maus explained why Geronimo had fled. Robert Tribolet, an operative of the notorious Tucson Ring—"a group of merchants who wished to keep the Indian war going in order to grow rich on military contracts"[23]— dispensed liquor to the belligerents, who, in turn, became inebriated. Tribolet then told them they would be executed upon their return to Arizona from Mexico.[24]

Before Crook could act, a message arrived from Washington. Deeming the March 27 surrender terms unacceptable, President Grover Cleveland ordered Crook to renegotiate. There was only one condition. "If they came in and all gave up their weapons, their lives would be spared; if not, they would be hunted down and killed." For Crook, this was an untenable situation.[25] Chihuahua had not joined Geronimo on March 29, and were this stipulation laid before him and his seventy-six followers (who were sent to Fort Marion as prisoners of war on April 7 under General Sheridan's April 5 order),[26] they would most likely flee and advise Geronimo that Crook had lied—with the consequence that none of the fugitives would ever trust him again. Never again, therefore, would they consent to renew negotiations.[27]

Subsequently, Crook advised Sheridan of Geronimo's escape. A two-day frenetic telegraphic exchange followed. Sheridan implied that Crook had exercised poor judgment in utilizing Chiricahua scouts. Crook defended his methods. Exasperated, however, Crook suggested on April 1, 1886, that Sheridan assign someone else to complete the task of subduing Geronimo. Although he believed his strategy was the "one most likely to prove successful in the end," Crook noted that he might be "too much wedded to my own views in this matter." Crook then asked to be relieved of his command.[28]

Crook's request provided Sheridan with the "opportunity he sought for years."[29] Disagreeing strongly with Crook's use of scouts, Sheridan insisted that only "white troopers using standard tactics would be effective." For Sheridan, the stakes were enormous—perhaps even the White House might not be out of reach. On April 2, Sheridan ordered his disciple, Nelson Miles, to take over.[30] Ten days later, General Miles arrived at Fort Bowie. Shortly thereafter, the general, whose avidity for fame and fortune was at least the equal of his mentor's aspirations, considered how his Arizona tour of duty could advance his personal ambitions. One way to attain such sought-after acclaim was to relocate the Chiricahuas in their entirety. Miles believed that even if Geronimo surrendered, other Chiricahuas might well revolt.[31] Therefore, both envisioning himself as Arizona's savior and believing that this accomplishment would fling open the doors to the military establishment's highest echelons, Miles deliberately falsified facts to make more palatable the suggestion that the Chiricahuas who had not taken to the field be removed from the Southwest altogether, thus enabling

Arizona's settlers, who for two decades had prayed that just such a policy might be pursued, to exploit the territory's resources. Perhaps the Chiricahuas could be sent to the Indian Territory.[32] Conveyed through proper military channels, this intelligence quickly reached President Grover Cleveland, who, rejecting Miles's suggestion, eventually ordered the Chiricahuas' removal to Florida as prisoners of war— despite, ironically enough, the general's prophetic protestations that the region's humid subtropical climate would in time take its toll in death and hardship on a people attuned to the dryness of desert and mountain air.[33]

On July 3, Miles attempted to put his plan into effect. Accordingly, he "requested permission to send a delegation of headmen to Washington to discuss such removal." On July 7, Sheridan advised Secretary of War William Endicott of his doubts about this proposal. From Sheridan's perspective, interestingly enough, Indian wars were caused by government removal of tribes from their original homelands. He believed that instead of pleading to have Indians relocated to less troubled areas, those sections of the country containing belligerent Indians ought to take responsibility for their control. Even so, Sheridan consented to allowing a Chiricahua delegation to travel to Washington.[34]

Later that month, Miles and Lucius Quintus Cincinnatus Lamar, Jr., son of the secretary of the interior, selected Chatto, one of Crook's most trusted Indian scouts, and twelve other Chiricahuas for this purpose. The party arrived in Washington on July 18. Earlier, Miles's superiors had explained to him why the proposal to relocate all Chiricahuas to Indian Territory was impossible. Federal statutes enacted in 1879 prohibited any removal there of Arizona and New Mexico Indians. Miles suggested that the law be modified. Cleveland, Endicott, and Lamar considered the idea but believed this legislative change to be unattainable. Although ordered to abandon this idea, Miles insisted that there existed precedents for locating Indians where laws forbade such placement. Furthermore, Miles advised Sheridan, who concurred with this view, that if the government objected, he discerned no rationalization that could be employed to prevent sending the Chiricahuas to Fort Riley, Kansas, or Fort Union, New Mexico.[35]

Interestingly enough, after the Indians' arrival in Washington, the matter of the Chiricahuas' possible removal from Arizona was never discussed with Chatto and the scouts. Indeed, on July 19, Chatto received a silver peace medal. By July 26, Captain John Gregory Bourke, well acquainted with Chatto and the scouts, arranged an interview with Secretary of War Endicott. Chatto, who spoke of his trust in the secretary of war, said he desired his own land in Arizona. He believed Endicott would ensure that his request was granted. Chatto considered his medal a token that the Indians should remain in Arizona. On the following day, Bourke escorted Chatto and the entire scout delegation to confer with President Cleveland. Cleveland insisted there was no need for further discussion, as both Lamar and Endicott had on paper everything the scouts had already told them.[36]

Yet, on July 31, a special conference was convened at the White House. In attendance were Secretary of State Thomas F. Bayard, Interior Secretary Lamar, Bourke, Endicott, Cleveland, and Captain Joseph Dorst, who accompanied Chatto's delegation as their officer-in-charge. Cleveland came directly to the point: could the Chiricahuas in their entirety be sent to Fort Marion? If so, how might Chatto and the other scouts "be detained, prevented from returning to Arizona," and subsequently routed to Florida? Bourke protested against this scheme because the Chiricahuas remaining on the reservation conducted themselves peacefully and engaged in agricultural pursuits. If the Chiricahuas were sent away, other remaining Apache tribes would feel aggrieved and might consequently bolt their reservations. Dorst strongly disagreed. He maintained the other Apaches had "long disliked the Chiricahuas and would be glad to see them go." Even so, Cleveland and Endicott apparently had their minds made up. At the conference's conclusion, Endicott, taking Dorst aside, enquired "about the mechanics of gathering the Indians together."[37]

Indeed, the Cleveland administration initially proposed that the entire Chiricahua tribe be sent to Florida before Chatto and his group were ready to return home. By the time the Indians left Washington, the only question remaining was how to carry out this removal. Sheridan, erroneously believing that Chatto's delegation thought the government was determined to expel the Chiricahuas from Arizona, wanted to act expeditiously. He felt that if Chatto and the scouts were permitted to go back to their reservation, the rest of the tribe would be warned, causing many of them to join Geronimo and Naiche. Therefore, on July 30, Sheridan suggested that they be sent directly to Florida. Simultaneously, the remaining Chiricahua males residing at San Carlos were to be arrested and placed on a train for Fort Marion.[38]

On July 31, Sheridan requested Miles's opinion of his proposal. Promising to provide details as to the plan's advantages and disadvantages later, Miles, on August 1, equivocated. In the meantime, he suggested that Chatto and the scouts be taken to Carlisle, Pennsylvania. Miles stalled for time because he "still hoped to locate all the Chiricahuas to the Indian Territory." Indeed, "as the summer wore on, it became crucial to Miles that the Indians be sent" there. Serving a twofold purpose, not only would such enable Miles to receive southwesterners' undying gratitude, but, as the most favorable surrender inducement available, it also was his "best chance to end the Apache war quickly and reap the entire credit for settling the Chiricahua problem."

Furthermore, by late July, the general realized "he was no closer to capturing" Geronimo and his fellow belligerents "than he had been when he relieved Crook during the first part of April." Under the circumstances, therefore, Miles was forced to conclude that the employment of Crook's methods might well be the "only way to induce the hostiles to surrender," which, in turn, meant offering them "conditions, the very idea" that Cleveland, fearing renewed outbreaks, had "adamantly rejected" earlier. Miles also believed, regarding his relocation proposal, that if all the Chiricahuas were evicted from San Carlos, the combatants most likely could be cajoled into joining them. Consequently, Cleveland might be convinced that "permanent exile was proper punishment," not to mention that such "would eliminate any danger from them in the future." Thus, for Miles, who continued to pursue the proposition that the Indian Territory presented the best choice, the area adjacent to Fort Sill was the appropriate place to locate the Chiricahuas because not only was it "much like parts of their" Arizona reservation, but it would also offer them "one less reason to be dissatisfied." Also, it was "far enough away from Arizona to suit the people of that territory, as well as suggest that Miles's Oklahoma plan had succeeded where Crook's Florida plan had failed." Miles's scheme was only partially successful. On August 2, Dorst's superiors ordered him to transport Chatto and the scouts to Carlisle and subsequently back to San Carlos, after which Sheridan said they could then be arrested.[39]

On August 6, Miles transmitted orders to retain the Chatto delegation at Carlisle indefinitely. Were its members returned to Arizona, they would then believe that they would be permitted to remain there. Thus, it would be exceedingly difficult to gather the entire tribe when the appointed time for removal arrived. But it was too late to keep them at Carlisle because they were already in Kansas. On August 11, Dorst received a message to take his charges to Fort Leavenworth, arriving there on the same day.[40] On September 12, War Department officials instructed General Joseph Potter, Fort Leavenworth's commanding officer, to send Chatto and the scouts to Fort Marion.[41] On September 14, they and Captain Dorst departed by train for Florida,[42] arriving there on September 17.[43]

Meanwhile, by late August, the Cleveland administration had come to a final decision concerning those Chiricahuas remaining at San Carlos. They would be removed to Fort Marion. Indeed, War Department officials queried Colonel Loomis Langdon as to whether that installation might be able to accommodate some 400 additional Indians. Responding, Langdon explained that "conditions were already crowded." He therefore "recommended that no more Indians be sent." Even so, if necessary, room for seventy-five could be found were sufficient funding provided. Adamant on this matter, Cleveland, Endicott, Lamar, and Sheridan insisted that arrangements be made. On August 25, they decided to relocate the entire tribe there. Miles was then ordered to begin the Chiricahua roundup.[44]

As for the belligerents who had yet to surrender, on August 24, Geronimo told Lieutenant Charles Gatewood that he was agreeable to discussing peace with Miles. On September 3, at Skeleton Canyon in southeastern Arizona, an uneasy Miles met Geronimo.[45] Such a meeting was possible only because Miles had covertly resorted to the use of Indian scouts. Miles found himself faced with a direct order from President Cleveland to "bring in the hostiles unconditionally." Blatantly disregarding this command, Miles instructed Gatewood to offer terms. Simply, "if they surrendered, they would not be harmed." Instead, not only would the belligerents "be sent to Florida with the other Chiricahuas," where they "would rejoin their families," but they would eventually be returned to Arizona once sentiment against them had dissipated.[46]

On September 4, discussions continued. Miles induced the belligerents to journey to Fort Bowie "with promises he seriously doubted he could keep." Indeed, the combatants "agreed to be sent out of Arizona only when Miles confirmed what Gatewood" had previously told them. Besides, Miles warned, the territory remained "unsafe for the band" because Arizona's civil authorities, after adjudging the belligerents guilty of rapine and murder, were most anxious to execute them for their crimes.[47] On September 5, the combatants arrived at Fort Bowie,[48] whereupon Miles arranged for their rail transport to Florida.

Meanwhile, Miles gave the impression that their surrender was unconditional.[49] Phrasing his comments to this effect, Miles wired General Oliver Otis Howard, Pacific Division commandant, on September 6.[50] That same day, Howard conveyed this intelligence to Washington, advising his superiors that the surrender was unconditional. In his telegram, Howard asked, "What should be done with Geronimo and the hostiles now prisoners of war?"[51] On September 7, Cleveland ordered the captives held until tried for their crimes.[52] In turn, Miles suggested alternative solutions, warning of their possible pretrial escape or slaughter by that territory's irate citizenry.[53] But the War Department remained steadfast. On September 8, Cleveland issued the final order: guard against their escape and incarcerate them at the closest garrison.[54] Although this decision reached Fort Bowie while Miles was still completing preparations for his departure with the belligerents, he was not informed until too late. Captain William Thompson intercepted the telegram, which was not delivered[55] until after they entrained eastward on September 8.[56] Traveling with them were the loyal scouts Kayihtah and Martine, seized by Miles shortly before leaving the post. Such perfidy eventually proved a stupendous miscalculation, for "seven months later, the War Department would be badly shaken up by public reaction."[57]

Miles journeyed with them as far as Deming, New Mexico, from which he proceeded to Albuquerque on business.[58] While there, Miles advised Howard on September 9 that Howard labored under "an erroneous impression" about the prisoners. They had submitted only on the understanding that they would be exiled.[59] Miles then informed the War Department that he had complied with the nearest post or prison incarceration order.[60] Although he had sent them to Florida, they could be intercepted at Fort Sam Houston in San Antonio, Texas, or rerouted to Fort Leavenworth. On September 10, a suspicious Acting Secretary of War Richard C. Drum ordered the train stopped at San Antonio, where the Chiricahuas were detained for six weeks.[61]

Meanwhile, both the Pacific Division headquarters staff in San Francisco and War Department officials in Washington frantically searched for several pivotal communiqués. One of these telegrams, so

Miles claimed, purportedly authorized the general to negotiate surrender terms; the other supposedly directed him to transport Geronimo and his fellow belligerents to Florida.[62] These putative dispatches were never located for the simple reason that they were never sent.[63] President Cleveland, on September 23, ordered Howard to transmit forthwith a detailed report concerning the "immediate circumstances surrounding the capture."[64] On the same day, Howard advised his superiors that he was unable to locate the particulars attendant thereto. Miles, Howard surmised, gave guarantees to Geronimo and the other belligerents that they would be unharmed and sent to live with their families in Florida.[65]

Two days later, the War Department ordered Miles to enumerate the exact conditions he had given.[66] On September 29, Miles transmitted a detailed report lacking any substance.[67] Consequently, War Department officials ordered Fort Sam Houston commandant General David Stanley to interrogate the former combatants to ascertain the exact capitulation conditions proffered the captives. Stanley filed his report on September 30. Geronimo and Naiche were examined separately. Both of them gave the same account, which supported Howard's conclusion. In violation of direct presidential orders, terms had indeed been given.[68] Meanwhile, Miles forwarded his annual report which, subsequently discussed by Cleveland and Endicott, the War Department received by October 1.[69]

On October 7, 14, and 15, Cleveland's entire cabinet convened to consider the prisoners' disposition. Members rejected outright Miles's suggestion that the Chiricahua prisoners be located at an installation west of the Mississippi River. They also immediately spurned those spiteful efforts designed to ship them to Fort Jefferson on the Dry Tortugas off the Florida coast. Fort Pickens, situated on Santa Rosa Island in Florida's Pensacola Bay, seemed the better option. In addition, Cleveland found himself faced with Arizona officials demanding that the belligerents be returned there for trial, as well as territorial citizens screaming for vengeance.[70]

Subsequently, on October 19, Cleveland arrived at a decision: the belligerents' families would be broken up. Their women and children were to be sent to Fort Marion; the men would be located at Fort Pickens. Public safety demanded this, said Cleveland. Hence, not only would they be removed far from the scenes of their past depredations, but they would also be "guarded with the strictest vigilance."[71] Departing San

Antonio on October 22, the former combatants arrived at Fort Pickens three days later.[72] Justifying this solution, Cleveland insisted that he acted as he did out of concern for the attitude of the southwesterners. Indeed, in November, Governor Conrad M. Zulick assured the president that Arizona citizens felt secure because the belligerents, now under close observation, were so far removed that it was impossible for them to repeat their outrages in that territory.[73] Cleveland therefore considered the Chiricahua issue resolved.

CHAPTER

2

An Exile of Despair
in Florida and Alabama

▼   ▼   ▼

*I*ntelligence regarding the rapidly deteriorating conditions confronting the Chiricahuas held at Fort Marion soon caught the attention of Indian activist organizations. Their reaction to this information quickly caused the Cleveland administration to conclude that far from being fully settled, the Chiricahuas' case required immediate reconsideration. For one thing, the Chiricahuas at Fort Marion were decimated by disease. Indeed, by the time they arrived at this installation, they were already infected with malaria.[1] Other medical afflictions included dysentery bacteria, bronchitis, and tuberculosis.[2] A damp climate, inadequate housing that was both crowded and improperly ventilated, as well as initially sited on a location lacking suitable drainage,[3] a dearth of suitable clothing, and poor nutrition—even abject hunger—exacerbated the situation. Food supplies were clearly inadequate: the Chiricahuas generally lacked fresh meat, fruits, and vegetables.[4] An adult's daily meat ration was one pound, while a child received only half that. Such rations were not only insufficient, but they also consisted of far too much pork—a serious problem in that Chiricahua dietary laws (which also excluded ingestion of fish) proscribed its consumption.[5] Ironically, these privations caused even General Miles to proclaim that Fort Marion was a "second black hole of Calcutta."[6]

At the start of 1887, complaints reached Herbert Welsh and the Indian Rights Association. A well-known reformer, Welsh was determined not to let the government rest until the Chiricahua captives in Florida received justice. On the basis of letters received describing their appalling situation, Welsh decided to visit Fort Marion, a journey he undertook at the end of January 1887. At the same time, he approached Captain John Gregory Bourke as his entree to War Department officialdom. Bourke proposed that Welsh enlist the aid of the Boston Indian Citizenship Committee to find prominent and influential Bostonians willing to write letters of introduction to Secretary of War Endicott. Of course, Endicott did not want an investigation and tried to prevent it, knowing full well that the War Department both imprisoned the Chiricahuas indiscriminately and administered their incarceration improperly. On March 7, after finally obtaining the requisite authorization, Welsh, in Bourke's company, departed for Florida, arriving at Fort Marion on March 8. Everything he had heard and read about the Chiricahuas' plight at this installation was true. What Welsh saw there made him "determined to expose the neglect, injustice and general hopelessness" they suffered.[7]

Although Welsh did not publish his report until the end of April 1887, word of its contents, leaked in late March, caused War Department officials such great discomfort that they were forced to devise remedial measures.[8] Welsh's action also convinced other Indian rights societies, such as the Women's National Indian Association, the Boston Indian Citizenship Committee, and the Massachusetts Indian Association, to petition the president, War Department officials, and other general government functionaries for improvement of the Chiricahuas' circumstances. In addition, these organizations sought to ascertain the reasons not only for the government's imprisonment of innocent people, but also for its failure to keep faith with Chatto and the scouts. By the second week of April, due to the intense pressure, President Cleveland assured the activists that the Chiricahuas would be removed eventually but claimed that "he was having difficulty finding the proper place to locate them."[9]

On April 9, Secretary Endicott summoned Bourke to discuss this matter. He advised the captain that Cleveland was upset over the Florida situation. For several weeks, the president consulted with his cabinet. Cleveland concluded that the Chiricahua prisoners should be removed from Fort Marion and that the prisoners at Fort Pickens should be reunited with their families. Mount Vernon Barracks, Alabama, was suggested as a possible relocation site for the Fort Marion prisoners. Even so, this post required inspection as to its suitability. Endicott detailed Bourke, who arrived at Mount Vernon Barracks on April 11, to conduct this examination.[10] Located in Mobile County, Alabama, the post, at 224 feet above sea level, consisted of 2,162 acres situated in a dense pine forest surrounded by countryside whose topographical features included swamps and low-lying hills traversed by numerous creeks and bayous. There was very little arable land. Indeed, much of the soil, composed as it was of white sand, clay, and calcareous material, was quite poor and thus unsuitable for either crop or livestock raising—although Bourke noted that it possessed potential for prime poultry production.[11]

Employment, therefore, would be a problem. Because the area's forests contained an abundance of oak and cypress, Bourke believed the Chiricahuas could secure work in such timber-related industries as manufacturing cypress shingles, felling lumber, gathering "red oak from which tannic acid for curing hides" was procured, and extracting pine sap for production of turpentine. Bourke also suggested that some of the men be enlisted as scouts. Of course, the government would have to supply the tools and other materials required to undertake these occupations. In addition, once the Chiricahuas cleared a sufficient amount of land, they could raise cotton, the one sustainable commodity, considering the surrounding soil conditions.[12]

Bourke described the installation's structures as sound and observed that "sanitary conditions were good." Regarding health concerns, malaria could pose a problem. Still, "the air was pure and sweet, the temperature was mild except in the mid summer when the days were hot, but the nights were cool and pleasant." Furthermore, "water was in ample supply, pure and cool."[13] He informed Endicott of the results of his investigation on April 14. On the same day, Endicott, who concluded that this post was ideal for their resettlement, detailed Bourke to discuss with Cleveland the possibility of removing the Chiricahua prisoners to this location—a proposal that received the president's approval.[14] With the exception of thirty-five children sent to Carlisle, 354 arrived there from Fort Marion on April 28.[15] After their arrival, post officers placed them under the leadership of six chiefs and permitted each group to select its own campsite.[16]

As an improvement upon their previous location, Mount Vernon Barracks failed to meet the Chiricahuas' expectations. According to Eugene Chihuahua, they "didn't know what misery was" until the army "dumped us in those swamps." Contrasting Fort Marion with

Eugene Chihuahua. *Courtesy Fort Sill Museum.*

Mount Vernon, Chihuahua said they soon discovered the latter to be quite inferior to the former.[17] Army officers in charge of these Indians made every effort to maintain a healthful and comfortable camp environment. Yet, the moist climate of this region continued to take its toll in victims of tuberculosis. Indeed, within two years of their arrival at this site, 25 percent of their original number had perished from this disease.[18] So appalling was the mortality rate that, years later, Marian Stephens, an observer of great sensitivity as well as an early missionary to the Chiricahuas, wrote, "No matter what these people have done, Government has been ahead in dealing out punishment." As far as Stephens was concerned, given the degree of their suffering, one might well have considered it a humanitarian act were the army ordered to execute the Chiricahuas, as opposed to permitting their death, "one by one, of that most hopeless of diseases, consumption."[19]

After publication of his report, Welsh made plans to plead his case during the fall meeting of the Lake Mohonk Conference of Friends of the Indian. Meanwhile, during the summer of 1887, reports reached both the Indian Rights Association and the War Department that the Chiricahuas fared poorly at Mount Vernon. According to the officer-in-charge, Major William Sinclair, the military establishment exerted no effort to improve the Chiricahuas' conditions after their arrival at this installation. Sam Bowman, their interpreter, wrote to both Welsh and Bourke that the prisoners were idle. There also loomed the immense danger of yellow fever from nearby swamps.[20] Throughout the summer, Sinclair and the post surgeon advised General Howard that because the Chiricahuas continuously lacked enough to eat, hunger and weakness existed among the prisoners.[21] In August 1887, Dr. Walter Reed, arriving for a tour of duty as post surgeon, found bronchitis spreading. Before summer's end, ten had died—mostly of tuberculosis.[22] Immediately protesting the shortage of rations, Reed, supported by Sinclair, strongly urged that they be increased. Reed also discovered that many of the Chiricahuas were in poor health due to constant hunger induced by the dietary prohibitions that forbade consumption of, among other things, pork. To alleviate their hunger, the Chiricahuas sold their personal effects to purchase food items more amenable to their tastes at the local store. On October 12, General Sheridan ordered an increase in food rations to a full soldier ration for each adult and half that for each child.[23]

Due to the adverse conditions confronting the prisoners, Welsh intensified his exertions on their behalf. Unable to attend the October Mohonk Conference, Welsh requested various Indian activists

in Massachusetts to pressure the government to move the Chiricahuas
to a more suitable home. Meanwhile, dire reports concerning the Chiricahuas' circumstances continued to pour in. These discussed the shod-
dy housing that lacked sun and air and noted that the captives generally
experienced demoralization and dissipation. By the end of January 1888,
everyone agreed that the Chiricahuas had to be removed from Alabama.
Even so, Endicott ignored Welsh, fearing that Welsh merely wanted to
attack the administration. Instead, Endicott turned to Captain Richard
Henry Pratt at Carlisle and General Samuel Armstrong of Hampton Institute in Hampton, Virginia, for advice.[24] On January 21, 1888, Pratt recommended that the Chiricahuas be relocated to Fort Sill, Oklahoma.[25]

During the spring and summer of 1888, Welsh continued his efforts to get the administration to act. At the end of May, he conferred
with George Crook in Chicago. Crook suggested that the matter might
be resolved by relocating all the Chiricahuas to Fort Sill. On June 11,
1888, Welsh advised Endicott of Crook's views and asked what the government thought about this proposal. Cleveland ignored Welsh out of
pique at earlier Indian Rights Association criticism. In late June, despite this rebuff, Welsh launched his unsuccessful campaign to have
the Chiricahuas removed to the Indian Territory. By the end of 1888, he
was "convinced that the government was determined to do nothing."
Though Welsh forged on with such resettlement schemes, these efforts
fared no better through the close of the Cleveland administration in
March 1889.[26] Perhaps the new Harrison administration might be convinced to take remedial action.

Meanwhile, by January 1, 1888, the Chiricahuas' overseers had
completed construction of thirty-five cabins for the captives' use, as
well as a storehouse and a medical dispensary. Each was built of peeled
pine poles with a clapboard roof and installed plank flooring. These
dwellings had a living space of 144 square feet and featured a small
window and a sheet-iron stove for heating. They were erected on a high
and thoroughly drained tract of land.[27] Such endeavors paved the way
for the May 13, 1888, arrival at Mount Vernon of those Chiricahua prisoners—Geronimo and his followers—held at Fort Pickens.[28]

At the onset of 1889, the educational needs of the Chiricahuas
not sent to Carlisle were finally addressed. On February 14, 1889, two
teachers—whose services were contracted for by the Boston Indian Citizenship Committee on the basis of their instructional experience with
western Indians—arrived at Mount Vernon Barracks. Previously, Vincen-
tine Tilson Booth had taught at Carlisle, and Marian E. Stephens had

taught at Hampton. While at Mount Vernon Barracks, they also served as Christian missionaries. Classes began on March 4 with one young student in attendance. Enrollment later expanded to sixty children. Marian Stephens, who emphasized instruction in English, taught the adult classes. At first, only the men attended. Booth taught the children. Booth was later replaced by Sophie Shepard, a Mobile County, Alabama, native who installed Geronimo as the school disciplinarian. She believed "his influence 'as an element of terror' was too valuable to risk losing." Construction of the one-room schoolhouse was completed in late 1889.[29]

After President Benjamin Harrison's inauguration, there appeared to be a change of attitude toward the Chiricahuas. Harrison's secretary of war, Redfield Proctor, decided to send someone to examine possible sites for relocation. Regarding this matter, Bourke, Crook, and General John M. Schofield, commander of the army, discussed the Chiricahuas' situation on March 29, 1889. Later, while Herbert Welsh urged a prompt resolution of the issue, the Boston Indian Citizenship Committee and the Boston branch of the Massachusetts Indian Association petitioned the War Department to send Captain Bourke to inspect a potential Chiricahua relocation site in North Carolina. On June 14, the War Department ordered Bourke to examine this state's western region for a suitable resettlement location.[30]

During the spring of 1889, Colonel Robert Patterson Hughes, inspector general for the Atlantic Division, toured Mount Vernon Barracks, which were now under the command of Major Charles T. Witherell, who arrived there in May. While there, Hughes observed that no favorable opportunities existed for the application of the Chiricahuas' energies. When the Indian Rights Association learned of this situation, it exerted pressure on the Harrison administration to effect a positive change in conditions for the captives. This organization assigned Charles C. Painter to tackle the Chiricahua problem. Painter led the movement to purchase a tract of land in the East for the captives. Military officials appointed Captain Bourke to represent the War Department's interests in this matter.[31]

On June 23, 1889, Bourke and Painter arrived at Mount Vernon Barracks to evaluate the Chiricahuas' situation and ascertain their views regarding the proposal to remove them eastward. The pair met with twenty-nine of the prisoners, including Chatto, Geronimo, Naiche, and Loco. Also present, representing the War Department, were General Richard A. Jackson, Major Witherell, Dr. Walter Reed, and, significantly, Lieutenant Zebulon B. Vance, son of the North Carolina senator, who was stationed at this post. After pointing out that the Indian Rights Association planned to buy land for them, Painter advised the Chiricahuas of "what would be expected of them before any land would be provided." Speaking bluntly, he told his audience that there no longer existed any place in the country "for Indians, but there was land for men." Simply, Painter desired the Chiricahuas to "quit being Indians, to lose their identity, and be like white men." Although there was no "more land for hunting purposes," there was "land available for farming and for those who wanted to make a living like white people." Furthermore, the "old Indian road was shut up because the white man" had constructed railroads that traversed it, causing what remained of the "Indian road to lead only to ruin."

Consequently, Painter explained to "his listeners, who knew well the harsh remarks were painfully true," that there was "nothing open any longer but the white man's road," which not only led to schools, where "he must educate his children, and to the fields, where he must work for a living," but also to the "shops where he makes his clothes, and all he needs for the comforts of life." Continuing, Painter said that "those whom I represent today believe that you can walk in a path just the same as a white man; that you are men just the same as we are." Painter's associates were both "ready to open the road to you and help you walk in it and . . . ready to put our hands in our pockets and buy you a home." Of course, such required that the Chiricahuas, for their part, be prepared to forsake the past—the maliciousness of which whites were also responsible for—and "begin anew and work for your living in the new path."[32]

The general consensus among the Chiricahua conferees was that they desperately desired an opportunity to definitively improve their lot through agricultural pursuits in a healthier location than their current environment, where, victims of disease, they found themselves "melting away like ice in the summer." Other Chiricahua leaders agreed, "pointing out that they had farmed successfully in Arizona and mastered many of the white man's tools." In addition, they desired to be where rivers flowed and where it snowed.[33] Before departing, Bourke reminded them that the promised land purchase was not yet a reality, but that efforts would be undertaken to make it so.[34]

Subsequently, during the last week of June and the first week of July 1889, Bourke and Painter proceeded to North Carolina, where they first examined the 100,000-acre Eastern Cherokee Reservation, located in western North Carolina's Great Smokey Mountain region.[35] Bourke especially liked this area because it had the potential to provide the Chiricahua prisoners with adequate economic sustenance. During a discussion with the Cherokees regarding the Chiricahuas' possible relocation to that region, Bourke discovered they were "agreeable to the idea of the Chiricahuas living near them." They also "were willing to sell land to the Indian Rights Association" for this purpose in the amount of 12,000 acres.[36] Bourke then examined the area surrounding Wilmington in extreme southeastern North Carolina. He rejected it as unsuitable because of its proximity to the Green Swamp.[37] Upon his return to Washington, Bourke advised his superiors that due to its superior advantages, the tract offered by the Cherokees was the site to which the Chiricahuas should be relocated.[38]

On July 5, Bourke submitted his report. He recommended that the government accept the Cherokees' offer and suggested that the military "continue to look after the Chiricahuas after they were settled." Schofield and General John C. Kelton approved Bourke's recommendation. This proposal also received Secretary Proctor's most enthusiastic support because he believed that the Cherokee offer was the long-sought solution to the Chiricahua problem.[39] Unfortunately, the Indian Rights Association failed to purchase the North Carolina tract.[40]

Consequently, during the first week of August, Proctor journeyed to Boston to arrange purchase of this particular parcel by friends of the Indian in Massachusetts. The Boston committee comprising these allies, however, only guaranteed money for purchase of lands owned by a Reverend Woodworth situated near Wilmington—precisely the tract that Bourke had earlier deemed unsuitable. This Boston committee would therefore have to be assembled to consider the western North Carolina proposal and authorize the purchase from the Cherokees. Proctor thus had nothing to show for his efforts.

On September 6, 1889, the Boston committee met and decided to send a representative with Bourke to re-examine the Cherokee site. Were their representative to concur with Bourke's assessment, the purchase from the Cherokees would be made for the Chiricahuas. Indeed, earlier, on September 2, Bourke, Proctor, and Commissioner of Indian Affairs Thomas Morgan discussed the purchase proposal. They agreed that when the Boston people bought the land, the War Department would transfer the prisoners there.[41]

Meanwhile, War Department functionaries officially released Bourke's report—the salient details of which had caught journalists' attention several weeks earlier—to the public during the last week of

July. Despite a July 20 *New York Times* editorial noting that the Harrison administration had under advisement a proposal to relocate the Chiricahuas on the Eastern Cherokee Reservation, a rumor started that these Indians were to be sent back to Arizona. Strenuous protests from southwesterners immediately ensued. For their part, though, western North Carolinians were initially receptive to the idea, foreseeing a potential monetary windfall.[42]

Yet on September 7, Proctor's enthusiasm for this plan appeared somewhat diminished. He was now more concerned about North Carolina press attacks against this scheme. During early September, at least one western North Carolina editor protested the proposal, observing that "if they were good Indians, they would be free." Thus, political considerations once again overrode humanitarian concerns. These protests did not abate, making Proctor even more cautious in the matter.[43] On September 27, Governor Daniel G. Fowle said the Chiricahuas were not welcome in his state. North Carolinians, he maintained, did not want any more Indians, explaining they vividly recalled the difficulty of expelling the Cherokees more than half a century earlier.[44] But at Bourke's suggestion, Proctor attempted an alliance with North Carolina senator Zebulon Vance of Asheville. Supporting Proctor, Vance assured Asheville journalists that their fear for public safety was unfounded. By the end of October, Vance's campaign reversed public opinion: the Chiricahuas were now welcome.

Even as Vance's efforts gained momentum, Proctor hesitated.[45] In late September, he noted the existence of a statute mandating confinement of Indians held as prisoners to a military installation. Consequently, "there was no better place" than Mount Vernon Barracks to retain the Chiricahuas until they were someday released from their prisoner-of-war status.[46] Despite this setback, the Boston Indian Citizenship Committee prodded him to send a new commission to make yet another inspection of the lands in question. Meanwhile, Proctor waffled yet again and "hoped that Congress might vote to move the Apaches onto land offered by the Cherokees."[47]

While War Department officials vacillated over removing the Chiricahuas from Alabama, reports continued to surface that little opportunity existed for the Chiricahuas to train in the agricultural arts through which they might become self-sufficient. Small wonder, then, that by fall's end, War Department officials, once again prodded by Indian rights organizations, decided a change was indeed necessary.[48] Consequently, during the winter of 1889–1890, they revisited the issue of where to locate the Chiricahua prisoners. As did earlier inquiries, their latest investigation concluded that both Fort Sill and the mountainous region of western North Carolina were ideal sites for Chiricahua resettlement. Interestingly enough, President Harrison recommended that Congress enact legislation to permit their resettlement in the Indian Territory.[49]

In December, the War Department ordered Lieutenant Guy Howard to Mount Vernon Barracks to prepare a detailed report on the Chiricahuas' condition. Howard prefaced his findings by noting that the Chiricahuas were in a "condition which needs prompt action to avoid positive inhumanity." Their state of health was abysmal, and numerous deaths resulted from consumption—a state of affairs induced by the highly humid climate. Additionally, in that they were prisoners, whatever work the men performed amounted to prison labor. Chiricahua women, having little to occupy their energies, lacked incentive for self-improvement. Furthermore, "no arable land for cultivation" existed in the surrounding region. Finally, Howard explained, although several missionaries taught school, the "good of these short steps toward education is not apparent without giving the Indian child some better outlook on the future than he now has." Accordingly, Howard recommended requesting congressional funding to provide adequate acreage and to provision the Chiricahuas with both "materials and tools to build cabins" and "simple farm utensils, cattle and seeds." He then suggested that they be placed on this land by March 1, 1890, because "another year's delay would be criminal."[50]

While Howard investigated conditions at Mount Vernon Barracks, now commanded by Major William Kellogg, General George Crook continued his campaign to have the Chiricahua captives relocated westward to a drier climate. On December 30, 1889, he, Lieutenant Lyman Kennon, and Senator Vance inspected the proposed Cherokee site. Although Crook believed that the country was much like that of the White Mountains in Arizona, he did not believe there was sufficient available land to support nearly 400 Chiricahuas.[51] On January 2, 1890, Crook and Kennon arrived at Mount Vernon Barracks on a fact-finding mission.[52] They conferred with the Chiricahua headmen Naiche and Chatto. Crook and Kennon saw that the Chiricahuas' current situation was hopeless.[53]

As the Chiricahuas' tale unfolded, Crook learned that not only had Geronimo and his fellow belligerents not been forced to surrender, but also that without the Apache scouts (such as Martine and Kayihtah), their stronghold would not have been located. Yet, acting in bad faith, Miles and his War Department accomplices had removed the scouts eastward for no other reason, according to Noche, a former scout, than White Mountain Apache opposition to the Chiricahua presence. Subsequently, Crook and Kennon departed for Fort Sill. On January 6, Crook prepared a report detailing his observations, which both favored the Chiricahuas' removal to that post and impugned the "wisdom, the motives and the actions of General Miles and the government toward the Apache captives."[54]

Arriving in Washington on January 7, Crook let it be known publicly that the belligerents never would have been captured without the help of the scouts. It was an outrage that they now languished without work and were victims of disease. Crook believed that the Chiricahua prisoners should receive farms in the Indian Territory.[55] Crook's recommendations quickly ignited a heated confrontation between Crook and Miles partisans over whether to relocate the Chiricahuas at Fort Sill or in North Carolina. Arguing in the press for Fort Sill as the only appropriate site for Chiricahua removal, Crook appealed to Congress for a resolution that would first transfer them to Oklahoma and then ultimately settle them as a free people on the Kiowa and Comanche Reservation.[56]

Subsequently, Secretary Proctor advised President Harrison to remove the Chiricahuas from Alabama.[57] Although Miles vehemently opposed this plan, on January 13, Secretary Proctor, despite his recent temporization on the issue, submitted two proposals to President Harrison—one to relocate the Chiricahuas to North Carolina, the other to place them in the Indian Territory.[58] Although he believed that their settlement in North Carolina might produce the desired results, Proctor considered the Indian Territory a far more suitable relocation site.[59] Reiterating his preference for the latter, the secretary proffered his support for the Fort Sill plan, provided that Congress authorized both the transfer of the Chiricahuas to that location and negotiations with the Kiowas and Comanches to purchase the post and other reservation lands needed for resettlement upon the Chiricahuas' eventual release.[60]

In this respect, there was only one obstacle: the 1879 statute forbidding any Arizona or New Mexico tribe from living in Indian Territory. It would take an act of Congress to change the law. Even so, Proctor believed there was nothing to prevent the Chiricahuas from staying at Fort Sill until Congress took the necessary action.[61] By January 21, 1890, Senate Indian Affairs Committee Chairman Henry Laurens Dawes succeeded in gaining the passage of Senate Resolution 42, which directed the War Department to transfer the Chiricahuas to the

Indian Territory.[62] Two days later, this matter was referred to the House Committee on Indian Affairs.[63]

At this point, a heated controversy ensued over this resolution. Indeed, Senate approval of the measure caused no little anxiety among southwestern residents. Led by Miles, the Arizona, New Mexico, and California press attacked the plan with endless protests.[64] No less bitterly opposed to this relocation proposal, both the region's residents[65] and such organizations as the Society of Arizona Pioneers launched vituperative remonstrations against the proposition.[66]

House of Representatives members who protested any consideration of the measure demanded a public hearing. Acceding to these demands, House Indian Affairs Committee chairman Bishop W. Perkins of Kansas conducted hearings on the issue in February 1890. To forestall any furtherance of the army's Chiricahua relocation scheme, Arizona territorial delegate Marcus Aurelius Smith quickly subpoenaed Nelson Miles's testimony regarding the matter of moving the Indians to Fort Sill. During his strenuous protestations against the proposal, Miles, contradicting the evidence at hand, lied under oath. Protecting his image as Arizona's savior, the general insisted that at the time he suggested removing the Chiricahuas to Fort Sill, he did not think he would be able to remove the Chiricahuas as far east as North Carolina.[67] Arizona territorial governor Louis Wolfley also vehemently testified against the proposition.

Perkins, however, needed no additional prodding. His committee was also charged with supervision of matters pertaining to the Indian Territory—much of which was about to be reorganized as Oklahoma Territory. Removal of the Chiricahuas to this location would quickly disrupt the purchase of prime agricultural acreage by land-hungry white farmers. In addition, George Crook, the Chiricahuas' champion, suffered a fatal heart attack on March 21. With his demise, the Chiricahuas' latest hope for a significant improvement in their conditions also died, bottled up in Perkins's committee. For the moment, then, opponents of Chiricahua removal to Fort Sill won the day.[68] Its relocation plans temporarily checked, the War Department bided its time for another three years.

Meanwhile, Herbert Welsh and the Indian Rights Association pushed yet again for the North Carolina location. During the spring of 1890, Proctor cooperated with these efforts by preparing a bill whereby Congress would appropriate money to buy the land, and the government would be reimbursed from the sale of the Chiricahuas' Arizona reservation. As Representative Perkins was about to submit this legislation for passage in the house, Lieutenant Guy Howard, General Oliver O.

Howard's son, suggested that something be done for the Chiricahuas where they already were. He intended this proposal as only a temporary measure until a more suitable location could be found. But with this suggestion, the younger Howard inadvertently destroyed the North Carolina plan in that the House Indian Affairs Committee seized on this idea as a way to "postpone more discussion on a sensitive issue." Through June 1890, the Indian Rights Association pressed the issue to no avail.[69]

Responding to Welsh's accusations that he was responsible for the failure of the latest North Carolina relocation plan, Proctor advised Senator Dawes on June 25, 1890, that he had never labored under the impression that the scheme to remove the Chiricahuas to North Carolina was abandoned as a result of Lieutenant Howard's recommendation. Insisting that his views remained constant concerning the previously proffered proposal to relocate the Chiricahuas to North Carolina, Proctor advised Dawes "that if they could not be removed to Fort Sill, we ought to provide a good location in North Carolina, or elsewhere, for them." Yet because he saw "little prospect of action in any direction by Congress," Proctor said he "took steps to do the best we could for them where they are." Such measures were not "intended to check or discourage Congressional action." Indeed, reiterating his earlier stance, Proctor told Dawes that he would be pleased to lend his assistance were there anything else he could "do in the matter."[70] Even so, now quite weary of the Chiricahua Apache prisoner-of-war issue, the government contented itself with attempting to ameliorate the Chiricahuas' situation at Mount Vernon Barracks.[71]

Unhappily biding their time, War Department officials who supported the Chiricahuas' relocation to Fort Sill were forced to redouble their efforts toward improving the prisoners' conditions at Mount Vernon Barracks. In June 1890, Lieutenant William Wallace Wotherspoon, who replaced Major William Kellogg, arrived at Mount Vernon as the Chiricahuas' new officer-in-charge. He demanded that they cease speculating on possible removal from Alabama. Convinced that they would never be relocated, Wotherspoon insisted his charges make up their minds to work like white men. Wotherspoon promised to find them jobs. By summer's end, many Chiricahua men were employed either at the post cutting wood or laboring for nearby farmers. In this manner, a step was taken toward solving the employment problem.[72]

The following March, a number of these Chiricahuas found themselves involved in an experiment conceived by Secretary Proctor the previous summer as at least one means of easing the assimilation

of Indians into white society. On March 8, Proctor ordered the recruit-
ment of Indians to replenish the ranks of such skeletonized units of the
army's infantry regiments as Company I. Arriving at Mount Vernon
Barracks on March 20, 1891, Proctor inspected the Chiricahuas and personally enquired into their progress with a view toward having a complement of Chiricahua men enlisted in Company I. Proctor later
rationalized this project, explaining that he "attempted to turn these Indians over to the Department of the Interior but could not do it." Therefore, he tried to accomplish what he could, both under the law and in
view of available funding, to enable them to become self-sufficient.
Simply, he desired to "lead the Indians from the present idle life they
are now leading and endeavor to civilize them," so that as many of
them as possible might "reap the benefits of civilization."[73]

Believing that Mount Vernon Barracks provided an ideal opportunity to put his plan into operation, Proctor ordered Wotherspoon to
form an Indian company.[74] Every inducement was offered to join. Thus
was born Company I of the U.S. Twelfth Infantry Regiment.[75] Despite
Wotherspoon's earlier doubts about Proctor's scheme, this unit, comprising fifty-five Chiricahuas, achieved great success.[76]

One of Company I's primary tasks was the construction, completed by the end of 1891, of a village situated on higher ground in
more healthful surroundings.[77] Seventy-five houses were built, as well
as a combination mess hall and kitchen, a new hospital, and barracks
designated for Company I. These buildings represented a slight improvement in the Chiricahuas' lot. In addition, the children's education
progressed well, encouraging the Massachusetts Indian Association to
continue its support of this endeavor.[78] Yet, such efforts did little to
turn the overall tide of misfortune experienced by the Chiricahuas.

In late March 1893, Charles Painter journeyed to Mount Vernon.
Conferring with Wotherspoon, he learned that no more could be done
for the prisoners. Painter therefore concluded that the time had arrived
to settle the Chiricahuas' future permanently and that the Indian Rights
Association was the organization to initiate this action. Consequently,
he urged the Indian Rights Association's executive committee to give
President Harrison and Secretary of War Proctor no peace until the captives were sent where they could support themselves. In addition, on
October 11, 1893, Wotherspoon addressed the Lake Mohonk Conference, advising attendees that in terms of Chiricahua assimilation into
white society, these Indians were, in their present circumstances,
"about at the limit where they can be carried." He recommended that

the Chiricahuas be sent to North Carolina, given individual farms, and "left to work out their own salvation."

Thus, in December, accompanied by Richard Henry Pratt, Wotherspoon visited the proposed Cherokee location for yet another examination. On December 14, Wotherspoon reported that although it was previously thought that the Cherokee offer was best for the Chiricahuas, renewed scrutiny revealed that only one-eighth of the proffered parcel could be cultivated. Of course, the officers made this observation when snow covered the landscape. Not surprisingly, the Indian Rights Association protested Wotherspoon's change of mind, a futile remonstration in light of current congressional refusal to fund any Chiricahua relocation proposal.[79]

Despite such setbacks, at the beginning of 1894, supporters of Indian rights intensified their efforts to resolve the Chiricahua problem. From their perspective, they had good reason to increase their level of activism because in March 1893, Grover Cleveland had returned to the White House. Both the president and his secretary of war, Daniel Lamont, initially displayed "no inclination to settle the matter." Although Painter demanded that the Indians be removed to North Carolina immediately, Lamont simply waited for the Interior Department to retake custody of the Chiricahuas. Yet, by February's end, doubtless feeling besieged by Indian rights organizations' pleas, Lamont charged Captain George W. Davis with the task of arriving at an effective resolution of the question.[80] Given the degree of discomfiture experienced by military personnel at the hands of Indian activists, Davis's charge came not a moment too soon.

3

Vigorous Protests Are Raised Against Locating the Chiricahuas in Oklahoma

▼   ▼   ▼

*B*efore his transfer to General Howard's staff on February 17, 1894, Captain Wotherspoon reported that since September 1886, 246 Chiricahuas had died in captivity, a death rate far exceeding that of "any nation in the world." Of the slightly more than 300 Chiricahuas then in War Department custody, 165 were prisoners of war by virtue of having been born into captivity. In addition, more than "two hundred surviving women and children were being held for crimes largely committed by men." Under the circumstances, the Chiricahua captives became an onerous stigma on an otherwise benign government that found it increasingly difficult to justify maintaining custody of them.[1]

Therefore, suffering acute embarrassment caused in large measure by the incessant pressure that Indian rights activists exerted, the War Department badly desired to have them transferred to Interior's jurisdiction.[2] With an eye toward this goal, General Howard visited Mount Vernon Barracks on March 24. After conferring with Lieutenant Charles C. Ballou, the Chiricahuas' new officer-in-charge, and his assistant, Lieutenant Allyn K. Capron, he suggested that the Interior Department take charge of the Chiricahuas as expeditiously as possible.[3] However, because government bureaucracy in general—and the legislative branch in particular—were far more attuned to southwestern desires than

Captain Allyn Capron. *Courtesy Fort Sill Museum.*

Mount Vernon Chiricahua wishes regarding relocation, the transfer was not to be.[4]

Even so, a potential opportunity to relocate the Chiricahuas elsewhere soon presented itself, although the captives would remain under the War Department's jurisdiction as prisoners of war. By 1894, for reasons of economy, the War Department evinced a desire to abandon such installations as Mount Vernon Barracks because they no longer served national defense needs. Swiftly seizing on this situation, General Howard recommended the Chiricahuas' removal to a reservation in the West.[5] His superior, Major General John M. Schofield, the army's commanding general, agreed but stipulated that none of them be removed to Arizona, New Mexico, or Texas, "where resentment toward the captives was too strong to tolerate a return to those areas."[6]

This time, though, the War Department insisted on only one location: Oklahoma. By spring, military officials were convinced that of all installations, only Fort Sill satisfied the criteria of appropriate climate and sufficient agricultural land for permanent resettlement. Entrenching themselves to combat any vigorous opposition that might arise, certain key officers prepared to wage a strenuous campaign that ensured the Chiricahuas' removal to this site. In the event of opposition, the argument could be made that Fort Sill not only contained a garrison sufficient for their control, but also was nearly 600 miles away from the region in which the former belligerents had perpetrated their criminal acts.[7]

Consequently, army officials vigorously lobbied for Fort Sill as their sole objective in Chiricahua removal. On May 19, the Senate subcommittee dealing with military appropriations advised Captain George W. Davis, military secretary to Secretary of War Daniel S. Lamont, that members had inserted legislation in the fiscal 1895 army appropriation bill that directed the secretary of war to place the Chiricahuas at Fort Sill.[8] Upon learning of this provision, Miles, ever on the alert to prevent the slightest tarnishing of his image among Arizonans, as well as congressional opposition to Chiricahua resettlement at Fort Sill, suggested revision of the proposed legislation so that it authorized the secretary of war to remove the Chiricahuas to any installation he might select.[9]

This recommendation came not a moment too soon. Shortly after Miles received the original proposal, Congress amended it to exclude Oklahoma, thus leaving the original 1879 proscription intact.[10] Word of this legislative revision reached military officials at the same time Miles's proposal crossed Lamont's desk. To salvage the military's Chiricahua resettlement plan, the secretary hastily dispatched to the Hill emissaries who assuaged the House and Senate military affairs panels. Officers chosen for this task assured them that the secretary of war had no desire to be coerced into apportioning the Geronimo belligerents among various military installations or to release them from prison. Rather, the army intended to place the women and children at various posts, where they would remain under observation.[11] Thus appeased, committee members supported the secretary's proposal. As revised, the amendment authorized Lamont to remove the prisoners to any military reservation he deemed appropriate. Including this provision, the army appropriation bill went into conference in early July.

That the military proceeded if not a little covertly, then in a prudent and timely manner concerning the preservation of its plan to relocate the Chiricahuas at Fort Sill was amply demonstrated by the furious floor fight over Amendment 19 that followed in the House after the conference report on the army appropriation bill was submitted for approval on July 28. Miles had correctly anticipated the subsequent objections and obstructionist tactics that resulted from this revision. Indeed, the debate that began in the House chamber on that hot and humid July day was no less steamy and stifling than the suffocating and stultifying weather conditions outside the Capitol.

Importuned by Arizona territorial delegate Marcus Smith, Oklahoma territorial delegate Dennis T. Flynn immediately called the House's attention to the conference revision of Amendment 19. Originally, Flynn explained, Fort Sill was designated the location where all the Chiricahuas, generally acknowledged as "Geronimo's band of murderers," would be sent. In the Senate, Flynn continued, legislators offered an amendment that omitted any mention of Fort Sill and only authorized the Indians' resettlement by the secretary of war at locations not forbidden by existing law. But, Flynn said, in a manner unknown to him, House conferees saw fit to delete the Senate's language. Instead, the matter was left "discretionary with the Secretary of War as to where these Indians shall be removed."[12] Imploring House members not to pass the conference measure, Flynn pleaded with his colleagues not to "place upon the many feeble settlers who are now striving to eke out an existence in that new country . . . that band of Indians whose records are well known in every schoolhouse" throughout the land.

At this juncture, Joseph H. Outhwaite, chairman of the House Committee on Military Affairs, defended the measure, skillfully maneuvering around Flynn's objections. In the first place, Outhwaite said, this amendment did not specify any particular place, such as Oklahoma, to which the Chiricahuas might be removed. Furthermore, its only purpose was to relocate those—namely women and children—who posed no danger. They would be sent to various military installations throughout the United States and would not be placed on Indian reservations. Supervised by army officers, they would have an "opportunity like human beings to make their own way and to establish themselves in life." Were the secretary of war to "deem it proper and wise to send one or two families" to a military installation in Oklahoma, the bill authorized him to do so. As far as Outhwaite was concerned, Oklahoma was "certainly no more sacred than any other part of the country."

Flynn insisted the measure amounted to nothing less than a recision of the 1879 act prohibiting the removal of Arizona Indians to the Indian Territory. Outhwaite, who with great adroitness carefully made the distinction between an Indian reservation and a military reservation, emphatically replied in good conscience that Amendment 19 did not repeal this law. Of course, Outhwaite added sardonically, if his colleagues considered it appropriate to continue to confine women and children "simply because they are the women and children of men who committed crimes many years ago, and that is the only reason they are there," then the House would defeat the conference report.[13]

No sooner was this said than Marcus Smith, burning with rage and indignation, leaped to the floor and launched a vituperative rejoinder. Smith lodged his protest against this measure both in the "name of the murders" committed by them and in the "name of humanity." Were this provision passed and "these Indians scattered, my word for it, they will come together and renew their depredations. . . . Tell me," Smith demanded, "that they will not come back!" Had they "truly been subjected to the horrors" that Outhwaite described, they would return "all the more aggrieved." Sympathy might be better expended, Smith believed, upon those "poor white people who will certainly become the victims of these murderous Indians if you allow them to go back into that country." As time would soon reveal, Smith little realized that he had, at that moment, unwittingly played into the hands of his hero, Nelson Miles.

Of course, Smith made no distinction between the noncombatant Chiricahuas and Geronimo's belligerent followers. Outhwaite attempted to differentiate between the two groups by explaining that one of the assurances given was that the latter would not be removed. This served only to intensify Smith's unreasonable tirade. Demurring further, Smith remarked that "this honest," though "mistaken sentiment of sympathy" for Geronimo's people would again "force that calamity" on southwesterners, consequently sending them out once more "upon that beautiful crow hunt," in a renewed attempt to recapture Apache Indians on Sonora's mountain fastnesses. According to Smith, there never "lived a more desperate, bloodthirsty, cunning villain than the Apache Indian . . . in all the history of Indian warfare." Geronimo's band was "imbrued in the best blood of American men, women and children, not one of whom ever did him or his any harm."

Unfortunately, Smith maintained, when Geronimo's adherents "were captured and brought back they were not taken to the reservation and made a proper example of." All of them "ought to have been hanged as a plain warning to others that when they violated the law," they would receive the same penalty. Instead, determined "to set these Indians to cultivating some rocky reservation," Outhwaite proposed "an appropriation for that purpose!" Outhwaite simply had no "idea how that suggestion strikes a man from that portion of the country. An appropriation to put an Apache Indian to work!" Smith then exclaimed, "My conscience! One dollar" spent on such a ludicrous enterprise was "thrown away: a cent put into it is squandered." Smith then asked his colleagues not to permit the conference report's passage. Had this piece of legislation been "met directly as an independent measure," it would have been defeated. Those who supported the amendment were well aware that as a separate proposition, it would fail to receive House approval. Thus they placed it in the army appropriation bill. Concluding his remarks, Smith said that those interested in having this legislation passed certainly "knew that this was their safest course. They took the surest route to their end."

At this, John A.T. Hull, one of the conference report's floor managers, rushed to assist Outhwaite with his defense of Amendment 19. Rationally remonstrating against Flynn's and Smith's arguments, Hull began his rejoinder by explaining to his colleagues that Flynn had expressed satisfaction with that version of the amendment originally accepted by the Senate. Hull then suggested a reason for Flynn's former position. As initially passed, Amendment 19 prevented the secretary of war from resettling the Chiricahuas at any location forbidden by law. Oklahoma fell under this statutory prohibition. Elucidating further, Hull noted that Flynn would assent to the measure only if none of the Chiricahuas were sent to his territory. Therefore, the House would not "act from very high motives" were it to limit the secretary's discretion "so that he may send these Indians to any place in the United States except Oklahoma."[14] Besides, the cause of humanity dictated that the time had come for remedial action on behalf of the noncombatants— "not the old criminal who was sent there as a punishment, but the great number of children born into captivity." Actually, none of "these criminals, the old Indian prisoners," would be removed from Alabama. Agreeing with Hull, Outhwaite explained that the War Department did not "wish to keep over two hundred women and children in prison all their lives because of the sins of their fathers." With the debate concluded, Outhwaite demanded a vote on the conference report, which the House approved.[15]

During the first week of August, President Grover Cleveland signed into law the army appropriation bill. With its passage, the War Department began preparing for the Chiricahuas' removal from Alabama. Yet so narrow was the military's victory that despite its triumph, the War Department moved gingerly in implementing its Chiricahua resettlement plan. In mid-August, George W. Davis advised Miles that

Secretary Lamont desired Miles's views on how best to carry out the Chiricahuas' relocation because the general's familiarity with Apaches and knowledge of the Indian problem, especially regarding that aspect debated by Flynn and Smith, entitled his opinion and recommendations to special consideration.

Although the secretary of war now had a broader range of authority under which to act in the matter, assurances given to the House Military Committee chairman during its deliberations on the army appropriation bill conference report were still to be respected, insofar as practicable. However, Davis noted that although his superiors believed a general resolution of the difficulty might be achieved in the manner outlined by Outhwaite, the War Department was not bound by assurances given to individual congressmen.[16] Indeed, in a report later prepared by Davis, the major revealed just how broadly the army intended to interpret Outhwaite's remarks regarding Amendment 19. Essentially, Davis explained, the August 2, 1894, Army Appropriation Act repealed the 1879 prohibition against relocating the Chiricahuas to Indian Territory.[17] For the moment, though, Davis directed Miles to conduct a thorough examination of all aspects related to the relocation issue. Furthermore, Miles was to send an officer to Alabama to fully examine the Chiricahuas' situation at Mount Vernon Barracks. Miles was then to forward his recommendations, along with the information gleaned from the inquiry, on how the statute might best be executed.[18]

Cautiously biding his time, Miles wired Davis for authority to send Captain Marion P. Maus, a participant in the late Geronimo hostilities, and Lieutenant Hugh L. Scott, who had experience with the Kiowas and Comanches, to Mount Vernon Barracks to conduct the Alabama portion of the inquiry. Their goal would be to recommend that a certain number of the Chiricahuas be sent to Fort Sill.[19] On August 29, 1894, Maus and Scott arrived at Mount Vernon Barracks and conferred with the Chiricahua prisoners. Maus reported them as "most anxious for a change." They desired to go "where they can cultivate the soil and follow the foot steps of the white men." Maus believed a great change had taken place in their attitude. Their "savage spirit" appeared broken; their fierce countenance of long ago was no more.[20]

Chatto and Loco, both of whom participated in the Apache wars, made two of the more poignant pleas. "If anything I could say . . . would hurry up the farms," said Chatto, "I wish it would. Most of the old people are dead." Once Miles referred to him as "brother." Chatto clearly remembered that. Perhaps the general had already selected a suitable site for them. "None of us like this country." Loco said he was "tired and sick, but since I heard what you say about a farm, I am getting better." He desired land where he could live and raise crops at some other location. "We thought when we came here we would do well," but most had died of sickness since coming to Alabama.[21]

Despite their circumstances, the Chiricahua prisoners presented a "respectable and industrious appearance." They lived in a village of seventy-four well-built houses constantly maintained in a neat and clean manner. The local inhabitants neither feared them nor lodged complaints against them. Still, there was every reason why the Chiricahuas should go where they might "become useful and progressive citizens." Since first taken into captivity, "their record . . . has been excellent for such a class of people." Many of the incorrigibles were now deceased. Yet, numerous others were born after the conclusion of hostilities who, perpetrating no harm, suffered equally with the guilty. Discontented with their situation and fearing an imminent demise, the Chiricahuas pleaded for removal from Alabama to safeguard their children from further episodes of fatal diseases.

Maus believed they had "cause to fear when they have suffered in eight years a loss of 262." As to a place of removal, Maus recommended Fort Sill. This post was situated on good land with an adequate water supply. Because "his wide knowledge of the Indian character and great experience eminently fit him for such duty," Maus also suggested that Hugh Scott be placed in charge of them.[22]

No sooner had Maus submitted his report than Miles quickly forwarded his recommendations to Davis. "Congress having passed the law authorizing the Secretary to move the Indians," Miles believed this removal should be executed according to the statute's "general purpose and language" rather than attempt compliance with "assurances made by any . . . members of Congress" upon the House floor. Indeed, Miles had already carefully read those materials on the subject previously sent by Davis. Miles paid special attention to remarks made during the course of House debate on Chiricahua removal. There can be no question that the general particularly focused on the objections of Marcus Smith. Taking a page from the vituperative Arizonan, Miles deftly used the territorial delegate's argument to good advantage in advancing his own interests in the Chiricahua relocation matter. For to Miles, it was quite obvious that "the assurances of individual members of Congress could not be carried out with safety." Simply, Miles believed "it would be gross injustice and refined cruelty" to separate "innocent Indian women and children from . . . their kindred and tribe . . . and scatter them over the country at different military posts" where they would be cast among those unable to speak their language and to "whom they could not communicate their wants or necessities." Thus, were there "anything that would make their fathers, brothers and sons desperate outlaws, it would be such an act of injustice."

Besides, the law was now upon the statute books, and the military's only responsibility was to execute this law as it saw fit. Therefore, the army's sole constraint was to carry out its mandate in a "faithful and judicious manner." In this respect, the Chiricahuas were to be treated with absolute justice. Officers were to do everything possible to improve these Indians' condition. Of course, military personnel were to take the appropriate precautions to prevent Chiricahua disaffection or escape. Had Congress's intention been to scatter the Indians on military reservations throughout the nation, the law could have been so amended.[23]

Of course, Miles's superiors were initially a bit more cautious. Schofield suggested to Lamont that the Chiricahuas be sent immediately to Fort Sill "to be encamped there in the vicinity of the post under the protection and control of the garrison" so that neither danger nor injury could be inflicted upon anyone through their presence. After more considered deliberation, the Chiricahuas could then be relocated from that point either to one or several installations where, "under the control of the troops," all the aims intended by the "Act of Congress providing for their removal may be satisfactorily accomplished."[24] Subsequently, Davis invited Maus's attention to Schofield's recommendation and, counseling the captain not to become anxious over any possibility that the plan to remove the Chiricahuas to Fort Sill might be quashed by congressional opposition, explained the real reason behind the general's suggestion. "In procuring the final order for the movement," Davis said military officials purposely constructed its language to indicate that Fort Sill was only an expedient. Therefore, referring to Outhwaite's assurances and the outcry made in Congress, Davis said a later dispersal was not precluded. If they had to, War Department functionaries could still declare that Fort Sill was not the Chiricahuas' final destination.[25]

In truth, neither Miles nor his superiors had any intention of relocating the Chiricahuas to a military reservation other than Fort Sill. Although he would never know the extent of the role played by his hero-savior of Arizona regarding Chiricahua removal to this post, Marcus

Smith's prophetic assessment of the impact of Amendment 19 was quite correct. For the War Department most definitely knew what it was about. Accordingly, it did indeed take the safest and surest route to the realization of its Chiricahua relocation project.

By mid-September, Secretary Lamont approved Miles's recommendations.[26] Early on the morning of September 18, General Oliver O. Howard prepared the order for the Chiricahuas' relocation to Fort Sill.[27] Lieutenant Scott was to take immediate charge of the Chiricahuas upon their arrival at that post.[28] Upon receiving a copy of this directive, Miles instructed the commandant at Fort Sill to provide for the Indians' health and welfare.[29] Later that month, the Chiricahuas were issued winter clothing, food rations, and other necessary supplies for both their journey to and later use at Fort Sill. On October 2, 1894, the Chiricahua Apache prisoners of war departed Mount Vernon Barracks, Alabama.[30] They arrived at Rush Springs, Indian Territory, on the morning of October 4 en route to the military installation that would be their home for the next twenty years. They remained overnight at Rush Springs to recover from the initial leg of their journey.[31]

During their first night on the open Oklahoma prairie, a whole new generation of Chiricahuas, unaccustomed to such cacophony, encountered the howls of coyotes plaintively echoing about the landscape. Yet, there were those among them who dimly remembered such doleful cries. Reminded thus of times long past and places far away, a number of the old women began to cry. In a sense, they felt the people had come home at last.[32]

CHAPTER

4

The Chiricahuas Settle in
at Fort Sill

▼   ▼   ▼

*W*elcomed the next morning, October 5, 1894, by the Kiowas and Comanches, who helped them transport their property to Cache Creek, the Chiricahuas proceeded from Rush Springs to Fort Sill, arriving there later that day.[1] Although many of them walked to their new home, they arrived encouraged and in good spirits. Many expressed pleasure at being there.[2] Indeed, Scott had not deceived them. As he promised, they saw the mountains. Of course, "they weren't tall like ours but they were mountains." No one had to climb the trees to view the sun. Furthermore, the water flowing in the creeks was "clear sparkling mountain water."[3] At their new home, the Chiricahuas breathed more freely,[4] as attested to by the observation that the "smell of sage was good to us."[5]

By October's end, the War Department received reports that the Chiricahuas lived well and appeared "quite content with the change." In all of Oklahoma, Fort Sill was certainly the best possible site. Other military reservations possessed defects such as overly sandy soil unsuitable for agriculture, and a white population that pressed "around on every side," so that "whiskey could be sold in any quantity." By any standard, therefore, Fort Sill was most definitely a superior location for the Chiricahuas' establishment because it was "absolutely removed from any bad influences." Furthermore, by engaging in agricultural endeavors, the Indians could accomplish much at this post. Cattle raising would also be certainly profitable for the Chiricahuas. One thousand head would not be too much to start with. Agricultural planning would take into consideration that large quantities of oats, corn, and other produce could be raised; in time the prisoners might even supply the post with forage. Elated over the Chiricahuas' future prospects, officers involved with their resettlement at Fort Sill optimistically believed the captives would remain contentedly at the military reservation. Within three years, they predicted, the Chiricahuas would "be in a prosperous condition, and in time very well off."[6]

Throughout October, the Chiricahuas busily prepared for winter. They immediately undertook well and road construction and cleared grounds in the timber bottoms for winter camps.[7] Unfortunately, the Chiricahuas' Alabama dwellings, disassembled for train transit to Fort Sill, were inadvertently sidetracked to a New Orleans freight yard, where, in a mysterious conflagration, they burned to the rail line.[8] Consequently, fabrication of suitable habitations became a prime concern. Ironically, although the Chiricahuas had dwelt in houses for nearly eight years and learned to "like some kind of roof," initial proposals for replacement lodgings suggested that "conical wall tents without hoods, and the fresh arbors" that the Chiricahuas proficiently assembled, were far more conducive to health than the typical frame houses because the latter were extremely difficult to ventilate properly. Furthermore, the frame houses would prove "exceedingly cold in winter and hot in summer." A second benefit to traditional Chiricahua dwellings was that the "wick-i-up can be burned and its site thoroughly disinfected."[9]

In addition, the Chiricahuas were counted twice daily. While given every reasonable liberty, they generally labored at quarrying stone, filling lime kilns, and cutting timber. Plans for future endeavors included preparing for a successful spring planting. A large, arable plain containing a sizable quantity of bottomland was located on the military reservation, between Cache and Medicine Bluff Creeks. Before winter set in, this land had to be plowed and sowed with oats and other crops. Once this was accomplished, attention could be focused on the purchase and development of a Chiricahua cattle herd. Scott believed this enterprise would become their only viable economic mainstay.[10]

Despite such glowing prognostications for the Chiricahuas' future, a nearly insurmountable obstacle loomed on the horizon: who would fund the various programs outlined for Chiricahua "civilization" and acculturation? In the ensuing argument between Scott and the quartermaster general's office, Scott, a shrewd and capable officer, intimated that no future progress could be expected and, indeed, that sharp reversals with "grave consequences" would result unless the quartermaster general supplied those provisions that Scott understood were not covered by the $15,000 allocated by Congress in the fiscal 1895 army appropriation bill.[11] To ensure the success of his Chiricahua acculturation program, Scott was not above utilizing strong-arm tactics, especially in this case, because the quartermaster general believed that all expenses incurred on behalf of these Indians should come out of the $15,000 appropriation.[12]

Scott believed his aggressive approach to the problem was necessary because the military planned to transfer custody of the Chiricahuas to the Bureau of Indian Affairs sometime within the next two years, when all could feel certain that the prisoners were "no more dangerous than other Indians in the neighborhood."[13] Forcing the matter to a head, Scott advised his superiors in the Department of the Missouri that he had suspended purchasing any materials with money from the special fund until a decision was reached on the quartermaster general's ruling. Scott believed this ruling inconsistent with the legislation that passed the special Chiricahua appropriation (in addition to other funds designated for their benefit).[14]

Scott also maintained that because the cost of subsistence, clothing, and transportation had totaled more than $20,000 the previous year, he did not understand how cattle, lumber, and seeds might also be purchased to help settle these Indians. Scott reminded his superiors that the $15,000 appropriation was in addition to those sums expended under the usual allocation granted the secretary of war. Were Lamont to uphold the quartermaster general's ruling, then another plan would have to be devised for advancing these Indians. Otherwise, the results that Miles expected from Scott could not be accomplished. Therefore, the sooner Scott could secure a "ruling according to the meaning of the Act the better it will be for all parties concerned."[15] Failure to obtain such, Scott explained, would cause dissatisfaction among the prisoners.[16]

Perusing the correspondence generated by this issue, Miles fixed upon that section of Scott's entreaties dealing with prisoner disaffection and began to do some arm-twisting of his own. Writing to George W. Davis, Miles trotted out his favorite threat and advised the major that if the quartermaster general's decision was allowed to stand, the

Chiricahuas would "all be on the warpath in Arizona or New Mexico inside of twelve months." Had the military forgotten that several hundred thousand dollars were expended to "subjugate them and put them where they now are?" Furthermore, the citizens of these territories spent "millions of dollars before they were rid of them." Therefore, from the standpoint of security, the only alternative was to not only "hold them under close military surveillance," but also to provide them with food, clothing, and other care until the time the government's military arm could be safely withdrawn.[17]

No further prodding was necessary. On November 10, Secretary Lamont revoked the quartermaster general's ruling.[18] On November 12, George D. Ruggles, the adjutant general, advised Richard N. Batchelder, the quartermaster general, that transportation, rations, clothing, and medical attention for the Chiricahuas were to be charged to army appropriations other than the $15,000 allocation for their acculturation.[19] Deeply gratified by the successful outcome of this issue, Scott approached his labors among these Indians with renewed vigor as 1894 drew to a close.[20]

Severely cold, dry, and blustery conditions ushered in the dreary January of 1895. Temperatures that plummeted to zero caused Scott to wax anxious over the Chiricahuas' temporary shelter of tents and wickiups. Fortunately, there were no complaints of suffering. Located in the timbered areas, the villages were well protected. Even so, Scott considered suitable housing the most serious challenge immediately confronting his charges. As the new year unfolded, the lieutenant resolved to make this problem his first priority. Despite a subordinate's earlier suggestion that for health considerations alone, the Chiricahuas were better off in their wickiups, Scott finally opted for dwellings of frame construction.[21] Beginning January 1, Scott engaged a master carpenter to manufacture window and door frames. Although Scott estimated that the Chiricahuas' housing needs required the fabrication of seventy-three structures, he initially contracted for lumber sufficient to construct only twenty houses.[22] Each dwelling consisted of two rooms, 196 square feet each, divided by a covered passageway. Walls were constructed of pickets laid on sills, which, in turn, rested on a loose foundation. Each house also had two doors, four windows, and tile chimneys.[23] Most of the materials needed for the dwellings' erection were shipped in and used in conjunction with timber already cut on the military reserve. The buildings were constructed on various Chiricahua village sites. Scott spent much of 1895 overseeing completion of this task.

Chiricahua wickiups, Fort Sill. *Courtesy Fort Sill Museum.*

Numerous delays during the first half of 1895 forestalled completion of the Chiricahua housing project. Because the winter of 1894–
1895 was not only the coldest and windiest but also the stormiest one
"known here for many years past," the fuel supplies issued to the Chiricahuas by the chief quartermaster were exhausted by mid-February.[24]
Rectifying this situation required the withdrawal of a "considerable
portion of the able-bodied men . . . from regular work in order to cut
and haul the necessary fuel."[25]

Another chore that considerably curtailed the time scheduled for
housing construction was soil preparation for cultivation. Had plows
been available and the ground not so hard due to excessive lack of moisture, this task could have been accomplished by the end of the previous
fall.[26] Despite these difficulties, Scott managed to have 100 acres of sod
broken for planting. Of this, fifty acres were harrowed with the disk and
sowed with oats. Ten acres were utilized for a "garden and about twenty
acres sowed with corn on the sod." Of course, if rain did not come soon,
there would be no harvest. Even so, despite a potential crop failure,
Scott consoled himself with the fact that at least the land was in good
enough condition for the following farming season.[27] Fortunately, during June, several good rains fell, "sufficient to ensure the grass crop and
probably to make hay."[28]

Chiricahuas milling pickets at their sawmill in preparation for constructing their houses at Fort Sill, 1895. *Courtesy Fort Sill Museum.*

Picket house construction used for Chiricahua housing at Fort Sill.
Courtesy Fort Sill Museum.

Still, Scott reported some progress in the area of housing construction. Eight houses were "erected near a spring not far from the post for Geronimo and his immediate relatives." Scott now believed the time had come to "locate the houses for the others in various parts of the reservation near springs and suitable arable land and wood." Scott said such building should be undertaken because he believed the Chiricahuas' "present contentment and freedom from breaches of discipline" suggested that this endeavor entailed little risk.[29] Despite these gains, building continued at a slow pace. In June, the Chiricahuas expended a great deal of time and labor erecting fences around recently planted crops.[30]

While attending to housing and agricultural matters, Scott implemented his Chiricahua cattle program in mid-June. Unfortunately, this operation did not get off to a good start. Bids for cattle were opened and subsequently rejected as exorbitant. Scott later procured cattle at a more reasonable cost from an individual he considered trustworthy.[31] Secretary Lamont subsequently approved this action.[32] At a cost of $10,271, a total of 580 Hereford cattle consisting of 560 heifers and 20 bulls were delivered to Fort Sill by August 1. These animals were later distributed among the Chiricahuas on an individual basis.[33] This done, Scott doubtless believed that as far as this aspect of the Chiricahuas' welfare was concerned, he could settle down to establishing the herd on a profitable basis. But alas, no sooner had most of the Herefords been paid for than some of the herd began to sicken and die. Believing the contractor to have defaulted on the terms of the purchase

Naiche's village, located near Four Mile Crossing, Fort Sill.
Courtesy Fort Sill Museum.

agreement, an irate Scott demanded an investigation. Pending the results of this inquiry,[34] Scott requested authority, later granted, to hold in abeyance any further payments.[35]

At the secretary of war's request,[36] the secretary of agriculture, Julius S. Morton, launched an investigation of the mysterious illness. He ordered an inspector to conduct an inquiry at Fort Sill.[37] Early that September, Agriculture Department inspector Albert Dean discovered the cause of the current cattle malaise. *Boophilus bovus,* or the southern cattle tick, was responsible for the splenetic cattle fever, otherwise known as Texas fever, suffered by the Chiricahuas' Herefords. An otherwise healthy herd became infected when they were placed in the same pen occupied by an already contaminated semi-monthly beef issue shipped to Fort Sill from southern Texas. Should there be future cattle purchases, Dean suggested that these transactions be made in the open market from those parts of the country where cattle were immune to this disease.[38] Fortunately for the Chiricahuas, this incident proved only a minor setback.

Even so, the care and safekeeping of the Chiricahuas' cattle was the most pressing problem for some time to come. As summer became a mere memory, a not-so-benign fall unleashed upon southwestern Oklahoma severe storms that arrived earlier than at any time since Fort Sill's establishment. This weather had a decidedly disruptive effect on the cattle project. In sheer frustration, Scott noted that the cattle refused to stay where they were placed. Every storm caused them to scatter. He therefore devised a plan whereby the herd would be driven into deeply timbered ravines, where they would remain in the event meteorological elements turned tempestuous. Were the weather favorable, they would "not get so far away before daylight" and thus could be "more easily checked." It is clear Scott well understood that if the Chiricahuas were to enjoy future economic success, his first priority must be to preserve the cattle herd. Thus he spared "no pains . . . to accomplish this result."[39]

This project was of vital importance because Oklahoma's climate was such that "only a few special food products" could be successfully "cultivated in average years. Stock raising must be a principal reliance." In five years, Captain Scott predicted, the Chiricahuas would "have as many thousands of cattle as they now have hundreds and the increase should support them in comfort." Even so, the soil was fertile and promised good crops of corn, especially South African kaffir corn, "recently introduced with marked success in the semi-arid regions of

Winter range at Fort Sill used for grazing the Chiricahuas' cattle herd, 1897.
Courtesy Fort Sill Museum.

the West."[40] Among its particular advantages, kaffir corn was drought
resistant and contained the same nutritive value and ease of digestion
for cattle as a mixed combination of cracked corn and chopped hay.[41]

Not only did the bad weather hamper the cattle and crop endeavors, but it also put a damper on any quick completion of the Chiricahua housing project. Still, seventeen houses were constructed that
fall. Within the next year, the Chiricahuas erected one comfortable
dwelling for each of some seventy families. These dwellings were arranged in "groups of four to six" and distributed across many miles of
scenic hill and valley country. By the end of 1895, Scott noted that the
Chiricahuas, "formerly so wild and intractable," made great strides toward establishing themselves on a self-sustaining basis. Thus, they
possessed a "better opportunity for quickly attaining the end sought
than any Indians" he knew of.[42] Furthermore, the improvement in
health induced by a "salubrious climate" alone justified the "wisdom
and humanity of their removal to this Territory."[43] Indeed, as Blossom
Haozous later poignantly observed, the climate, surroundings, and
mountains were "much better than the swamps in Alabama; the people were much better when they got to Oklahoma."[44] Yet although
progress was made and there transpired no "insubordination or man-
ifestation of disposition to molest the settlers or to return to their
former haunts in Arizona and Mexico," military officials believed the

Chiricahuas required army supervision for an additional year or two, or at least until all "danger of their outbreak is passed" and people inhabiting the region adjacent to Fort Sill were convinced of their immunity from harm.[45]

Although the military deemed such supervision expedient for a while longer, so confidant were they of a promising future for these Indians that the War Department began to look toward the time it could relinquish control of the Chiricahuas. Major Davis therefore suggested that a thoroughly developed Chiricahua policy be devised by both the War and Interior Departments. As soon as no military necessity existed for holding them captive, the War Department would terminate the Chiricahuas' prisoner-of-war status. Their supervision would naturally fall to the Indian Office. Davis strongly recommended that an annual examination of the Chiricahuas' situation be conducted by a special Indian Agent. This agent would then advise the Indian Office of the War Department's policy toward the Chiricahuas. Interior officials would then consult with the military so that the War Department could ensure that its policy comported with Interior's jurisdictional procedures for other tribal groups. This would allow Interior to more readily retake custody of the Chiricahuas when the time arrived.[46] During the course of the next four years, a number of the military's efforts on behalf of these Indians would encourage just such a change.

Blossom Wrattan Haozous, mother of famed Chiricahua artist Allan Houser, as a young girl at Fort Sill. *Courtesy Fort Sill Museum.*

CHAPTER

5

Enlargement of Fort Sill for the Chiricahuas' Eventual Allotment

▼   ▼   ▼

*A*s 1896 began, the initial item on the War Department's Chiricahua prisoner-of-war agenda was to implement their release. Once freed, the Indians were to be placed under the Interior Department's jurisdiction. In January, George W. Davis informed Hugh Scott that Davis's superiors believed the Chiricahuas' status as prisoners of war must end soon. Were conditions to remain satisfactory, there was no doubt that the Chiricahuas could be turned over to Interior by June 30, 1897. With this goal in mind, the War Department advised Interior of its views. Military officials urged Interior to send a representative to Fort Sill to examine the Chiricahuas' situation. During this investigation, the representative was to familiarize himself with the efforts made "to bring these Indians forward to a condition where they will be self supporting" and then formulate proposals respecting their eventual discharge. The agent would then forward his recommendations to Interior, which would in turn would communicate them to the War Department. Furthermore, Davis said, a matter of extreme urgency requiring immediate resolution had arisen: the area of Fort Sill occupied by the Chiricahuas had to be sequestered in such a manner that it would be acknowledged as their property in the event of certain contingencies.[1]

Indeed, such an exigency had surfaced several years before the Chiricahuas' arrival at Fort Sill. Article 11, Section Seven, of the October 21, 1867, Treaty of Medicine Lodge stipulated that the Kiowas and Comanches agreed not to oppose military installations already erected on lands both formerly held and currently possessed by them.[2] Situated on the Kiowa and Comanche Reservation, Fort Sill was founded by the army on January 8, 1869.[3] Because Fort Sill replaced Fort Cobb, which at the time of the Medicine Lodge Treaty was an active post thirty miles east of the reservation's western border, the War Department interpreted the compact to mean that Kiowa and Comanche consent to its establishment was unnecessary.[4] Consequently, the War Department effected this station's legal formation on October 7, 1871.[5] Even so, title to the land on which Fort Sill stood remained vested in the Kiowa and Comanche Reservation because the War Department, when it created Fort Sill, believed that, in time, this facility might well be deemed unnecessary and thus abandoned. However, on October 6, 1892, in conformity with provisions contained in the 1887 Dawes Severalty Act, the Jerome Commission, whose principal task was the liquidation of the Kiowa and Comanche Reservation, concluded—under somewhat questionable circumstances—an accord known as the Jerome Agreement with the Kiowas and Comanches. This agreement, pending congressional approval, provided for both individual land allotments and the sale of surplus reservation acreage.[6] Legally, therefore, accession by Congress to the Jerome Agreement's terms would cause Fort Sill to become the War Department's property in fee simple. This is precisely what happened. Legislation passed on June 6, 1900, ratifying the Jerome Agreement stipulated that none of the surplus acreage occupied by the military—in this case, Fort Sill—would be opened to homesteading.[7] Such a change potentially jeopardized Chiricahua rights to Fort Sill in that military officials might still find a use for this post and remove them. If ever an opportunity presented itself to preclude such a possibility, that moment had arrived. Perhaps, before Congress ratified the Jerome Agreement, the Kiowas and Comanches might be persuaded to part with that portion of the Fort Sill military reserve designated to be the Chiricahuas' permanent home upon release from prisoner-of-war status.

Accordingly, on January 6, 1896, Secretary of War Lamont advised Interior Secretary Hoke Smith that in view of the War Department's policy of establishing the Chiricahuas on a self-sustaining basis, the army had no desire to control them any longer than military considerations demanded. Because supervision of the Chiricahuas would naturally devolve upon Interior, it was only proper that Smith be informed of War Department policy in this regard. Lamont suggested that an Indian Service officer be detailed to Fort Sill to consult with the Chiricahuas' officer-in-charge about future plans for these Indians. Interior's representative would report any matters of interest to that department, because, in all probability, it would again have charge of these people within a year or two. Lamont suggested that June 30, 1897, be designated as the target date for Interior's takeover, at which time Fort Sill's western end would be turned over to the Chiricahuas for permanent occupancy.[8]

Months passed before Interior took any definitive action. C. C. Duncan, the new Kiowa and Comanche Agent at Anadarko, Oklahoma, reported the results of his inspection on June 20. Duncan, however, completely evaded the issue of whether Interior should resume custody of the Chiricahuas who were to be allotted at Fort Sill as suggested by the secretary of war. Scott's work on the prisoners' behalf, Duncan explained, added "daily to the value of the reservation." During councils held with the Kiowas and Comanches, Duncan discovered that "they had caught on to this, and now say they do not care to dispose of this reservation at any price." Unless Congress approved the Jerome Agreement, the June 6, 1900, ratification of which extinguished the Kiowa and Comanche Reservation, the government could "expect to pay well for this reservation" and might be unable to procure it at any cost. Although an outright purchase of enough Kiowa and Comanche land for Chiricahua settlement was the best solution to the problem at hand, the government would be well advised to seek other lands for the Chiricahuas.[9]

On July 3, Commissioner of Indian Affairs Daniel M. Browning received Duncan's findings. On August 3, Browning, who greatly understated the case, explained that although Duncan's report failed to address Lamont's suggestions, Browning nevertheless had the "honor to recommend that it be transmitted for his [Lamont's] information."[10] Browning's and Smith's responses of August 3 and 6, respectively, surely indicated to Davis and Lamont that, deliberately hedging on this issue, Interior had not only no interest in retaking charge of the Chiricahuas, but also no intention of doing so.[11] With Chiricahua welfare in the balance, Interior permitted a prime opportunity to provide these Indians with full justice to pass by, as future events all too vividly demonstrated.

Scott experienced some degree of frustration at this turn of events. Davis, Scott speculated, would doubtlessly discover Duncan's report to be valueless. Scott knew the real reason for the vehement objections raised by the Kiowas and Comanches to the sale of this military installation. Both he and the Indians believed the Jerome Agreement of October 1892 to be a fraudulent transaction.[12] In truth, Scott's view of the matter was no exaggeration. Article 12 of the Medicine Lodge Treaty stipulated that no agreement for the "cession of any . . . part of the reservation . . . shall be of any validity . . . unless executed and signed by at least three-fourths of all the adult male Indians occupying the same."[13] But the Jerome Commission had failed to obtain the three-fourths consent that the Medicine Lodge Treaty mandated.[14] Furthermore, Scott argued, were it "ratified against their protest already made, these Indians will feel always that they have been cheated out of their country." Both Kiowas and Comanches feared their rights as allottees would be "checked in a way they will never recover from if this country is settled up by whites prematurely."

Scott personally believed the Kiowas and Comanches might consider it advantageous to sell the military reservation soon, provided, of course, a fair price could be obtained. They would benefit by "having the Apaches . . . as neighbors rather than the hostile white man." Were he empowered to bargain with these Indians, based on a selling price of $1.25 per acre, Scott was certain that a sale could be quickly consummated, "notwithstanding their present attitude as reported by Inspector Duncan." In truth, Scott said, he did not believe anyone else could conclude the arrangement.

In terms of bringing about the desired sale, Scott was heartened to learn that Davis understood the importance of procuring title to this land for the Chiricahuas before the end of winter. Simply, the incoming William McKinley administration would "know little and care less about it." Were the title issue not decided immediately, Scott said, it would "end in a few years in the Apaches being dispossessed and thrown out on the world without a protector."[15] If Interior insisted on maintaining its obstructionist position, then another tack would have to be taken. Therefore, Scott, Davis, and their War Department superiors spent the remainder of summer and fall searching for a new approach to resolving the dilemma of Chiricahua release and allotment at Fort Sill.

As the War Department spent the first half of 1896 attempting to negotiate the Interior Department's takeover of Chiricahua affairs, Scott began this year with a routine more hectic than ever as he guided his charges along the road to white standards of civilization. Very little rain fell during the calamitous summer of 1896. Southwestern Oklahoma experienced relentless searing heat, with the mercury soaring to more than 100 degrees between July 20 and August 17. Larger streams slowed to a bare trickle or even dried up; smaller ones had ceased flowing months earlier. So serious was the lack of moisture that cattlemen in Oklahoma and northern Texas feared a hay famine for the coming winter. Several cattlemen predicted that this commodity would command the unheard-of price of $20 per ton. Perhaps the Chiricahuas might profit if they could lay in a surplus of fodder. Scott wrote that hay was nearly unobtainable. A large area had to be cut to obtain a mere ton of forage. Even then, this operation almost required a "razor and a fine tooth comb."[16]

On the other hand, discretion decreed that surplus forage be retained in the event of an exceptionally severe winter. In light of the long-term goal of making the Chiricahuas self-sustaining by the summer of 1897, laying in adequate stores of feed was especially important to maintaining the cattle herd as their economic mainstay. Although Scott did not advocate completely cutting off the army food ration at this time, a gradual decrease was to be implemented to prepare them to live off the fruits of their labor. Rations might be eliminated altogether when the "calves born this year are large enough to kill without loss and to have a series of cattle coming on thereafter." Of course, such a reduction in rations depended heavily on next year's crops, and Scott

Chiricahuas baling hay for delivery to the Fort Sill quartermaster, 1897.
Courtesy Fort Sill Museum.

therefore planned to double the area under cultivation. Also, Scott had yet to reap the remainder of the current year's harvest.

On August 1, despite the seemingly insurmountable obstacles brought on by drought, Scott reported with cautious optimism on the Chiricahuas' morale. They seemed "happy, contented and pleased with the country and their prospects for the future." Not "one complaint . . . has been . . . lodged against them for a wrong committed against a white man or an Indian since their arrival." Furthermore, newspapers "of this section which opposed their coming here most bitterly" now, "having seemingly forgotten their existence," lacked any "mention of them whatever."[17]

Throughout the remainder of the summer and early fall, the Chiricahuas found themselves mainly engaged in harvesting their major crops of kaffir corn and hay. Although the kaffir corn ripened early, promising a substantial yield, lack of moisture was so severe that by November 1 the Chiricahuas realized only 400 tons of hay valued at $8 per ton. This was 100 tons less than that produced the previous season. Other harvests were 31,500 cantaloupes (valued at $.10 each), 11,000 watermelons (also worth $.10 each), 2,500 bushels of sweet potatoes (priced at $1 per bushel), 200,000 pounds of kaffir corn (quoted at $.20 per fifty-six-pound bushel), and 400 tons of kaffir corn forage (valued at $3 per ton). By November 1, the Chiricahuas also had a total of 300 calves worth $8 per head.[18]

With the summer's harvest completed, the Chiricahuas were at long last able to concentrate on readying their new dwellings for habitation. Not only had they performed much of the construction of the buildings themselves, but they had also built beds, tables, and other necessary furnishings. Upon completing these tasks, the Chiricahuas moved into their new homes by December.[19] These houses were not all grouped together; rather, they were placed in clusters of twelve widely scattered villages "according to kindred or intimate friendship."[20] Each village had a chief, headman, or other important personage in charge. The previous year, these individuals had been instructed to "select within certain boundaries a site for his village, having reference to both its scenic and sanitary attractions." Each headman was "held responsible for the general condition and police of his community."[21] All that remained to ensure the permanency of this aspect of Scott's Chiricahua acculturation program was to procure for them title to the land upon which they were now situated.

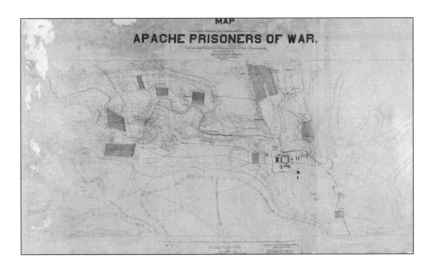

Map showing location of Chiricahua Apache prisoner-of-war villages at Fort
Sill, 1897. *Courtesy Fort Sill Museum.*

Kayatennae's village. *Courtesy Library of Congress.*

During the summer, Scott had carefully labored on a scheme that he believed would achieve exactly that result. By October's end, Scott had fine-tuned his plan and prepared to argue its merits before his superiors. Were the War Department to realize its goal of having the Chiricahuas attain economic independence within the next two years, their cattle herd would have to number at least 3,500 head. A herd this size required 36,000 acres of grazing land for its maintenance. Experienced Oklahoma cattlemen allowed a minimum of ten acres per animal on the range. Factoring in the acreage needed to grow supplemental crops for the cattle herd's maintenance, an allotment of at least 116 acres per head of household was needed for cattle raising alone. Although the usual Indian allotment in the West was 160 acres each, Scott believed this "none too large where the main dependence must be on stock raising."

Yet, few of Fort Sill's 23,040 acres were arable, the remainder being somewhat rocky and "cut up by ravines, or high, dry and rolling" countryside. Of Fort Sill's land area, 10,000 acres was certainly suitable for stock-grazing purposes. However, this amount fell far short of the 36,000 acres needed to support a projected cattle herd of 3,500. Therefore, the 26,000 acres sought as grazing lands for the Chiricahuas' cattle would have to be additional to the current acreage because Fort Sill, as it was then constituted, could not be "equitably subdivided on the checker board plan." If such lands were not provided, this plan would leave one family "on arable land and the next one far from water on a network of ravines where it could not maintain itself." Topography and soil conditions had been a major consideration in locating the Chiricahuas' houses "in small communities . . . upon arable land sufficient for gardens and cornfields which are fenced in."

Scott's idea, then, was to maintain this arrangement on a permanent basis. Therefore, the Chiricahuas were to retain all the arable lands on the original post for purposes of cultivation. What land remained, as well as the proposed 26,000-acre grazing addition, would have its outside borders enclosed. In this way, stock could be permitted to range over the reserve according to the season, water supply, and amount of grass available. Each family would look after its own cattle.

Reminding his superiors that title to Fort Sill remained vested in the Kiowas and Comanches by congressional authority and that "when no longer required for military purposes it must revert to them," Scott turned to the matter of how title to such lands might actually be procured. Again referring to the Jerome Agreement, Scott recommended appointment of a new commission to renegotiate the sale of Fort Sill to the United States, "together with a strip on its borders where it would not interfere with Indian locations or vested rights, sufficient to make up the 36,000 acres" required for the Chiricahua cattle herd. He then suggested that a patent for the lands comprising Fort Sill's current acreage, as well as the 26,000-acre addition, be issued to the Chiricahuas. Scott believed that an "offer of $1.25 an acre . . . made through the right persons would speedily result in a satisfactory agreement." The title issue was a most important one. Were it not settled immediately, it would be a "source of friction among these tribes, a cause of anxiety to their white neighbors," and would "likely . . . have a disastrous and costly ending."[22]

With this warning of possible catastrophe, Scott's superiors hurriedly summoned him to Washington in November to discuss his proposals in detail, planning to modify his suggestions where necessary and subsequently see the new plans through to fruition. Although Scott's superiors believed his solution to the Chiricahua title and allotment problems sound enough, President Cleveland thought it inadvisable to recommend an outright purchase "lest it . . . jeopardize the whole reservation of the Kiowas and Comanches on account of the fraudulent agreement." Actually, the basic outline of Scott's design remained the same. The only major change was that when the Kiowas and Comanches consented to the sale, the lands would be added by executive order rather than outright purchase.[23] Indeed, so confident was the War Department that Scott would successfully remove any objection these Indians might have to the continued occupation of their lands by the Chiricahuas,[24] that the president himself, in the presence of Lamont and Davis, instructed Scott to obtain the "consent of the Kiowa and Comanche Indians to the addition of enough of their land" to Fort Sill to allow each Chiricahua a 160-acre allotment upon the installation's abandonment,[25] or a total of 26,987 acres, compensation to be made when Congress purchased the remainder of the Kiowa and Comanche surplus acreage.[26] Although Fort Sill's abandonment would take place in the not too distant future, lamentably, and with tragically ominous implications for the Chiricahuas' future welfare, no actual date was set.[27]

Notwithstanding the lack of an immediate target date for Fort Sill's abandonment, Lamont instructed Adjutant General George D. Ruggles to advise General Wesley Merritt, commanding general of the Department of the Missouri, that the project to enlarge Fort Sill should be undertaken immediately. Inasmuch as the cattle herd "required a wider range and more extensive pasture" than Fort Sill could supply, Scott's suggestions "for extending the limits of the reserve . . . should be carried into effect." In this way, a total area of 50,000 acres would be made available for the Chiricahuas, thus permitting an allotment of 160 acres for each Indian. Adjutant General Ruggles further explained that because the United States would possess ownership of surplus Kiowa and Comanche lands upon the Jerome Agreement's ratification, the Chiricahuas would "ultimately be given title to the lands whereupon they have been established." Scott was not to include any land occupied as a homestead by the Kiowas and Comanches.[28]

During the latter part of December, Commissioner Browning directed Frank D. Baldwin, acting Agent for the Kiowas and Comanches, to assist Scott in this matter. In January 1897, Baldwin informed the Kiowas and Comanches that a council to discuss the proposed addition to Fort Sill would be called the following month. On February 16, 1897, Baldwin, opening negotiations, stated that the government did not intend to use this land for any purpose except as a military reservation and to provide homes for those Chiricahuas under Scott's charge. Baldwin assured them that although an addition of approximately 27,000 acres was needed, no land would be taken upon which any individual Indian claims existed. At first, Quanah Parker, a Quahada Comanche chief whose ancestry included white blood, was skeptical about the government's designs, although he was certainly sympathetic to the Chiricahuas' plight. Recalling all too vividly the fraudulent Jerome Agreement, the Kiowas and Comanches were willing to make a temporary loan of the land for the Chiricahuas' benefit, but they would not relinquish one acre outright unless they received just payment.

Scott salvaged the situation the following day. Stating that the agreement under negotiation did not permanently take away the land as Quanah Parker believed it would, Scott claimed that it added to the original military reservation and that this attachment would hold the same legal status as the original military reservation. While the government certainly desired to place the Chiricahuas there on a permanent basis, it was not "going to take anything for good without paying for it." Scott also recalled the Jerome Agreement: had not the president heeded the Indians' petition and advised Congress not to ratify this accord because "it was not made straight?" If these Indians were to finally succeed in breaking the Jerome Agreement, a fresh purchase agreement could be forged on better terms than the $.87 per acre offered by the Jerome Commission. Meanwhile, if Oklahomans succeeded in any attempts to force both the army and the Chiricahuas from Fort Sill in an effort to procure the installation for themselves, then, as provided by this new arrangement, the land, when no longer utilized by the military and the Chiricahuas, would be returned to the Kiowas and Comanches to prevent white people from obtaining it. Such would be the case unless Congress ratified the Jerome Agreement.[29]

Satisfied that Scott clearly and truthfully stated the situation, Quanah Parker agreed to the addition of new lands to Fort Sill by executive order "for the permanent settlement thereon of the Apache prisoners of war, who are now located on the original Fort Sill Military Reservation by Act of Congress." On February 17, 1897, Quanah Parker and the principal chiefs and headmen of the Kiowas and Comanches signed the agreement, which stipulated that the addition, as well as the original post, was to be utilized "only for military purposes and for the permanent settlement thereon of the Apache prisoners of war." A "just and adequate compensation" was to be made both for the addition and the original post in the event Congress purchased surplus lands on the remaining portion of the Kiowa and Comanche Reservation. If, in the meantime, such lands were not sold by Congress, the original post and its newly acquired addition would revert back to the Kiowas and Comanches unless the United States purchased these particular entities in fee simple.[30] Commissioner Browning later approved this plan and recommended that the executive order receive the president's approbation. Furthermore, he understood that the addition made to Fort Sill was procured for the purpose of placing the Chiricahua prisoners "permanently on the reservation thus enlarged."[31]

In a February 26 letter to the president—accompanied by a draft of the executive order that activated this agreement—Interior Secretary David R. Francis quickly reiterated Commissioner Browning's recommendations. Grover Cleveland approved and signed this document on the same day, and on March 15 the adjutant general published the executive order as General Orders No. 14, wherein the Eastern and Western Additions, comprising a total land area of 26,987 acres, were officially added to Fort Sill "for exclusive use for military purposes, and for the permanent location thereon of the Apache prisoners of war."[32]

In theory, at least, the Chiricahuas were now not only promised permanent homes but were indeed permanently established upon what would be their future allotments. Reflecting upon this accomplishment, Scott triumphantly remarked that despite a certain Indian inspector's

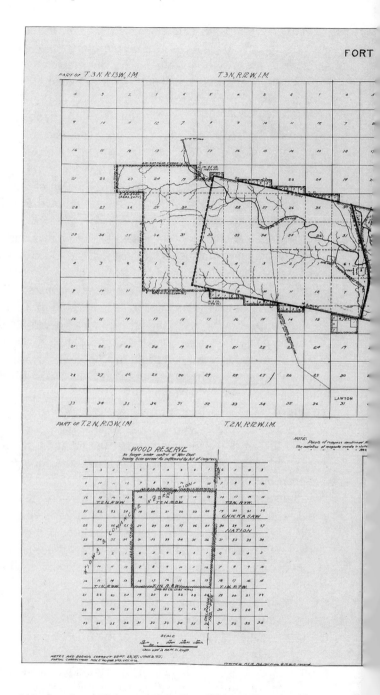

Map showing additions made to Fort Sill in 1897 to provide acreage
sufficient for grazing of the Chiricahuas' cattle herd.

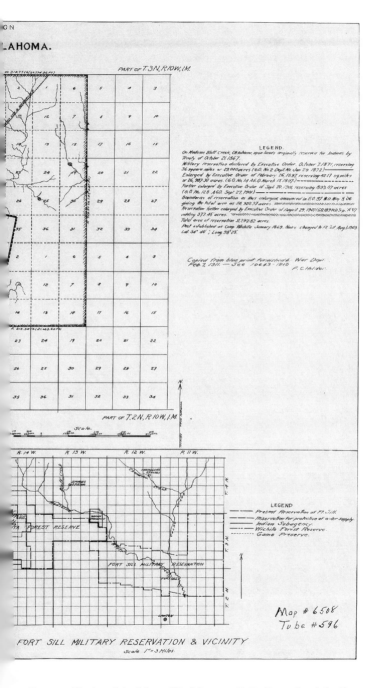

Courtesy National Archives, Washington, D.C. (Records of the Bureau of Indian Affairs, Record Group 75, Central Map File, #6508.)

report of violent opposition among the Kiowas and Comanches to the Chiricahuas' "remaining in their country," when "this proposition was made to them by the proper persons in whom they have confidence, they agreed at once without a particle of opposition in the most willing manner."[33] Indeed, they believed that this and this alone was what they had consented to.

6

Daily Routine, a False Alarm, and Missionaries

▼   ▼   ▼

*W*ith the Chiricahuas apparently well placed on a path that would not only lead to full assimilation into white society but also secure for them a prosperous future, Hugh Scott concluded during the summer of 1897 that the administrative reins of Chiricahua affairs could be safely entrusted to his subordinates. In August, he recommended that Lieutenant Francis H. Beach be accorded this responsibility.[1] Although Scott had found supervising the Indians to be fully rewarding, he decided the time had come for his children to receive the eastern education he believed they so desperately needed. Thus he successfully sought a billet in Washington and, on November 27, 1897, was relieved as the Chiricahuas' officer-in-charge.[2] On the same day, Beach assumed the duties of this office.

Of Scott and his work with the Chiricahuas, Francis Leupp, an Indian Rights Association agent, observed that "he was fortunate in one respect of having the War Department to deal with." This "Department, always presuming that an Army officer" was a "gentleman and a man of honor," embarrassed Scott "far less with red tape" than Interior, which transacted "its business on the apparent theory" that every agent was "either an incompetent or thief."[3] According to Scott's final report on his stewardship of Chiricahua affairs, the captives' reservation lands were doubled. They were established "therein as firmly as it is now possible to accomplish it—leaving it to the future to obtain for them patents for this land as soon as practicable," as well as to "protect them from . . . attempts to defraud them of it which will undoubtedly be made by unscrupulous white men."[4]

Scott's departure did not lessen the Chiricahuas' labor routine, nor did it diminish the amount of care and concern expended over their affairs. One of the first matters the new regime undertook was an attempt to mitigate the ravages of disease inflicted upon their 1,200 head of cattle. During the previous three years, many of the finest calves had perished from black leg, a fatal disease afflicting cattle. This loss cost the Chiricahuas $1,000 annually. Fortunately, although there was no cure, the disease could be prevented by use of Pasteur's Black Leg Vaccine.[5]

In early 1898, several Chiricahuas attempted to add a once-only innovation to their already diversified routine of agricultural chores. At the end of February, Allyn Capron reported that local newspapers were replete with accounts of the explosion that sank the USS *Maine,* which was docked at Havana. This was one of the incidents that led to hostilities between Spain and the United States. Talk of war had "at last aroused even the Apaches." A number of them told Capron that were he compelled to join the fray, they wished to accompany him and "whip those Spaniards."[6]

These eager volunteers, however, were not destined to participate in the Spanish-American War. Rather, certain hysterical whites expressed

Chiricahuas' cattle herd at Fort Sill, 1897. *Courtesy Fort Sill Museum.*

fear that once Fort Sill was evacuated of all but a token complement for combat in Cuba, the Chiricahuas, under Geronimo, planned to execute a campaign of terror against both the soldiers that remained and those settlers inhabiting the surrounding region. On April 19, 1898, with the departure of the post's garrison—excepting, of course, Beach and only enough military personnel "to guard the store houses"—events began breaking rapidly due to the circulation of numerous unsubstantiated reports of an imminent Chiricahua uprising.[7] No sooner had the troops gone than an informant advised Beach that in their absence, trouble might well be expected. Although the state of alarm was simply a product of the local rumor mill, the danger seemed real enough to the lieutenant. According to Beach, an educated Indian woman said the Chiricahuas were "making medicine and holding war dances." An investigation by the Chiricahuas' interpreter purportedly confirmed the probability of an "attempt to escape to Arizona." There were also indications that once the troopers left, a party of Comanches intended to attack the Chiricahuas.[8]

At Fort Sill, the soldiers' families were on the verge of panic. One post resident, Mattie Morris, said they were quite fearful when, at the onset of the Spanish-American War, most of the troops stationed there departed for battle. The families believed that "Geronimo and his band would harm us, as they were held prisoners on the reservation." On one occasion, "all the women and children were sent to the old guard house. My mother took us children and stayed all night."[9]

Grace Paulding, wife of one of the officers, provided a vivid description of the foreboding she remembered as permeating the military reservation during that time. "It began to look as if we were the ones in danger, not the troops going to war." Only two officers remained behind. They commanded a "rather inadequate guard" whose duty was to both "protect government property" and watch over the Chiricahuas. Evidently, Paulding wrote, "this looked to wily old Geronimo as a heaven-sent opportunity to make one last stand for freedom" and at the same time demonstrate his "defiance of his captors by massacring" what remained of the garrison. "It was late morning when the rumor started. . . . Early evening" was believed to be the "most probable time of attack." Upon receipt of this information, Grace mused, "we put in a long and nerve wracking afternoon" getting "everything in readiness." Although "we . . . tried to behave in the best tradition of army wives, it was impossible not to think of the dreadful possibility ahead." About midnight, Paulding wrote, there "came the faint notes of a cavalry bugle. No sound was ever more beautiful and the relief almost too great."[10]

In reality, Reverend Robert Chaat explained, the whites' panic was born of rumors and the prospect of being completely defenseless; the Chiricahuas had absolutely no intention of causing trouble.[11] Indeed, they were quite loyal despite their status as prisoners of war. Blossom Haozous maintained that there was not a shred of truth to the story: "somebody just made that up."[12] Raymond Loco also believed the rumor to be unfounded. "When Geronimo settled down, that was it. He done hung up his bows and arrows and was just as peaceful as I am right now."[13] Yet so intense was the whites' belief in some quarters that in order to prevent both his people and the Kiowas from being implicated in this purportedly planned affair, Quanah Parker took a few Comanche headmen with him to the Chiricahuas' villages and emphatically threatened them: "If you'd like to start trouble, we'll take care of you."[14]

After the dust raised by this episode began to settle, Beach apologetically explained that according to information provided by supposedly knowledgeable individuals, the Chiricahuas, like many tribal groups, believed that sometime in the future a general conflict with the whites would cause white extermination and conclude with the Indians' repossessing the entire country. Among the unfounded pieces of intelligence Beach received, one item suggested that at the time the garrison withdrew from Fort Sill, Indians living adjacent to the post thought the moment ripe for such insurgence. It was this report that Beach sent to Fort Sill commandant Edgar R. Kellogg before the departure of Kellogg's detachment from Rush Springs. Actually, as Beach subsequently discovered, the report had no factual basis, particularly as far as the Chiricahuas were concerned. Simply put, discipline among them was excellent. Furthermore, Beach noted, they were peaceably disposed. Therefore, he strongly doubted that they would ever again take to the warpath. To substantiate his opinion, he observed that as a tribe, they were willing to work.[15]

Indeed, adhering to the policies and goals set by Beach's predecessors, the Chiricahuas were too involved with achieving subsistence to contemplate engaging in insurrection, even had they been so inclined. Actually, self-maintenance required greater effort in 1898 than during the previous season. For the most part, their endeavors were successful, despite extremely dry conditions and a general invasion of grasshoppers. Each family possessed a ten-acre farm. One acre was dedicated to garden crops, one to cotton, and eight to kaffir corn. Garden crops included sugar corn, melons, sweet potatoes, onions, peas, and pumpkins. Although the Chiricahuas attempted to irrigate, drought devastated most of these vegetables. Despite the dearth of moisture, there was a large crop of kaffir corn, far more than necessary to provide grain and fodder for their cattle during the normal Oklahoma winter.

Of course, Beach encouraged the Chiricahuas to rely on cattle raising as their means of economic self-sufficiency. This, he said, was their chief industry. He reported that the herd was divided among them "to the extent of branding each animal with the number of the family to which it" belonged. Beach also reported an increase of 333 head. Despite the minor difficulties still encountered in making cattle the Chiricahuas' economic mainstay, Beach remained optimistic about the Indians' future.

Even so, the captives continued to have a number of pressing needs. Among these were a schoolhouse and church. Because it would be a long time before the Chiricahuas could spare enough from their earnings to build them, Beach intended to request permission to enlist the help of a missionary society.[16] His wait for a mission church for his charges was not long.

It was almost by chance that Beach enabled the Reformed Church in America's Women's Board of Domestic Missions to minister to these Indians. In 1895, the Women's Executive Committee, the Board of Domestic Missions' predecessor, had sent the Reverend Doctor Frank Hall Wright to Lawton, Oklahoma, to labor in the Comanche mission field.[17] While working among the Comanches, Wright learned of the Chiricahuas' plight and became sympathetic to what he perceived as their unjust treatment.[18] For four years, his heart burning with "zeal to reach these discouraged people with the hope-filled message of the Gospel of Christ," Wright's "way was blocked by . . . military authorities who, for some time, refused the missionary entrance to the prisoners of war."[19]

By August 1898, Wright was about to cease his efforts. On August 25, as he prepared to leave Fort Sill for the last time, Beach, returning to the military reserve, passed him, pausing long enough to discuss the nature of Wright's business. In a mood bordering on despair, Wright explained that he had received nothing but the "run around" concerning his attempts to establish a mission among the Chiricahuas.[20] Wright doubtless was surprised by the unexpected pleasantness of the lieutenant's reply. Beach told Wright that he wanted him to preach to the Chiricahuas.[21] Were the evangelist to return on the morrow, Beach promised to support the minister's effort to establish a mission for his charges.[22] Beach then consulted the Chiricahua headmen. They expressed a desire that such a mission be "established . . . to comprise religious instruction, a school for the younger children," and training in domestic pursuits.[23]

Wright needed no second invitation. On August 26, he returned to Fort Sill, whereupon a council was called.[24] Although the Chiricahuas believed themselves "too old to learn new ways" or "walk in new paths," they wished to have their children "taught 'the Jesus road.' Send someone here to teach them and we will be glad."[25] The plea "come and help us" was sent the following month to the Women's Executive Board by the Reverend Doctor Walter C. Roe, of Colony, Oklahoma, who in future years was himself to play an important role in the Chiricahuas' affairs. The Reformed Church in America then began planning its missionary endeavors among them.[26]

During the summer of 1899, as this denomination busily prepared for the full operation of its Apache Mission, Lieutenant Benjamin B. Hyer replaced Beach as the Chiricahuas' overseer. Upon his departure, Beach reported the captives as "prosperous, well disciplined and contented, engaged in stock raising and agricultural pursuits and living in villages well policed and in excellent sanitary condition."[27] Hyer continued his predecessor's policies, especially those concerning the Chiricahuas' cattle.[28] At the conclusion of his tenure in office, Hyer's efforts were assessed by Colonel Frank D. Baldwin. Visiting the Chiricahuas' camps, Baldwin found these Indians "all in houses, with indications of prosperity and improvement everywhere about their surroundings." Their cattle herd numbered 1,898 head. Though the "old Indians" continued to yearn for their former homes, Baldwin believed their offspring were quite contented at Fort Sill. Simply stated, as contrasted with their current state, "no one who knew of their condition" prior to their arrival at this post could advocate their return to the Southwest.[29]

Despite such optimism, ominous issues loomed on the horizon that did not bode well for their future weal. By the spring of 1900, pressure so intensified to open the Kiowa and Comanche Reservation that General George W. Davis felt compelled to advise the adjutant general of his belief that if "legislation looking to disposal of the Kiowa and Comanche lands" did not contain a title provision for the Chiricahuas, "all lands not occupied by Kiowas and Comanches" would "be sold to settlers," thereby dispossessing the Chiricahuas "of their houses and improvements." If this happened, these Indians would have nowhere to go. As matters stood, Davis said that the Chiricahuas had "as good a right in equity to the lands" they now occupied "as their neighbors" did.[30] Indeed, the next officer-in-charge, Captain Farrand B. Sayre, exerted every effort to preserve this right. His endeavors provided Interior with one last opportunity to safeguard the Chiricahuas' right in equity to the Fort Sill military reservation.

CHAPTER

7

A Subtle Policy Shift

▼   ▼   ▼

*W*hen Captain Farrand B. Sayre assumed his duties as the Chiricahuas' officer-in-charge during the early summer of 1900, he soon discovered they had numerous pressing needs that he was unable to remedy given the meager resources at his disposal. Despite their rapid progress on the road to white civilization, the Chiricahuas were in no position to provide themselves with all necessities. Houses constructed in 1894 required repair and improvements. Cookstoves and other appliances needed replacement. Many items were completely unserviceable. Although several Chiricahuas were skilled as blacksmiths and carpenters, they lacked the appropriate shops and equipment to repair their wagons, farm machinery, and other agricultural implements. Sayre therefore requested additional appropriations to mitigate these needs.[1]

A related issue also required prompt resolution. During the spring of 1901, preparations were made to throw open to settlement the surplus acreage of the now-allotted Kiowa and Comanche Reservation. Although allotment agents basically completed their tasks by May, General Land Office registrars and receivers had not yet begun entering homesteads on the books. As matters stood, once settlers took up their lands, potential disputes might arise regarding Fort Sill's northern and southern boundaries, and these disputes could impact the Chiricahuas.

Captain Farrand Sayre and Chiricahua scouts, 1902. *Courtesy Fort Sill Museum.*

Sayre devised a plan to eliminate these difficulties: the fractional parts of those quarter-sections containing Kiowa and Comanche reservation lands that bordered Fort Sill's northern and southern perimeters would be added to this installation for the Chiricahuas' benefit. Sayre requested that President Theodore Roosevelt be petitioned to take appropriate action.[2] On September 20, 1901, Roosevelt approved the Northern and Southern Additions to Fort Sill.[3]

Such developments availed the Chiricahuas little in terms of cementing their settlement and allotment at Fort Sill. On June 6, 1900, when Congress ratified the infamous Jerome Agreement, thus opening the Kiowa and Comanche Reservation to white settlement, Fort Sill legally became War Department property in fee simple. Within two years of the military reservation's change of status, War Department officials decided that Fort Sill ought to be retained as a military installation, and the Chiricahuas discovered they would not be allowed to keep the homes they believed had been promised them permanently. Simply speaking, the Chiricahua prisoners would have to go.

While attempting to prevent the eviction of his charges, Sayre busied himself resolving boundary problems and salvaging the Chiricahuas' agricultural situation. During the summer of 1901, southwestern Oklahoma again experienced protracted drought punctuated by searing, incessant winds. Except for the kaffir corn and hay, the

Group of Chiricahuas branding a calf during a roundup.
Courtesy Fort Sill Museum.

Chiricahuas suffered a total crop failure. During the 1902 growing season, their crops were somewhat more successful, although a good rain was needed for complete maturation.

In terms of the cattle herd, by mid-1902, the Herefords had increased to 3,755 head, a number greater than that believed necessary to sustain these Indians on a somewhat self-sufficient economic basis. In December, 247 steers sold in Kansas City reaped $9,103.41. Sayre stated that this was the most profitable cattle sale ever made by the Chiricahuas. Proceeds were distributed on an individual basis.[4]

Although the cattle herd began to earn money for the Chiricahuas, the Indians' needs were so great that in 1901 Sayre tried to launch other revenue-producing measures for his charges. One such enterprise, suggested by Sayre in late June, was the leasing of Fort Sill's wood reserve. In this matter, he had the full cooperation of Major George L. Scott, post commandant. Scott requested an early decision on the matter.[5]

In July, Brigadier General Henry C. Merriam, commander of the Department of the Missouri, recommended approval.[6] A decision on this issue, however, was not reached until October. Regarding the propriety of using funds derived from grazing leases on Fort Sill's wood reserve for the Chiricahuas' benefit, Judge Advocate General George B. Davis said that an erroneous understanding existed that Fort Sill's wood reserve continued to be an Indian reservation. This belief was ill-founded because on August 6, Kiowa and Comanche lands were thrown open to settlement. Whatever jurisdiction Interior once had in the matter, Davis said, was now eliminated. According to Davis, although the secretary of war possessed authority to lease for grazing purposes any part of Fort Sill not required for military use, the secretary could not expend moneys derived from such leases for the Chiricahuas' benefit. Extinguishment of Indian title, he explained, caused all lands comprising Fort Sill to become U.S. property. Davis therefore suggested that because much of the installation had been created for the Chiricahuas, Congress be requested to authorize use of the proposed leases' revenues for Chiricahua betterment.[7] Despite Davis's recommendation, the damage had been done. Reflecting an apparent change in attitude on the War Department's part as to the proper utilization of Fort Sill, Davis had presented the possibility that the installation might be used for purposes other than permanently allotting those lands previously promised the Chiricahuas.

Acting on Davis's suggestion, Secretary of War Elihu Root advised Interior he would request from Congress the requisite authority to apply the proceeds of future leases on Fort Sill's wood reserve for the Chiricahuas' benefit.[8] Root submitted the matter to Congress on January 18, 1902. As an incentive to pass this measure, Root informed Congress that a fiscal 1903 appropriation bill for the Chiricahuas might be unnecessary were authority granted to allocate, for their benefit, revenues derived from grazing leases.[9] Root hoped favorable legislation would be forthcoming.[10]

Although Sayre, too, hoped for congressional approval of this legislation, it failed to pass.[11] Indications that such a fate might well befall this measure had caught Sayre's attention during the late fall of 1901. Thus, on November 7, Sayre requested a $5,000 appropriation for the Chiricahuas' continued support. Although they continued making progress toward the goal of self-maintenance, their needs remained numerous and included fencing materials, repairs, farm machinery, draft animals, and new issues of livestock other than cattle.[12]

Chiricahuas laboring near their sawmill. *Courtesy Fort Sill Museum.*

George Scott strongly backed Sayre's request, explaining that the appropriation was essential for the captives' welfare and advancement.[13] Unfortunately for Sayre and his Chiricahua charges, he received from superiors little support for and even less cooperation with his efforts on the Indians' behalf. Within several months, military officials transferred Major Scott to another post, removing yet another key individual who, like Sayre, constantly strove to protect the Chiricahuas' interests.

At the departmental level, signs were evident that support had slackened to the point of becoming grudging. George Scott's hearty endorsement of Sayre's request for an additional appropriation for the Chiricahuas received the rather unenthusiastic attention of the department's commander on November 11, 1901. Although the estimate was not unreasonable, Brigadier General John C. Bates observed that their status as prisoners of war was nominal because they lived much as other Indians. Therefore, the question that now presented itself was whether the Chiricahuas might be turned over to Interior.[14] With this suggestion, the door initially opened by Judge Advocate General Davis to the possibility that Fort Sill might be retained as a military installation per se was now thrown further ajar. Bates's suggestion also presented

Interior one last chance to ensure the Chiricahuas' permanent allotment at Fort Sill—an opportunity that Interior failed to grasp.

On November 25, 1901, Root submitted to Interior both Sayre's appropriation request and Bates's suggestion that the time had come for Interior to retake custody of the Chiricahuas.[15] Uncertain whether conditions were favorable for such action, Commissioner of Indian Affairs William A. Jones expressed several reservations. An investigation was launched concerning the advisability of such a transfer. Jones also reminded Root that it was always the War Department's intention to make Fort Sill the Chiricahuas' permanent home. Until now, Jones noted, active measures to allot lands in severalty to the Chiricahuas had not been taken because prior to congressional ratification of the Jerome Agreement, title to the lands occupied by Fort Sill remained vested with the Kiowas and Comanches. But title was now held by the United States, and lands sufficient for their needs could be allotted them under the 1887 Dawes Severalty Act. Jones suggested that the program of Chiricahua civilization and allotment at Fort Sill could more readily be completed by the War Department than by any program initiated by Interior as a result of transferred custody.[16]

Special Agent Frank C. Armstrong, who conducted the investigation into the advisability of such a transfer, said the Chiricahuas had made excellent progress in their agricultural endeavors. Furthermore, many of them had learned trades. Even so, they required another two years under military control, preferably under Sayre's supervision. Eventually, this approach would both encourage them to take allotments and place them in a "condition to be released from the nominal captivity they now undergo without realizing the change." Due to ever increasing white settlement and its attendant vices within the region, Armstrong continued, if the Chiricahuas were immediately released and allotted, they would become demoralized. Consequently, all the work of the last five years would come to naught. Although Jones supported Sayre's appropriation request, which eventually won congressional approval, he said Armstrong's report confirmed his belief that the time was not yet ripe to devise any policy changes in the government's treatment of these Indians. Until the time arrived when they would be able to "provide for all their wants, even though it" might well "take ten years longer," the Chiricahuas were to remain under military supervision.[17]

A group of Chiricahuas standing in front of the Apache Prisoner of War Office. *Courtesy Fort Sill Museum.*

As events later demonstrated, the Chiricahuas would not receive the promised Fort Sill allotments in two—or even ten—years' time. By the end of 1901, a faction developed within the War Department that initially agitated for retention of half of Fort Sill for purely military purposes. Soon thereafter, military officials pressed for the Chiricahuas' complete removal from this post.

8

Initial War Department
Maneuvers to Retain Fort Sill
as a Military Reserve

▼   ▼   ▼

*A*gitation for the Chiricahuas' removal from Fort Sill began during
the late spring of 1902, when Major William Stanton replaced
George Scott as post commandant. As Captain Farrand Sayre made
clear in a July 2, 1902, letter to the adjutant general, Stanton not only
refused to give Sayre the complete backing he had become accustomed
to in administering Chiricahua affairs, but he also refused to accept the
contention that Fort Sill now existed solely for their benefit. In his letter, Sayre expressed particular concern that those policies established
by his predecessors and supported by their superior officers that per-
tained to administration of Chiricahuas affairs might well be reversed.
Delineating the issue at hand, he requested an immediate decision respecting the extent to which the Chiricahuas would be allowed to utilize this installation for such purposes as stock raising and agriculture.

Briefly reviewing the history and purpose of the additions made
to Fort Sill, Sayre described his problem in a manner that would not
arouse undue antagonism among military officials in Washington. Despite such efforts, the meaning conveyed by Sayre's message was un-
mistakable (and revealed an officer extremely frustrated by the
situation at hand). Sayre wished to know whether he would continue

to enjoy the support experienced by his predecessors and whether the Chiricahuas would be justly dealt with. He anticipated the time when a post commander would in fact become hostile to the Chiricahuas' interests and attempt to prevent Fort Sill's utilization for their benefit. Sayre therefore believed it important that their right to use this land, especially the additions, be affirmed by higher authority. Furthermore, Sayre believed their officer-in-charge was—and should remain—free to use these additions in the same manner generally employed by agents for lands owned by other tribal groups.[1]

When Sayre's report reached Major Stanton, he doubtless viewed it as nothing less than a blatant usurpation of his authority. But whatever his feelings, Stanton, biding his time, held them in check. He believed that it was now time to arrange a permanent settlement of the Chiricahuas' situation. Because their placement on the original reservation interfered with its use for military purposes, Stanton thought it best to either remove them from Fort Sill or abandon it entirely to their use. Furthermore, of all the military installations in the country, Stanton maintained that only Fort Sill was best suited for use by the field artillery. Consequently, he would regret its abandonment. Therefore, because the army's interests would be well served by retaining Fort Sill for this purpose, he recommended that the Chiricahuas be turned over to the Department of the Interior and given lands in severalty elsewhere. If lands better than those at Fort Sill could not be procured, the Chiricahuas could, without seriously interfering with military functions, be situated on that section of the post located east of the Rock Island Railroad. Stanton said this matter required prompt action because it was "unjust to encourage these Indians to make improvements on land from which it might be necessary to remove them."[2] General John Bates concurred with Stanton's views and suggested that a board of inquiry be appointed to divide Fort Sill equitably between the military and the Chiricahuas.

Bates's superiors approved this proposal on August 15.[3] The public soon received word of what was planned for the prisoners. On August 16, 1902, the *Washington Post* advised readers that the army planned to send a board of inquiry to Fort Sill to determine the extent of this post's military needs. Surplus lands were to be allotted to the Chiricahuas.[4]

One officer who took notice of this news most definitely did not approve. Hugh Scott, chief architect of the original plan to allot the Chiricahuas at Fort Sill, believed that what actually was being contemplated was their removal to another locale, not a move to a different part of the military installation. Scott therefore wished to submit certain information to the War Department, believing that so much time had elapsed since the Chiricahuas were first established at Fort Sill that many pertinent facts were unknown to departmental newcomers. As authorized by the War Department, Scott explained, the Chiricahuas were told that if they "behaved themselves they would be protected in their improvements and eventually given their allotments." Were the board of inquiry to carry out its purpose, it would effectively destroy "their advancement." Furthermore, even a "mere agitation of the subject" would entail deleterious consequences, affording them just cause to view their relocation elsewhere as a "distinct breach of faith" by the War Department.[5]

Scott's admonitions soon came to the attention of Nelson Miles, who concurred fully. Strenuously supporting Scott's views, Miles believed "it would be injudicious and unjust to disturb these Indians. . . . For the past few years they have been perfectly passive, contented and prosperous." Miles earnestly recommended that the Chiricahuas be permitted to remain at Fort Sill.[6]

On November 18, 1902, the board of inquiry convened to determine which section of Fort Sill might be retained for military use and which portion could be allotted to the Chiricahuas.[7] It offered three major recommendations. First, 2,964.51 acres were to "be set apart for military purposes exclusively." Second, the Chiricahuas would be permitted to graze their cattle on the 22,000-acre wood reserve. Finally, the Eastern and Western Additions would become the Chiricahuas' reservation, with the stipulation that army personnel could still use the additions for military maneuvers and exercises.[8]

These recommendations were not exactly what the War Department had envisioned. On February 2, 1903, General Davis claimed they would lead to friction. Because Fort Sill was one of the few large installations that remained under military control, Davis recommended that it be retained in its entirety by the War Department. Dual occupation would continue until final provisions for Chiricahua removal could be made.[9] Several days later, the secretary of war, Elihu Root, approved Davis's proposal. As a result, War Department officials broached the idea that it might be best to transfer the Chiricahuas to Interior's jurisdiction and remove them to some other reservation.[10] In April, Root solicited Interior's suggestions on how this transfer might be accomplished, "due regard being had to the legal and equitable rights of these Indians."[11] From this point on, the Chiricahuas were held as pawns in the military's struggle to maintain Fort Sill's integrity and viability.

Meanwhile, in January 1903, believing he had retained both mastery over administration of Chiricahua affairs and retention of the majority of Fort Sill acreage intended for their permanent settlement, Sayre forwarded guidelines to departmental superiors that defined what he perceived to be the Chiricahuas' status, their relation to the post, and the duties of their officers-in-charge.[12] In taking this action, Sayre wished to ensure independent and absolute control over the Chiricahuas' interests. Unfortunately, his list of suggested regulations was forwarded to Fort Sill commandant Charles Morton without departmental approval.

Morton quickly discerned Sayre's ploy. On January 12, 1903, he advised superiors that Sayre's letter assumed Fort Sill's commanding officer expressed antagonism toward the Chiricahuas. Furthermore, its "general tenor is to control him rather than the Indian prisoners." Morton insisted there was no friction, nor would there be in the future, were there "one head and the consultations usual in transactions of business are observed."

Misinterpreting the relevant documents that substantiated potential Chiricahua legal claims to Fort Sill, Morton said that he could locate only those records pertaining to additions made to Fort Sill that were specifically designated for the Chiricahuas. Of course, Morton said, this assumed that Fort Sill was "a military post on an Indian reservation, rather than Indian prisoners upon a military reservation." Until this question was finally resolved, Morton believed the post commandant should have ultimate control over matters relating to the Chiricahuas. Besides, a commanding officer's supervisory acts were "open and public, while the details of the affairs that must be attended to by a subaltern officer are largely known to the latter alone." In churlish tones tantamount to spiteful innuendo, Morton insisted that after all, the large sums expended on the Chiricahuas' behalf provided considerable "opportunities for peculation and temptations to peculate." This was reason enough to insist that the Chiricahuas' overseer be held directly accountable to the post commandant in the administration of their affairs.[13]

Meanwhile, Interior acted on Root's request for suggestions on how to transfer custody of the Chiricahuas, remove them from Fort Sill, and allot them elsewhere: yet another inquiry was initiated to evaluate the Indians' situation. The conclusions arising from this inquiry were not what Root had hoped for. Essentially, Interior took the position that the Chiricahuas be given the lands promised them at Fort Sill. Dissatisfied with such lack of cooperation, Root chose to wait for an appropriate opportunity to exert renewed pressure for their removal from this installation.

Rather than bide his time over the matter, Bates pressed for Chiricahua removal in order to permit Fort Sill's use for purely military purposes. When his annual report became public knowledge in mid-September, a torrent of opposition to the mere idea of such a project was unleashed. One of the most vociferous objections came from George Bird Grinnell, the noted ethnologist. Grinnell observed that throughout the nation's history, "it has been the course of politicians to move tribes of Indians from one place to another." This done, they would then "spend money in trying to civilize them." Finally, when the "land . . . they occupied became of value to the white man," native peoples were once more pulled up "by the roots" and removed to some other location, "there to begin over again the work of learning to be civilized." According to Grinnell, the Indian came to believe he had a permanence nowhere, with the dire result that "all motive for self-improvement and home making has been taken from him."

Focusing his attention on the Chiricahuas' situation, Grinnell said that the degree of advancement they had obtained was remarkable. He then insisted that the additions made to Fort Sill were the Chiricahuas' property. As their guardian, the War Department only controlled this accretion. They had been, Grinnell argued, "frequently . . . assured by officers of high standing and character that this was their home; that they would not be moved again." Such assurances were made "in order to induce them to work and improve their homes." Removal from Fort Sill would discourage them to an excessive degree because this action would summarily destroy "the fruits of their ten year's industry," so that they not only would "never again attack the problem of civilization," but also "would be thrown back into barbarism and literally destroyed." Grinnell fervently hoped the War Department contemplated no change in their location.[14] Subsequently, attempting to quell the worst of Grinnell's fears, Assistant Secretary of

War Robert Shaw Oliver replied that after carefully reviewing this issue, military officials did not think the War Department would soon reconsider the Chiricahua relocation question.[15]

Of course, this was merely a ruse to dampen and ultimately extinguish opposition to such removal, for military officials had already reconsidered this issue. A confidential War College Board report, approved by the secretary of war on May 6, 1903, called attention to the necessity of preserving Fort Sill intact. Eventually, this post would be enlarged to accommodate two squadrons of cavalry. Thus, in his 1903 annual report, General Bates suggested that the Chiricahuas be transferred to Fort Reno, Oklahoma, where they would be given outright the land and buildings thereon.

Supporting Bates's recommendation, Colonel Enoch H. Crowder referred to both congressional ratification of the Jerome Agreement and the 1897 presidential executive order that officially attached the Eastern and Western Additions to Fort Sill for the Chiricahuas' permanent settlement. Of course, Crowder's arguments conveniently ignored the fact that procuring this land for the Chiricahuas was the reason for securing the 1897 Kiowa and Comanche agreement that obtained this acreage, which accord directly led to this executive order. Crowder also neglected to mention that it was obviated by the Jerome Agreement. According to Crowder, because consummation of the Jerome Agreement passed title of those former Kiowa and Comanche lands occupied by Fort Sill to the United States, the government could now retain this installation for military ends. Thus, determined to retain Fort Sill intact, Crowder insisted that no claim could be made that the Chiricahuas, who, he believed, were not parties to the 1897 agreement procuring approximately 27,000 acres for Fort Sill's enlargement, "acquired by virtue of it any legal right which they could assert against" the U.S. government. All that remained to be ascertained was whether removal to Fort Reno was "expedient" and at the same time accorded them justice.[16]

Lines of communication on this point were opened with Interior in late December. On February 6, 1904, Commissioner of Indian Affairs William A. Jones, temporarily backing down from the Indian Office's earlier stand, agreed to retake custody of the Chiricahuas somewhere other than at Fort Sill. Because lands at Fort Reno were definitely inferior to those at Fort Sill, Jones suggested that south of Fort Sill, 23,000 acres of grazing land, comprising a portion of an unallotted

400,000-acre tract reserved to the Kiowas and Comanches, be purchased from these Indians for this purpose. Farrand Sayre would be designated as their acting agent. Even so, Jones could not but "regret the necessity for any action looking to a change in their present status," because the Chiricahuas had been told repeatedly that the land they now occupied at Fort Sill was to be their permanent home.[17]

Despite Jones's suggestion that Sayre continue as the Chiricahuas' agent, Sayre emphatically disagreed with the Indian Office's position. Such action as was now being contemplated, Sayre said, would constitute a crime against these Indians. Jones's approval of this decision seemed to have been gained by statements that military necessity dictated their removal; however, no such necessity existed. Besides, Sayre insisted, the Chiricahuas possessed at least a "right of occupancy on the original" post and were the "rightful owners of the additions."

Sayre then focused his attention on the two removal plans previously suggested. Fort Reno, where they would have only 17,000 acres of land, lacked wood, water, shelter, and—other than sixty buildings that were wholly unsatisfactory for the Chiricahuas' needs—improvements. Respecting a potential $50,000 expenditure for purchasing some 23,000 acres south of Fort Sill for the Chiricahuas and making "improvements worth about half of what they have here" (assuming that congressional funding were available in the first place), the Chiricahuas would be given an inadequate start and subsidized for only several months. Deeply outraged that such suggestions should even be broached, Sayre bitterly said the only judgment he cared to render on such proposals was "that the first appeared more impossible and impractical than the second." Not only did they "involve the commission of the same needless crime, a breach of trust," but they also involved the "destruction of the Indians' work of ten years," as well as their probable "relapse into savagery and speedy extinction."

Regarding his continuance as the Chiricahuas' agent, Sayre claimed the Indians' relocation would destroy his usefulness "by branding me a liar among them." After all, he had constantly advised them that the "Government would keep faith with them and that this reservation was their permanent home." Simply, "they would never believe any more promises that might be made to them and would never improve another reservation."

Sayre was also well aware that "Indian service, even if creditably done," was of little or "no advantage to an officer." However, "if I were a thief," Sayre explained, "I would have, under the scheme proposed, ample opportunities to steal enough to pay me for my time, trouble and loss of comfort." By a "course of reasoning . . . precisely analogous . . . to that followed by Colonel Crowder," Sayre could justify his actions. For example, Sayre said, "if rations were sent to me 'for the use and benefit' of the Indians," or were lumber sent "to build houses 'for their permanent location therein,'" Sayre could readily assure his conscience "that the Indians were 'not parties to the agreement' and that I was consequently free to appropriate them to my own use." Even so, Sayre had "never benefited by the value of a dollar through" his work with the Chiricahuas. He would "regard it a sufficient compensation" for his "hitherto unremunerated work with these Indians" were his recommendations regarding them "given consideration and credence at the War Department."[18]

Later, Brigadier General Samuel S. Sumner, Southwestern Division commanding officer, commented on Sayre's reaction, saying that his "own knowledge and experience with the Indian character" led him to entirely agree with the captain. Sayre "could neither retain nor regain his influence with these people after once deceiving them." Were it deemed suitable to remove the Chiricahuas from Fort Sill, Sumner remarked that a sense of justice compelled him to strongly recommend that Sayre be released from "all further control of or connection with them."[19] In less than seven months, Sayre was relieved as the Chiricahuas' officer-in-charge.

While the War Department made ready for what it believed would be a smooth transfer of the Chiricahuas from Fort Sill to Fort Reno, word of this move soon attracted the notice of other army officers sympathetic to their cause. In a March 3, 1904, letter to Richard Henry Pratt, founder of the Carlisle, Pennsylvania, Indian School where many of the prisoners' children received their elementary education, William W. Wotherspoon pleaded for assistance. Wotherspoon believed the idea of removing them arose from either a "simple wish to be rid of the care of" these Indians or some "scheme of the Oklahoma land shark to get in his work."[20] Responding with alacrity to the call for aid, Pratt personally stated the Chiricahuas' case before Secretary of War William Howard Taft.[21] Pratt believed that such arbitrary removal would not only discourage these Indians but also eradicate the gains they had made over the past decade.[22]

For the moment, Pratt's efforts had the desired effect. Robert Shaw Oliver advised Interior officials that those closely connected with the Chiricahuas believed that their removal from Fort Sill "would be a serious menace to their welfare." Also, because the military's interests appeared not to be compromised by retaining the Chiricahuas at Fort Sill, the secretary of war said they "should be continued under the conditions which surround them." Oliver hoped Interior would "concur in the wisdom of this action which is based solely upon" the War Department's desire "to foster and promote the welfare of these Indians."[23] Concerning this decision, Commissioner Jones expressed no small degree of satisfaction.[24]

Meanwhile, a new commandant, Major Henry L. Ripley, arrived at Fort Sill, where the tensions regarding who possessed final authority over administration of Chiricahua affairs remained unresolved. Furthermore, Fort Sill was now under the immediate jurisdiction of the Department of Texas. Its headquarters staff was completely unfamiliar with what had earlier transpired at Fort Sill regarding the allotment promises made to the Chiricahuas. Department commanders would be far more sympathetic to the complaints of a post commander who believed his authority was being infringed upon by the officer-in-charge for these Indians.

Ripley did not take kindly to Sayre's belief that his role was an independent one. During the summer of 1904, Ripley tactfully requested a resolution of the problem. By the end of July, Major Walter L. Finley, adjutant general of the Department of Texas, asked Ripley whether he believed it advisable to effect a change in personnel to ensure a greater degree of permanency in the management of the Chiricahuas' affairs. This was doubtless another way of enquiring whether Ripley believed it advisable to relieve Sayre of his duties.

On August 4, Ripley suggested that it would be in these Indians' best interests if "a retired officer of experience and general fitness were detailed in charge of them."[25] Finley replied on August 21 that after careful reflection, the department commander had decided to assign Lieutenant George A. Purington as Captain Sayre's relief. Of special interest to Ripley, Purington's instructions specified that he was to be entirely subordinate to the post commander's orders.[26] On August 26, 1904, the War Department officially approved Purington's appointment as the Chiricahuas' new officer-in-charge.[27] With Sayre's transfer and the arrival of a new officer completely subservient—as would be Purington's successors—to the post commandant's authority, the Chiricahuas would never again have a spokesman who believed himself independent enough to seek, outside regular military channels, redress and the fulfillment of past promises on these Indians' behalf.

CHAPTER

9

Undercurrents of Chiricahua
Disaffection

▼   ▼   ▼

*G*eorge Purington's appointment as the Chiricahuas' officer-in-charge inaugurated a generally harmonious working relationship between Fort Sill's commandant and the Indians' immediate overseer. This liaison, which endured until termination of these Indians' captivity in 1913 and 1914, was especially effective in formulating appropriate Chiricahua policies. In turn, this relationship also facilitated the military's decision to maintain Fort Sill intact as a military post and embark upon a course that protected its interests and ensured a favorable resolution to the vexed Apache problem.

Subsequent attempts by the War Department to entice Interior into accepting custody of the Chiricahuas and allotting them elsewhere, plus published reports of plans to renovate and enlarge Fort Sill for purely military purposes, created undercurrents of disaffection among these Indians toward their environment. Manipulating such disaffection to its advantage, the military managed to demoralize the Chiricahuas so severely that many of them later clamorously petitioned for removal to homes they once knew in the West. Ultimately, this tragic development permitted the War Department to renege for all time on its earlier promises of permanent allotment at Fort Sill.

Successful realization of the War Department's desire to be rid of the Chiricahuas can be credited to subtle shifts in policy. Directly traceable to a secret War College Board report of May 1903 emphasizing the necessity of maintaining Fort Sill for military purposes, such policy shifts, particularly regarding the command relationship between the post commandant and the Chiricahuas' officer-in-charge, were formulated and implemented throughout the remainder of that year and during the course of 1904.[1] Were the outcome desired by the military to be eventually achieved, the officer placed in charge of these Indians could not be permitted to act independently of those directives issued by Fort Sill's commanding officer. Essentially, military officials wished to prevent any operation outside normal military channels whereby the officer having custody of the Chiricahuas might voice opposition to the post commandant's directives regarding them. Purington was the first to operate under such a policy.

At the outset of Purington's assignment in August 1904, Brigadier General Jesse M. Lee, commander of the Department of Texas, established guidelines to achieve and maintain tranquillity in the administration of Chiricahua affairs. Lee suggested that Purington be allowed appropriate latitude in their management so as to "afford every opportunity to further their best interests." He then instructed the post commander to counsel Purington in performing these important duties. Even so, Purington was to be directly subordinate to the orders of Lieutenant Colonel Henry P. Kingsbury, Fort Sill's latest commandant.[2]

Purington was not unknown to the Chiricahuas when he assumed control of their affairs: he had been one of Sayre's assistants, and Sayre recommended him as his successor. At the time he took over as their officer-in-charge, the 1904 summer growing season was well under way. Already in cultivation were 1,100 acres of land, 700 of which the Chiricahuas seeded with kaffir and millet corn. For once, the weather worked to their advantage. Their crops, Purington reported, were in excellent condition. In addition to raising 240,000 pounds of corn and 1.3 million pounds of hay, they also grew sweet potatoes, tomatoes, melons, and other small vegetables.

The Chiricahuas also experienced increased success with their cattle herd. Especially encouraging was news that winter cattle losses were small. To minimize any future loss, Purington inaugurated a breeding program designed so that calves would arrive during the late spring rather than in February or March. Purington said there were 4,076 head on the range, and he expected an increase of 2,000 head in

Jason Betzinez *(far right)* and four unidentified Chiricahuas baling hay,
circa 1904. *Courtesy Fort Sill Museum.*

1905 and 2,500 in 1906. Furthermore, the Chiricahuas sold 498 steers
for $16,888.

When the harvest was completed, the Chiricahuas returned to
their normal routine of repairing buildings and fences, and Purington
noted that his charges passed the winter of 1904–1905 uneventfully.[3]
The following spring, however, a disconcerting incident transpired. On
May 15, 1905, General Lee conducted his annual inspection of Fort Sill.
He took advantage of the occasion to speak with Geronimo and other
Chiricahuas who sought an audience. Lee reported that Geronimo, who
did not hesitate to express his discontent with Fort Sill, requested that
Lee ask President Theodore Roosevelt to send his people back to their
old homes in southeastern Arizona. In addition, Geronimo said that
Fort Sill was an unhealthful place to live. Commenting on their griev-
ances, Lee observed that those Chiricahuas longing to return to Arizona were the "old timers" who, "common to their class," held the
"desire of living in the country of their ancestors."[4] Of course, much of
their disaffection resulted from uncertainty about whether they would
receive the allotments promised them at this post.[5]

Observations notwithstanding, Lee did not take their complaints lightly. He instructed Purington to prepare a report elucidating
his ideas regarding both the Chiricahuas' transfer—along with their

reservation—to Interior and the advisability of allotting them land in severalty. Purington believed Fort Sill belonged to the Chiricahuas. They "knew a reservation was being sought for them and . . . were told" Fort Sill "was their reservation." They were given assurances "they would not be moved again."

Though Purington said their rights to Fort Sill should be respected, he also understood the need to retain this post as a viable installation and expressed concern that Chiricahua allotment thereon would hamper the post's utility for military purposes. Only a small portion of Fort Sill contained arable land. Allotment of Fort Sill in its entirety, which required exclusion of rocky and other worthless areas, would necessitate this post's immediate abandonment. Even then, "these Indians would not be as well provided for as the Kiowas and Comanches." Purington believed such a course inadvisable because Fort Sill was one of the War Department's most valuable reservations. He therefore recommended that the Chiricahuas remain under War Department jurisdiction. This would allow the military to retain control over that area of Fort Sill occupied by the Chiricahuas because their interests did not require the War Department to abandon the installation.

Furthermore, Purington perceived a very real danger to the Chiricahua's welfare were these Indians given allotments either within or outside Fort Sill's confines. "If allotted in the usual way," their cattle industry "would be immediately destroyed." This was certainly an important consideration. Although the cattle were owned individually, Interior, which opposed communal activities among Indians, might not allow for communal grazing in providing an adequate land base upon which to graze the cattle herd in its entirety.

In addition, as individuals died, family members would sell the deceased's allotment to land-hungry whites. Were this allowed to occur, Purington believed that Fort Sill would almost immediately begin to slip away from the Chiricahuas. Within twenty-five years, both they and the War Department would lose the entire installation. Purington also looked askance at the very suggestion of turning them over to Interior. He, too, did not think they should be returned to the Southwest.[6]

Major Henry L. Ripley, Fort Sill's commandant, not only disagreed with Purington's view that Fort Sill belonged to the Chiricahuas but also considered it inadvisable to sacrifice any part of this installation for their permanent allotment. Located in the neighboring vicinity, Ripley said, was a goodly amount of land of equal value on which the Chiricahuas could be allotted were such action deemed in their best interest. If the "question of returning these Indians" to the Southwest were ever "seriously considered," then "as a preliminary step," Ripley recommended "that a delegation be sent . . . to look over the country" not seen by the Chiricahuas for twenty years and compare it with Oklahoma.[7] General Lee, active years earlier as an agent for the Southern Cheyennes, believed the Chiricahuas ought to maintain their present status for several more years.[8] Allotment "would be suicidal and tend to their ultimate poverty and vagrancy as soon as they could dispose of their land to white men." As to a delegation journeying to the Southwest "to look over the situation," Lee suggested that a small contingent of Chiricahuas be allowed to travel there for this purpose, possibly because he believed the dissatisfied element among them would finally be convinced that Oklahoma was best for them.[9]

With one important exception, Lieutenant General Adna R. Chaffee, chief of staff, advised adherence to Lee's suggestions. Chaffee, who served in the 1882 Sierra Madre Apache campaign, did not condone Lee's proposal that a Chiricahua delegation be permitted to traverse the Gila River's headwaters region.[10] Chaffee believed nothing positive could come of such an endeavor. Rather, much damage would ensue because both the "restlessness of those Indians who might go and their discontent with their present surroundings" would intensify. Chaffee, who was personally acquainted with both the Chiricahuas' present location and the region they desired to visit, was convinced that Fort Sill was "best for them in every way."[11] Although he squelched this proposal, the time fast approached when the requisite authority would be granted for this expedition, an action that eventually set the stage for removal of most of the Chiricahuas to the West. For the present, however, they continued to be mistakenly identified as Geronimo's Apaches, and their removal to this region was therefore out of the question due to potential political backlash. Ironically, this situation safeguarded—at least temporarily—their interests at Fort Sill.

Meanwhile, despite occasional rumblings about a possible Chiricahua removal to New Mexico, Reformed Church in America personnel at the Apache Mission earnestly continued their labors among their spiritual charges. A significant 1905 event held great import for the Chiricahuas' future. On May 9, Reverend Doctor Walter C. Roe, who had worked for several years at the Reformed Church in America's mission in Colony, Oklahoma, accepted the position of superintendent of missions for the Oklahoma field.[12] In time, utilizing his newly won position to good effect, Roe would exert what pressure and influence he

View of the Dutch Reformed Church (Reformed Church in America) Fort Sill Apache Mission buildings, including the elementary school, orphanage, laundry, church, and camp meeting tent. *Courtesy Fort Sill Museum.*

deemed necessary to protect the Chiricahuas' interests to the fullest possible extent.

Although Reformed Church in America missionaries believed both the stability of their enterprise and the fruitfulness of their endeavors would continue, rumors resurfaced concerning a possible removal of the Chiricahuas from Fort Sill. On April 21, 1906, Fort Sill's newest commander, Major Charles W. Taylor, penned the first official explanation for the disaffection engendered among the Chiricahuas by recent developments that, they believed, had ominous implications for the prospect of receiving title to Fort Sill. There seemed to be, Taylor noted, "some feeling of unrest" among them resulting from newspaper accounts and numerous discussions respecting both Fort Sill's enlargement and the "opening of new lands for settlement."[13] But then, as Hugh L. Scott had presciently predicted on August 30, 1902, even the slightest agitation upon these issues would have a most deleterious effect.

Indeed, events increasingly adverse to the Chiricahuas' interests proportionately magnified their feelings of discontent. Ultimately, those who lost all hope of ever receiving allotments once promised them at Fort Sill begged to be returned to their old homes in the Southwest. Because they were principally concerned about their children's welfare, Taylor believed much would be added "to their permanent contentment if the matter could be definitely settled." Therefore, Taylor

The Apache Mission's Chiricahua Christian Endeavor Society, 1903.
Courtesy Fort Sill Museum.

suggested that a delegation of Chiricahuas be sent to Washington as a step toward finally resolving this issue. This recommendation received immediate approval.

As matters developed, the delegation proved unnecessary. During the second half of October 1906, Secretary of War William Howard Taft personally appeared at Fort Sill on a three-day visit, an event that did not lessen the Chiricahuas' apprehensions over being removed from this installation. While at Fort Sill, Taft remarked that of all the installations in the United States, this was the one best suited for long-distance cannon practice. Furthermore, it possessed ideal facilities to become both a regimental and divisional station. In short, Taft believed Fort Sill to be the finest military reservation in the country.[14]

Even so, Taft met with several of the Chiricahuas.[15] As the interview commenced, George M. Wratten, their interpreter since the mid-1880s, quickly underscored what he saw as the central issue: those Chiricahuas dissatisfied with current conditions who therefore requested a change of scene did so primarily because of the uncertainty they felt regarding their position at Fort Sill, especially concerning the permanent homes and allotments previously promised them

The Apache Mission's Chiricahua Women's Missionary Society.
Courtesy Fort Sill Museum.

there. Jason Betzinez, who continually pressed for allotment in Oklahoma, was one of the three Chiricahua spokesmen who discussed the
Chiricahua's future status with Taft. Betzinez stated that "we want to
stay at Fort Sill and have those homes and lands" thereon "given to
us."[16] Chatto and Toclanny asked for homes "near the head of the
Gila River in the vicinity of Silver City, New Mexico, somewhere near
the Black Range."[17]

After concluding this interview, Taft briefly conferred with Naiche, an important participant in the Apache wars, and Asa Daklugie,
who incessantly appealed for removal to New Mexico. Taft said he
could make no definite commitments regarding any relocation of the
Chiricahuas to that territory. He left instructions directing them to examine the Hot Springs region. Taft promised to act on the matter once
he received their report.[18]

Purington forwarded Naiche and Daklugie's report to Washington on January 7, 1907. Therein, Naiche explained that severe weather and a shortage of funds prevented them from traveling beyond the Mescalero Reservation, whereupon the Agent suggested they examine it as a possible place for future settlement. Naiche and Daklugie observed that there existed grazing land, plenty of water, a good school for the children, timber good for lumber, and 475,000 acres of tillable land upon which wheat, oats, corn, Irish potatoes, kaffir corn, alfalfa, and other vegetables could be raised. Neither Purington nor Chatto, Toclanny, and Betzinez were particularly convinced of the merits of these arguments. Upon further inquiry, Purington learned that they had failed to inspect the region as thoroughly as they should have. Instead, both had spent much of their time "hunting and visiting with other Indians." Chatto reiterated his earlier request that a delegation be sent to inspect the Warm Springs region.[19] Taylor suggested that such a delegation be sent but advised his superiors that he believed the land in question had been thrown open to settlement. Were this the case, there was no point in sending anyone to look at unavailable land.[20]

As it turned out, on the very day Taylor offered his recommendations regarding an inspection of the Warm Springs country, Purington reported that Jason Betzinez and another Chiricahua were already in the vicinity. While awaiting their findings, Purington received a list from Naiche and Daklugie of those Chiricahuas who wished to live on the Mescalero Indian Reservation in New Mexico. Purington said they wanted to bring their cattle and other property along with them. In addition, the tribe appeared "divided on the question as to where they wanted to settle." Purington said he lacked sufficient information on either location to make suitable recommendations in the matter. As to their cattle, he believed it was unsafe to ship them to New Mexico because of the Texas fever tick. Purington said he would ascertain the wishes of the other Chiricahuas as soon as possible. "If they would stick to one idea and not change with the tide, one could formulate some plan for them."[21]

Taylor endorsed these recommendations. Upon receipt of Purington's report, Taft conferred with Roosevelt on the proper course to pursue. During this conference, Roosevelt must have impressed Taft with the political utility of maintaining the Chiricahuas where they were. Thus, Taft believed it imprudent, for the moment, to consider their removal to New Mexico. When it became necessary to use Fort Sill for military purposes, it would then be time to discuss a new location for them.

For the time being, Taft thought it wise to inform them that relocation to New Mexico was not possible, and they therefore had to remain in a locale that had made them as prosperous as any tribe under the government's supervision.[22]

Thus, the propaganda campaign that erroneously identified the Chiricahuas as Geronimo's band of Apaches made removal of these displaced people to New Mexico politically inexpedient. In the main, this stigma would be removed only after his demise. Until Geronimo's death actually occurred, continuous western clamor—born of mistaken assumptions fraught with emotionally laden memories of past horrors—against the Chiricahuas' return to their former southwestern home was potentially ruinous to those politicians who had the audacity to even suggest such a project. On the other hand, the undercurrents of Chiricahua disaffection engendered by the uncertainty of their permanent allotment at Fort Sill provided an unexpected opening wedge that the War Department later utilized to both resolve the allotment issue and permanently retain Fort Sill intact as a viable military installation.

Despite the views of some officers that the Chiricahuas were better off in Oklahoma, during the summer of 1907 military officials launched yet another investigation regarding the feasibility of removing them to New Mexico. This investigation took place when Major General James Franklin Bell, chief of staff, visited Fort Sill in late June. During the course of a conference convened on June 27, Bell advised the Chiricahuas of his intention to recommend that a board of inquiry meet at this post to prepare plans for permanently placing them elsewhere. Bell proposed that, meanwhile, several of these Indians be permitted to examine potential resettlement sites in Arizona or New Mexico to ascertain their suitability.[23] Bell also promised to suggest that the captives be liberated. No Chiricahuas would be required to leave Fort Sill against their will. Even so, because he believed that Fort Sill must be retained by the War Department for purely military purposes, Bell recommended that the Chiricahuas not be given land in severalty at this installation. The government, he said, would encounter little difficulty in finding sufficient land to allot them at another location.[24]

Bell's recommendations reached Acting Secretary of War Fred C. Ainsworth on July 17.[25] Ainsworth did not want to act on Bell's requests without authorization from his superiors because he knew the "horror and detestation with which the people of Arizona and New Mexico regard this murderous band that ravaged their territories so long and so severely." It was "reasonable to expect a storm of protest from those people" were the War Department to return "members of the band to . . . scenes of their former depredations." Even so, Ainsworth believed the War Department should renew its efforts to have Interior retake custody of the Chiricahuas.[26]

President Roosevelt disapproved Bell's requests. At the same time, he approved the War Department's suggestion that all aspects of the Chiricahuas' status be thoroughly discussed with Interior Department officials.[27] Accordingly, military personnel referred this matter to Interior on July 27.[28] Here the issue remained in limbo until its revival in March 1908. Still, General Bell's recommendations did effect a definitive resolution of at least one aspect of the matter as far as the War Department was concerned: clearly, the Chiricahuas were not to be allotted at Fort Sill.

By the summer of 1907, the Chiricahuas' concern over their future at Fort Sill finally filtered down to the workers at the Apache Mission. Yet there was one missionary who remained undaunted by the dark future seemingly facing the Apache Mission and its spiritual charges. Later that year there came to the mission a teacher who, in time, would show herself to be especially devoted to the Chiricahuas' welfare.[29] From the moment of her arrival, missionary Hendrina Hospers took to her labors among the Chiricahuas with exceptional zeal. Well aware of her limitations, she recognized the need to develop an increased understanding of these people.[30] In time, the Chiricahuas not only bestowed on her their trust but also came to hold Hospers in high esteem.

When government pressure to vacate Fort Sill became too great to resist alone, those desperate Chiricahuas steadfastly desiring allotments in Oklahoma approached Hospers for help. They were not disappointed, for Hendrina Hospers upheld their trust. Even so, while the Apache Mission experienced a generally prosperous state of affairs throughout 1908, those sinister forces that cast a shadow over its long-term prospects again regrouped. Such forces would in time oversee both the mission's demise and the Chiricahuas' removal from Fort Sill.

In January 1908, military officials initiated a new effort to resolve the issue of permanent homes for these Indians. On March 7, Vincent Natalish, a Chiricahua educated at Carlisle and residing in New York City, requested Kansas Senator Charles Curtis's assistance in obtaining relief for his people. Natalish, who for a number of years had kept abreast of the Chiricahuas' situation, advised Curtis that on January 7, General Bell had personally informed him that the War Department intended to make Fort Sill a permanent post. This meant that his

Partial contingent of Apache Mission staff. Identified *(left to right)* are
Pastor James Bell, Miss Martha Prince, and Miss Hendrina Hospers.
Courtesy Fort Sill Museum.

people would have to be removed. Because it was the Interior Department's responsibility to locate a new home for the Chiricahuas, Natalish also called on Commissioner of Indian Affairs Francis E. Leupp.
Leupp asked him to ascertain their desires and then examine possible
relocation sites in Arizona.[31]

On March 7, Natalish reported the results of his investigation to
both Curtis and Leupp. So despairing had many Chiricahuas become
regarding the possibility of remaining in Oklahoma on the allotments
promised them that, because Fort Sill was to remain a military installation, a number desired to return not to Mescalero but to their original homes on the Warms Springs Reservation in southwestern New
Mexico.[32] According to Natalish, the land and country at Mescalero
was worthless for grazing and agriculture. At San Carlos, there was
"not enough farming land to go around among the Apaches who are
already there." With the "only strip of land which might be used for
grazing . . . fenced off by a cattle company," what remained of this

reservation was "all desert." In a moment of reflection, Natalish said he "often wondered" what the government's idea was "in forcing the Apaches off their old homes where they had farms and were contented" and then compelling "them to make" the "San Carlos desert their home, where they would have to be fed at the Government's expense forever." After all, said Natalish, taking the Chiricahuas from their homes was "the foundation of all the troubles which took place in New Mexico and Arizona."[33]

Such clamor for a resolution of this problem prompted Interior on April 27, 1908, to answer the War Department's July 27, 1907, inquiry as to whether Interior was willing to retake custody of these Indians. Interior's reply was somewhat vague. Because the Chiricahuas had "become a fairly industrious as well as prosperous race," Interior believed their removal from Fort Sill to be inadvisable. Their current status should continue until the president could again be consulted on this particular matter.[34] What was made clear, however, was that even though necessity might in time dictate the use of Fort Sill for solely military purposes, until a compromise solution presented itself respecting the availability of Kiowa and Comanche dead allotments for those Chiricahuas desiring to remain in Oklahoma, Interior would adhere to its 1904 position that these Indians should receive the permanent allotments promised them at Fort Sill.

On January 7, 1909, Vincent Natalish renewed his appeal for both the Chiricahuas' release and their return to southwestern New Mexico. Writing to Roosevelt, Natalish reminded the president that the Chiricahuas' removal from their Arizona and New Mexico homes to San Carlos was "the beginning of their outbreaks." Still, "in every uprising there always have been many who joined the United States forces and fought against their own people." Thus "many of the Apaches enlisted as scouts and fought faithfully with the United States Army against Geronimo." But, he asked rhetorically, "what happened to those Apaches that were loyal to the Government and fought for it?" After all the "hardships the scouts endured while fighting against their own people, the United States Government sent them and their families into exile." They suffered the "same penalty as those against whom they had fought." Many of them perished in captivity. Additionally, for "twenty-two long years they have been and are now held as prisoners of war." Did not "such treatment from a civilized government make a man's blood boil?" Natalish then noted there existed "other tribes of Indians who . . . fought the United States Government and were captured and sent away in captivity without losing their land." They were "allowed to return to their homes; if any part of their land had been taken away the Government paid them for it." Natalish hoped Roosevelt would give this matter his attention and deal justly with these people.[35]

Before any relocation to the Southwest could be contemplated, the undeserved stigma attaching to the Chiricahuas of being "Geronimo's Apaches" would have to be eliminated. This objective could only be realized through Geronimo's demise, which occurred less than two months later in February 1909, prompting the Mescalero Indian Agent to suggest that the Chiricahuas be removed to that reservation. This offer intensified the disaffection already felt by those Chiricahuas who despaired of ever receiving homes at Fort Sill. This feeling was used to good advantage by the War Department eighteen months later when it erected the Field Artillery School of Fire at Fort Sill and subsequently sought to remove the Chiricahuas altogether. Had Interior retaken custody of the Chiricahuas in 1897 as the War Department had requested, the bitter internecine struggle that ensued over the final disposition of these displaced people would have been avoided. Furthermore, Interior would not have been burdened by the heavy expense incurred as a result of this settlement.

10

Opening the Way to Removal From Fort Sill: Geronimo's Demise and Agitation for Relocation to New Mexico

▼   ▼   ▼

P iercing lamentations punctuated the still air during the predawn hours of February 17, 1909. Throughout the Chiricahua camps, old women, "wild with grief," began to mourn their fallen leader.[1] Such keening persisted late into the night. Geronimo, who decades earlier had repeatedly struck terror into the hearts of southwestern settlers, had passed away. From Fort Sill, telegraph wires carried the succinct message that he had died of pneumonia at 6:15 a.m.[2]

As far as many Lawton, Oklahoma, citizens were concerned, Geronimo's death "aroused as much commotion and . . . as deep an interest in this city as would have been occasioned by the demise of most any distinguished man." Indeed, Lawton's leading newspapers, piecing together Geronimo's obituary, vied with one another in the hyperbole of their coverage. "No Indian," said the *Daily News Republican,* "living or dead, ever was so famous, so generally known of, or constituted such a racy item of news." Though "he was perhaps the most cruel and bloodthirsty brave that ever scalped a victim," as a "world character," Geronimo would "ever live in history."[3] Not to be outdone, the *Lawton Constitution Democrat* topped its masthead with the following proclamation: "In the death of Geronimo, once the terror of all Christendom, but another milestone" was reached in the "'passing of Poor Lo,' the 'Original American.'" Furthermore, this journal noted that "even to the hour of his death he could not forget the great pleasures and excitement of the warpath." Hence, people who "knew him best were unalterably opposed to the proposition of allowing him to return to the Arizona fields of his former raids of rapine and murder."[4]

For this reason, Naiche, addressing his people after the burial service at Fort Sill, not only recalled Geronimo's prowess as a warrior but also declared that he was not to be followed in peacetime. Although Geronimo could fight, Naiche said, "he never learned to control himself and therefore never continued to control others." After Naiche's speech, a number of the old women again moaned in anguish. Pitifully wailing in the strange Chiricahua dialect, they cried, "Everybody hated you: white men hated you, Mexicans hated you, Apaches hated you; all of them hated you. You been good to us. We love you, we hate to see you go."[5]

On the part of some white men, at least, the hate lingered. This sentiment was especially strong in Arizona. Indeed, a perusal of this territory's journals suggests that most Arizonans were ecstatic upon being informed of Geronimo's death. Headlines screamed "bloodthirsty old savage dies of pneumonia at Fort Sill" and "died as lived—hating bitterly to the end the palefaces."[6] According to the *Tucson Citizen*, that "Geronimo should have been hanged twenty years before expressed well the limits of Arizona's sorrow over the demise of the red personification of murder, rapine and theft."[7]

Tucson's *Arizona Daily Star*, reporting Geronimo's death in equally lurid terms, said that although the "world loses through the death of good men," in the case of Geronimo's demise, the loss was a singular gain. Pandering to its readers' penchant for the sensational, this journal then titillated its clientele by advising them that he "died ripe in years, full of Sunday school literature and with as much deviltry as the fiend incarnate to whom he has just gone." As a "craftsmaster in the art of human deviltry," Geronimo could give "old Torquemada cards and spades and beat him with his own trumps." Of course, the "minister who buried him probably mourned his passing as a good man." But even so, "a good Indian is good when he is good and cold— otherwise he is bad."[8]

Notifying Tombstone's citizens that Geronimo had been "gathered to his fathers," the *Epitaph* proffered the suggestion that he "ought to have been gathered there in his early youth." Furthermore, that city's paper vehemently opposed the return of Geronimo's remains to Arizona, lest that territory's "matchless ozone . . . bring him back to life."[9] Bisbee residents were reminded that Geronimo, who continuously "contested with a dogged determination the coming of the white man to Arizona," ceaselessly fought the "march of civilization and industry in this Territory." Seen in this light, his death "removed from life a character" who, in the future, would figure prominently in Arizona's history.[10]

In New Mexico, reaction to Geronimo's demise was calm compared with the notice his passing attracted in Arizona's press. An Alamogordo newspaper, the *Otero County Advertiser,* was one of the few territorial journals to report the event. It coolly noted that Geronimo was once the terror of the West. Even so, readers learned, because he "professed religion three years ago," Christian missionaries would conduct the decedent's funeral.[11]

Such calm as many New Mexicans evinced upon learning of Geronimo's demise boded well for those Chiricahuas who eventually elected relocation to that territory. His death removed the one impediment that had prevented resettlement of those prisoners who wished to join their relatives and friends at Mescalero. Unlike Arizonans, most New Mexicans did not care whether these Indians removed to their territory.

Geronimo's death also allowed the military to play more easily upon the dissatisfaction experienced by many of the Chiricahua prisoners, thereby facilitating their removal to Mescalero yet further. These maneuvers made it equally difficult for those Chiricahuas desiring to remain in Oklahoma to do so, even were they not to be allotted at Fort Sill. Hence, the way was opened to retain Fort Sill as a viable military installation. Most Interior officials maintained their original position on the Chiricahua matter, attempting to force the War Department to adhere to previous promises of providing these Indians with permanent homes at Fort Sill. However, lacking the political clout possessed in abundance by the military, Interior lost this rather protracted struggle.

Interestingly enough, the opening salvo in the struggle between the War and Interior Departments over Chiricahua allotment at Fort Sill was initiated in Interior's lower echelons. This action resulted from the behind-the-scenes endeavors engaged in by James A. Carroll, the Mescalero Indian Agent, despite Interior's steadfast commitment to the policy that War Department officials allot the Chiricahuas as originally planned. Carroll's efforts certainly indicated the degree of southeastern

New Mexico's concern over potential Chiricahua removal to that location, otherwise Carroll never would have considered taking the steps that he did.

During the summer of 1909, Carroll advised Washington superiors that "certain numbers of Geronimo's Band at Fort Sill," closely related to Mescalero tribe members, ceaselessly pleaded to be allowed to reunite with their relatives. Now that Geronimo was dead, there was no longer any reason to deny their petition.[12] Actually, Carroll explained, Commissioner of Indian Affairs Francis E. Leupp had raised this issue several years earlier when visiting the Mescalero Agency. So interested was Leupp in seeing these people reunited that he conferred with Roosevelt on the subject. Roosevelt had appeared equally "anxious to aid the Indians," but ascertaining that opposition existed "to the movement on the part of certain citizens in Arizona—at least, opposition to the removal of Geronimo," the president deemed it "expedient . . . to defer action." Furthermore, Carroll noted, Geronimo's death caused those Chiricahuas desiring the change to renew their efforts to settle there.

Claiming to represent 155 of those Chiricahuas held at Fort Sill, Asa Daklugie, whom Carroll described as doubtless the "most influential member of Geronimo's band," was especially determined to effect consummation of such a project.[13] In May 1909, Daklugie, who envisioned himself as the Moses who would lead his fellow Chiricahuas out of exile at Fort Sill to the freedom of Mescalero, advised Carroll of his determination. Nobody "will change that which I had wanted to do for two years." The two men could discuss the situation during his impending visit.[14] This time, discussions with the Mescaleros would focus on the terms by which the Chiricahuas might be removed to this reservation.[15]

Arriving at Mescalero on May 10, Daklugie asked that a council be called. This meeting was convened on May 13.[16] During the conference, the Mescaleros appeared quite anxious for the Chiricahuas to be settled at their reservation. As a condition for relocation, the Mescaleros stipulated that they bring with them their cattle, which would become tribal property. Of course, were it impossible to carry out these provisions, the Mescaleros would still welcome the Fort Sill band and incorporate them "into the tribe with all the rights and privileges of full membership."

In late June, Carroll seized an opportunity to present his views before appropriate Interior officials. U.S. Indian Inspector James McLaughlin, on business at Mescalero, spoke with several members of

Asa Daklugie. *Courtesy Fort Sill Museum.*

this tribe, who requested that a council be called to discuss bringing their "friends here from Fort Sill." Accordingly, McLaughlin convened this conference on June 26. Magoosh, one of the leading spokesmen, said that the Mescaleros were "anxious to get those Fort Sill Indians over here." Furthermore, he had visited with the Chiricahuas at Fort

Sill. Consulting with them, Magoosh learned that "most of them wanted to move over here."

Near the conference's end, McLaughlin polled those in attendance as to whether they wished the Fort Sill Apaches to be relocated
at Mescalero. All present gave their assent. At the council's conclusion, McLaughlin explained that no promises could be made other
than to submit their request for the secretary of the interior's consideration.[17] McLaughlin forwarded this request with his observation
that if Interior, "now that . . . Geronimo is dead," were to contemplate
the Chiricahuas' removal from Fort Sill, the Mescalero Reservation
possessed "ample . . . capacity to provide desirable locations for all"
Chiricahuas, should they desire such relocation. McLaughlin recommended their transfer to Mescalero on condition that their wishes respecting this matter be fully ascertained.[18] Although McLaughlin's
report regarding Carroll's proposals to remove the Chiricahuas to
Mescalero was transmitted on July 6 to Commissioner of Indian Affairs Robert G. Valentine, who had replaced Leupp on June 19, 1909,
Valentine took no action on this matter until early 1910.[19]

Valentine also soon heard from Carroll. On July 28, 1909, Carroll
urged removal "to this reservation those members of Geronimo's Band
at Fort Sill who are pleading to come." In part, he based his proposal on
humanitarian considerations. Families who were "so long separated"
would be reunited. Furthermore, the "amalgamation would prove ben-
eficial to the physical condition of both . . . bands." Because each community was small, inbreeding had occurred. This caused their physical
condition to be "simply deplorable. Without an infusion of new blood,
each band must, sooner or later, become extinct."[20]

Samuel M. Brosius and Herbert Welsh, Indian Rights Association
representatives who outlined their own program for freeing the Chiricahuas, also besieged Valentine. For the next four years, this organization maintained constant vigilance over the issue. It did not cease
agitating until these Indians received at least a measure of justice regarding both liberation from their onerous prisoner-of-war status and allotments in Oklahoma for those not wishing to remove to New Mexico.

Brosius believed the original captives' descendants preferred to
remain in Oklahoma and receive their allotments at Fort Sill. Due to
"their continued serfdom under the military," Brosius said, "they have
become despondent and hopeless," a state of mind that paved the way
"for retrogression by steady steps into dissipation." They pleaded for
"allotment and an opportunity to better their condition." At least eighty

acres of land could be allotted to each Chiricahua without seriously diminishing that area of the post specifically dedicated to military use.[21] Having thoroughly studied Brosius's report, Herbert Welsh forwarded it to Commissioner Valentine on August 4 with the observation that the "simplest principles of justice" required the Chiricahuas' release. Once this was accomplished, Welsh said, the federal government should then provide for "their maintenance and welfare."[22] Responding, Valentine said that he was investigating the matter very carefully.[23]

While Valentine launched his own investigation regarding the feasibility of releasing and allotting the Chiricahuas at Fort Sill, his superiors forwarded McLaughlin's report and the papers that accompanied it to the secretary of war on August 9. Acting Interior Secretary Jesse E. Wilson said his department desired the views of military officials concerning the advisability of removing these Indians to Mescalero. Wilson suggested that their officer-in-charge prepare a complete account of their "present condition, their progress, resources and whether it is the desire of a majority of the band to join their relatives in New Mexico." Once Interior possessed this information, the department would carefully consider the matter further.[24]

In August, War Department officials ordered Purington to undertake this investigation and directed Fort Sill's commandant to offer appropriate recommendations on the proposed change. These recommendations were to take into account not only the Chiricahuas' best interests but also the "advantage from a military point of view in having them removed from Fort Sill."[25] On August 22, Purington conferred with the Chiricahuas to determine whether they wished to reside at Mescalero. Although thirty-eight of those attending opted for Mescalero, eighteen voted for Ojo Caliente. If they could not relocate there, they would prefer to remain at Fort Sill. About a third of those who had not yet despaired of being allotted at Fort Sill held out for homes at that installation.

In this regard, James Kaywaykla poignantly noted that "they haven't any home, no place they could call their own; today it appears as if it was right in front of us awaiting." Kaywaykla knew the "country around Fort Sill. . . . We have thought of this land here and want it. They say sometimes that it can't be ours—that they are going to put a lot of soldiers here." But, Kaywaykla said, "even if they put soldiers here, give us our homes here." While "some of these Apaches want to leave here, we want to stay on these lands. We don't ask for something we have not seen." That which was "over the hill and out of sight we don't want. What we ask for is land that we have seen and is . . . here in front of us." Were a man to live, "he must have something to live on. If I am here I know that I have something to live on, something that will take care of me." Kaywaykla urged Purington to "make a strong plea for this land for us." Echoing Kaywaykla's sentiments to a certain extent, Lawrence Mithlo said the Chiricahuas worked "very hard on this reservation and that is why we like it." Mithlo wished to know "why should we go away and leave it without making something from that labor? Please give it to us and make it so that it is ours."[26]

James Kaywaykla. *Courtesy Fort Sill Museum.*

Purington subsequently offered his recommendations on the matter. Fort Sill should not be taken from these Indians "without regard to their best interests." Yet, partially misinterpreting the 1902 Board of Officers' recommendations, Purington believed that army personnel possessed the right to reserve Fort Sill exclusively for military maneuvers and exercises. Hence, those Chiricahuas who desired resettlement at Mescalero and Ojo Caliente should be sent there. As for those Chiricahuas who elected to remain in Oklahoma, Purington proposed purchasing for them the allotments of deceased Kiowas and Comanches.[27] Regarding the War Department's eventual repudiation of its earlier promises of allotment at Fort Sill, Purington's suggestions ultimately sealed the Chiricahuas' fate. His ideas resulted in the removal of all Chiricahuas from the installation.

CHAPTER

11

Foreclosure of Chiricahua Rights to Fort Sill: Establishment of the U.S. Army Field Artillery School of Fire

▼　▼　▼

A ctually, inklings that their eventual removal was a foregone conclusion had arisen prior to Purington's August 1909 conference.
According to the *Lawton Constitution Democrat*, with "the passing of
Geronimo on to the 'happy hunting grounds,'" the War Department finally took notice of the Chiricahuas' pleas in this regard.[1] Only a day
after Geronimo's death, this journal electrified its readers with the
speculation that a new $20-million post was in the offing for Fort Sill.
Construction was to be spread over a ten-year period. When completed, the installation would "be the greatest military plant in the United
States." Current proposals dictated that the "post . . . be devoted exclusively to the artillery arm of the service."[2]

When Purington's recommendation that the Chiricahuas be removed to New Mexico crossed James F. Bell's desk for action, the chief
of staff could truthfully state that the Fort Sill Reservation, "not only as
originally bounded, but as bounded by the additions, is now deemed
by the War Department as necessary for military purposes." Therefore,
the military believed it desirable "to reduce the numbers of Indians

thereon to the least practicable number."[3] Clearly, one way or another, they would all have to vacate Fort Sill.

On November 18, 1909, Secretary of War Jacob M. Dickinson suggested that Purington's recommendation be approved and Interior be so notified. President William Howard Taft initially disagreed.[4] Acting Secretary of War Robert Shaw Oliver later suggested that Taft reconsider his decision because Purington's report was merely the information that Interior had called for in its letters of August 9 and December 18. Taft relented to the extent of instructing Oliver to leave any Chiricahua relocation proposal to Interior's discretion.[5]

On December 23, Oliver informed Interior Secretary Richard A. Ballinger that many of the Fort Sill Apaches appeared anxious for removal to the Southwest. Of course, a small number of Chiricahuas desired to remain at this post. However, military authorities wanted all of these Indians removed from Fort Sill. Still, the War Department decided the removal question should be resolved by Interior.[6]

Ballinger advised the War Department on December 31 that the time had come when the Chiricahuas "should no longer be held even nominally as prisoners." This was especially true because the demands of justice had been fully satisfied during the twenty-four years the Chiricahuas had spent as captives. Ballinger suggested that as soon as practicable, military officials take the necessary steps to release these Indians and transfer their jurisdiction to Interior. Should the War Department approve this suggestion, Interior would provide for their care and maintenance at Fort Sill until such time as it could "determine what disposition is to be made of those who wish to remove" from this post. Yet, when it came to the question of removing those Chiricahuas who wished to remain at Fort Sill, Ballinger said this was one issue that Interior desired to "investigate further before taking any decisive steps in that direction."[7]

Responding to Oliver's views of December 23, 1909, Indian Commissioner Valentine said on January 12, 1910, that the record showed that these Indians were promised Fort Sill "as their permanent home and that they would not be moved again." Furthermore, the "area of the original reservation appears to have been nearly doubled for the express purpose of settling them there permanently." Also, the War Department originally intended to "abandon the military post at some future time and allot the lands to the Indians in severalty." In any event, the Chiricahuas had "at least a right of occupancy in the lands of the original reservation" inasmuch as the additions would not have been procured "but for the presence of the Indians thereon." They also seemed to be the "rightful owners" of these additions. Hence, no change should be made in their present location.[8] Shortly, the Indian Office took an even stronger stand on this issue.

With cudgels taken up by the Indian Office, all parties having an interest in resolving the Chiricahua release, removal, and allotment issues immediately began maneuvering to ensure supremacy of their respective positions. In late January 1910, in a statement that in part closely paralleled Interior's stand, Samuel M. Brosius outlined the case as far as the Indian Rights Association was concerned. Regarding those Chiricahuas desiring to remove to Mescalero due to the disappointment of not receiving their promised allotments, Brosius believed that if younger members of the tribe were permitted to "select allotments at Fort Sill, few of the older members will then wish to return to Mescalero. . . . That they are held prisoners of war," Brosius said, "may incline the older members" to wish relocation at Mescalero, "but after they are convinced that they may take allotments at Fort Sill," they, too, would "decide to remain there, if their status is changed from prisoners to free men." Brosius suggested that Congress be exhorted to pass legislation allotting them at Fort Sill.[9]

Though not as adamant as Brosius on the matter of retaining all the Chiricahuas at Fort Sill, Walter C. Roe approved of pending legislation that provided for allotment of those Chiricahuas wanting to remain there.[10] Roe also supported the stipulation permitting the "non-progressives to join their relatives out West" because it allowed them to "live under conditions suited to their degree of advancement." In the ensuing struggle over how best to dispose of this problem, the Reformed Church, accepting Roe's views as its official stand and seeking a just solution that would redound to the benefit of all Chiricahuas, did not deviate from this position.

By the end of 1910, the Bureau of Indian Affairs publicly stated what it viewed as acceptable justice for the Chiricahuas. Because many were successful stock raisers who became attached to their lands, those so desiring were to be permitted to remain at Fort Sill permanently and be allotted lands at this location.[11] With the Indian Office having once again emphatically laid down the gauntlet respecting Chiricahua release, removal, and allotment, the War Department responded by exerting every effort to protect its interests, thereby ensuring Fort Sill's viability as a military installation.

But not all members of the military establishment shared the War Department's attitude. At Fort Sill there was at least one officer who understood the true nature of the dilemma besetting the Chiricahuas. Their friend when he was post commandant ten years earlier, Major George L. Scott, who replaced Purington in the late fall of 1910, returned as their new officer-in-charge. Writing sympathetically of their plight on December 14, 1910, he clearly outlined for Colonel Hugh L. Scott the conditions that confronted them.

Major George Scott said they appeared to have "lost their grip since active measures have been taken to move them" and thus did not appear as interested in their work as they had been ten years earlier. Continuing his analysis, the major then discussed the War Department's manipulation of these undercurrents of disaffection and despair, machinations devised to remove the Chiricahuas from Fort Sill altogether. He also observed that many of these Indians had inadvertently hastened their potential exodus by requesting a change. Evidently, the War Department wished to be rid of them. Therefore, those Chiricahuas seeking change only made it easier "for those who think they are in the way" to obtain their removal, a course of action that indeed seemed "to be on the slate."

Regarding the proposal to relocate them in the West, George Scott said that resettling this band in either Arizona or New Mexico with the expectation they would "succeed in making a living among people who are hostile . . . towards them because of their history" required more faith than he possessed. "It would be unfair to the nth degree with them." Still, he feared the matter had "gone too far to alter or amend." Therefore, one could only "meet conditions as they are imposed and make the best of them."[12]

Actually, matters had proceeded too far to prevent the Chiricahuas' situation from deteriorating yet further. At the very time the major described for Hugh Scott what he perceived as the deplorable circumstances arrayed against the Chiricahuas, Judge Advocate General George W. Davis prepared recommendations that led to their removal from Fort Sill. Regarding the 1897 executive order procuring the Eastern and Western Additions, Davis admitted the Chiricahuas had a legal claim to a large extent of Fort Sill and noted that the order created a permanent status for these Indians at this installation. But any attempt to allot them at this post was inexpedient. Therefore, legislation with such an objective "should not be favorably recommended to Congress."

Deliberately misconstruing the actual intent behind the phrases "only for military purposes" (as inserted in the February 17, 1897, agreement with the Kiowas and Comanches that procured these additions for the Chiricahuas' permanent settlement) and "for exclusive use for military purposes" (as incorporated into the February 26, 1897, presidential executive order officially attaching these tracts to Fort Sill), Davis devised a liberal interpretation of these phrases that he utilized to the War Department's advantage. There existed, Davis said, "a condition of fact, as established by executive and legislative action," which remained unaltered. "Since the . . . Eastern and Western Additions to the original military reservation were made," the War Department "found . . . the enlarged reservation . . . in the highest degree necessary for military purposes in the training and instruction of the troops, especially of the field artillery." Davis then suggested that the Chiricahuas be retained at Fort Sill until they could be removed to another reservation.[13]

Davis's explication of the situation ignored those implications inherent in Hugh Scott's 1897 statement to the Kiowas and Comanches regarding the stipulation "for exclusive use for military purposes." In no way was the term *use* meant to signify ownership. This was especially true because until Congress ratified the Jerome Agreement, both the additions and the original post were to revert back to the Kiowas and Comanches once the War Department ceased utilizing this land for military purposes—unless, of course, three-fourths of these Indians sold the tract outright to the United States.

In point of fact, the War Department's ownership of the land on which Fort Sill was located did not occur until the Jerome Agreement's ratification in 1900. According to George Scott, the aforesaid stipulation meant that the Eastern and Western Additions held the same legal status as the old military reservation. Of necessity, this provision was specifically formulated as a guarantee to assure the Kiowas and Comanches that the military would permit no part of Fort Sill to be aggrandized by white settlers because, Scott explained, in the words of Davis himself, this installation was merely a military reservation superimposed on an Indian reservation.

Even so, Davis's recommendations concerning the Chiricahuas' release, relocation, and allotment joined the battle over these issues. By so responding to the challenge earlier laid down by the Indian Office, the War Department, staunchly endeavoring to preserve intact its interests at Fort Sill, finally clarified its position by plainly opting for the Chiricahuas' removal. Thus, the War Department arrayed itself against the Interior Department, the Bureau of Indian Affairs, the Board of Indian Commissioners, the Indian Rights Association, and the Reformed Church in America, all of which were equally adamant in their insistence that the Chiricahuas be permanently allotted at Fort Sill as promised. Under the circumstances, the opposition experienced by military officials should have been overwhelming. But after four years of somewhat acrimonious struggle, the War Department found itself victorious.

Davis claimed that it was "in the highest degree necessary" that Fort Sill be retained for military purposes because during the fall of 1910, the War Department made arrangements to establish at Fort Sill the U.S. Army Field Artillery School of Fire. In fact, it was already in the process of spending the considerable sum of $1.25 million for the construction of a new post to house this facility. The school's first commandant, Captain Dan T. Moore, strenuously opposed the Chiricahuas' interests, possessing unmitigated antipathy toward them. Moore worked closely with Colonel Edwin St. John Greble, one of the Field Artillery School's most influential supporters. With utmost vigor, both officers zealously sought the quickest and most expedient method by which the military might remove the Chiricahuas altogether from this post.[14]

That the War Department refused to surrender a military installation possessing special advantages for such a school was evident throughout much of the correspondence conducted by Moore and Greble on the subject. On January 18, 1911, Greble said Moore should encounter no difficulty in formulating regulations that protected the prisoners' property. Simply, Greble's main objective was "to get the School started down there and then adjust the Indians after awhile."[15] Evidently, Moore did not take the hint, as demonstrated by his repeated fits of indignation that the school had to coexist with the Chiricahuas' need to herd their cattle on an extend range. Nor did fellow members of the Board of Officers (chaired by Lieutenant Colonel David J. Rumbough) when it convened to prepare special regulations governing the Field Artillery School of Fire's operation. Despite Greble's counsel, the board ignored the Chiricahuas' property rights.

At this point, a highly irritated colonel admonished Moore not to "for heaven's sake, do anything to antagonize the Indians now on the military reservation." Greble then strongly urged Moore to advise Rumbough that their property rights must be respected while they remained at Fort Sill, pointedly stating that "what we are after is to get them to move to some other place." Rumbough's "rules for fire . . . practically stated . . . that the firing would not be stopped even to drive the cattle off the range" and that their Indian Agent was repeatedly advised to this effect. Naturally, George Scott heatedly protested such transgressions,

Captain Dan T. Moore. *Courtesy Fort Sill Museum.*

leading Greble to sternly explain to Moore that if Indian rights organizations became aware of this, such action "would be a beautiful club in their hands to make us keep the Indians on the military reservation." Were more caution exercised in these matters, Greble believed the military could "get these Indians to go." Of course, it was "undoubtedly right to compensate them . . . well for such removal."[16]

Moore must have rankled at what he doubtless viewed as a restraint upon the Field Artillery School of Fire's effectiveness. In a somewhat defensive manner, Moore caustically replied on March 16 that the Chiricahuas' villages were situated in a way that prevented large stretches of the military reservation from being "used for target practice without shooting over or near one of them." Twisting the actual facts, Moore then suggested that "these so-called prisoners of war have more rights and privileges than free men." They were, he insisted, "too lazy to work. Hired men make their crops and cut hay for them." Furthermore, the government purchased this forage and reissued it to them to "feed to Government mules which are used in making" their crops. Moore concluded his tirade with the biting comment that the "Indian rights gang would be the first to howl if we gave these cut-throats exact justice."[17] The disgruntled captain then requested more specific guidelines, in terms of respecting Chiricahua property rights, for firing on the range.[18] Again admonishing Moore, Greble advised him to exercise patience. There was, after all, "no use of giving a weapon to the friends of the Indians."[19]

Several months later, Acting Secretary Oliver advised the opposition that, once again considering the Chiricahua question, the War Department hoped to arrive at a satisfactory resolution of this most complicated issue.[20] On July 20, 1911, Major General Arthur Murray, acting chief of staff, unveiled a plan that amply demonstrated that the military, for some time, had assiduously labored in search of just such an acceptable solution. Because large sums had already been expended on the artillery school's establishment, Murray believed "it would . . . pay the Government well to make such inducements to the Indians that they would be glad to take their land at some other place." As a preliminary measure, Murray thought it best to ascertain what might be offered the Chiricahuas, as well as the degree of amenability among "their white advocates" to such action. Of course, negotiations with the Chiricahuas would have to be opened and conducted carefully to avoid even the appearance of forcing them from Fort Sill.[21]

CHAPTER

12

A Promise "Broken to the Hope"

▼   ▼   ▼

*B*efore engaging in such negotiations, General Arthur Murray suggested that an officer the Chiricahuas had confidence in confer with Interior officials to ascertain what lands were available for occupancy by these Indians.[1] On July 20, 1911, War Department officials selected Hugh Scott for the task.[2] Scott now found himself in the unenviable position of having to accomplish that which he steadfastly opposed—namely, the complete removal of all Chiricahuas from Fort Sill. Were it any comfort to the colonel, his superiors also ordered him to carry out their directives in such a fashion that the Chiricahuas' rights and equities would be completely safeguarded.[3]

On August 8, Scott personally requested Commissioner Valentine's views on the Chiricahua matter. Valentine's reply reflected the Bureau of Indian Affairs' official response to the War Department's position. According to Valentine, the Chiricahuas' best interests required that those who desired to remain at Fort Sill be allotted there. Valentine said that "the furthest I would be willing to go would be to give them an absolutely voluntary option of rejoining their relatives on the Mescalero reservation."[4] In so saying, Valentine inadvertently provided the War Department with additional leverage to force a compromise on Interior and thus achieve the end it sought.

Scott then journeyed to Fort Sill, where he arrived on September 18.[5] At this point, the colonel attempted to convince the Chiricahuas that necessity dictated their relocation elsewhere. Assisting Scott in this assignment were Colonel Greble and Major George W. Goode, the new officer-in-charge. As Scott later reported, he undertook his mission with no small degree of trepidation—and with good reason. Earlier, rumors had reached the Chiricahuas that they were about to be pushed off the post. Naturally, those who expected and wanted allotments at Fort Sill were quite suspicious. Doubtless uppermost in the minds of these particular prisoners was whether the government was once again about to renege on its promises of freedom and homes for those who wanted them at this installation. Indeed, they were ready for Scott and asked him some tough questions.

Attempting to smooth ruffled feelings, Scott explained that he had heard about the Chiricahuas' discontent and came to Fort Sill to discuss their current concerns. But the Chiricahuas, especially those who wanted to remain at Fort Sill, were not readily disarmed. They believed his strategy was to drive a wedge between those who might elect to go to Mescalero and those who wished to remain, the ultimate goal being to remove all of them from Fort Sill. As one of their members, Lawrence Mithlo, so aptly stated, "We are not little children." James Kaywaykla, one of the partisans for allotment at Fort Sill, said that his people were not free. It was wrong for the government to hold his people as prisoners of war under military control. Rather, "it is right that they should set us free" and "give us our homes right here."

After all, they insisted, the Chiricahuas had been promised Fort Sill as their permanent home. Yet, recently, as Talbot Gooday, a Chiricahua prisoner of war who wished to remain at Fort Sill, explained, the army had constructed numerous buildings without asking their views on this matter. How would Scott feel "if something like that would be done on your land?" Furthermore, would the colonel be good enough to explain just exactly what his intentions toward them were? "What will you do with us?" asked Gooday. "Haven't we got any sense?" asked Mithlo. It seemed that Scott no longer wanted them to possess Fort Sill. Benedict Jozhe, a Chiricahua prisoner of war who also favored staying at this post, pointedly asked why, if the land was not to be theirs after all, they were told "not to have any mind for any other place for this is yours and you shall stay here for this is your home?" Did not the Chiricahuas have any "rights in the United States?" Just exactly what was the trouble? Were they not "human beings in the United States?" If not, Benedict plaintively inquired, then "what are we?"[6]

Talbot Gooday. *Courtesy Fort Sill Museum.*

Several days later, on September 21, Scott reconvened the conference. Actually, he needed several days to work out his next move on how to hammer home the idea that the Chiricahuas would have to leave Fort Sill. Scott decided to capitalize on the military's recent misinterpretation of the stipulation "for exclusive use for military purposes" by applying the latest construction of this provision's meaning to the whole of Fort Sill rather than confining it to the original post. These Indians soon grasped the true reason for Scott's visit.

Although the Chiricahuas wishing to relocate to Mescalero needed no convincing, Scott thought the time appropriate to drop his bombshell, to wit: Fort Sill had not been promised in perpetuity to the prisoners after all. Only the use and occupancy of this installation was guaranteed them until some other arrangements could be made for their care, permanent settlement, and release from prisoner-of-war status. Simply stated, their release from military custody rested upon their willingness to vacate the military reserve. Those who did not wish resettlement in New Mexico were welcome to remain at Fort Sill until they could be accommodated outside the post's confines, but they would do so under their current status. Scott then suggested that an expedition be organized to examine the lands on the Mescalero Reservation. Despite Scott's slick assurance that the government did not want "to take you by the hair of the head and pull you off out there," a stunned and not inconsiderable number of Chiricahuas who desired allotments at Fort Sill quickly realized that their earlier premonitions had proved correct. According to Eugene Chihuahua, Scott apparently had no intention of assisting them with their quest for freedom. As Talbot Gooday bitterly summed things up, there was "only one way out"—either remove to Mescalero and become free or remain as prisoners of war at Fort Sill.[7]

Upon concluding this late September conference, Scott prepared to examine the Mescalero Agency and the former Warm Springs Reservation.[8] On October 2, he arrived at Mescalero and began investigating various lands within its confines.[9] His objective was to find sufficient amounts of timber, grass, water, and land suitable for cultivation. Although there was timber and good grazing land, the fields available for agriculture were small and distant from existing springs, making irrigation difficult.[10]

On October 8, Scott convened a council of the Mescalero headmen, with Asa Daklugie as interpreter. Scott explained that some of the Chiricahuas were dissatisfied with Fort Sill. He then asked about their feelings toward the Chiricahuas. The headmen responded that they liked the Chiricahuas and would be pleased to accept them as their own.[11]

After briefly examining New Mexico's Warm Springs region,[12] Scott and those Chiricahuas accompanying him journeyed back to Fort Sill. Jason Betzinez described the Warm Springs area as a "depressing sight" because the former reservation, "once so fertile and green," was now devoid of vegetation and hence completely ruined.[13] On October 16, soon after their return, the colonel called another conference with the Chiricahuas, during which he reported the delegation's findings. Making a pitch for removal, Scott said that "if anybody feels that they must get away from the domination of the soldier, this is a good opportunity for them." As to when the military might abandon Fort Sill, no one knew. "But from the amount of money they have spent," Scott said, "it would not look as though they were going to give it up soon."

Bowing to the inevitable, the Chiricahuas voted on the matter. Upon Scott's departure, Talbot Gooday implored him "to help us get what we want." Because those who opted for Mescalero would receive their freedom once they arrived there, it was only right that the onerous prisoner-of-war status be lifted from those remaining at Fort Sill. "We ask the Government for this land . . . on the east side of Cache Creek." If the government desired the western portion of the military reserve, they could "have it and all the mountains. It looks like it is big enough for all the practice and all the shooting they want to do. . . . We want to be free here and we ask you to tell the Government to give us our homes. We ask with all our hearts that the Government give us homes."[14]

There was one task remaining that Scott felt compelled to accomplish. He believed that the views of those having frequent contact with the Chiricahuas were important in establishing a reasonable resolution of the Chiricahua problem. He therefore requested additional information from these individuals. Major Goode was the first to respond, strongly suggesting that the Chiricahuas be freed, placed under Interior's control, and given a "liberal allotment in some place where suitable land is available."[15]

Next came the observations of Walter C. Roe. He believed the Chiricahuas had become discouraged because they saw "no way out for themselves to freedom, separate holdings and individual progress." Furthermore, ever since a new "educated and civilized generation" came to the fore, the current manner of managing them and their interests was "worn out. . . . No degree of temporal prosperity," Roe said,

Jason Betzinez. *Courtesy Fort Sill Museum.*

could "compensate for the loss of freedom." This state of affairs was "anomalous and intolerable to the American spirit," particularly because several band members were "originally allies of the United States in the Geronimo hostilities, and others had nothing to do with those campaigns." Certainly, Roe said, "a general knowledge of the facts by the American people would result in deep indignation."

To avoid this, Roe suggested the Chiricahuas be freed, placed under Interior's control, and allocated 30,000 acres at Fort Sill east of Cache Creek. To Roe, who thought the only opposition would emanate from the vested interests of whites inhabiting the nearby towns and countryside, this program appeared both "just and feasible." Naturally, this plan's opponents wanted the land "settled with white people who pay taxes" and wished "to have the post developed to the utmost extent possible as a feeder" to area businesses. Because this problem was also a matter of justice regarding the "performance of our National promise to a helpless band" of Indians, these considerations, Roe maintained, should not dictate the manner in which a solution to the difficulty was arrived at.[16]

These views in hand, Scott returned to Washington and reported the results of his investigation. Indeed, he must have deemed the entire affair most distasteful. This attitude was evident throughout his opening remarks, penned on November 3, to Lieutenant General Leonard Wood, chief of staff. Realizing that the Chiricahuas had just cause to believe that "promises made to them had not yet been fulfilled," Scott said he had approached his task with some misgiving. These "promises were made by the direction of President Cleveland, who told" Scott in Secretary of War Lamont's presence "to get the consent of the Kiowa and Comanche Indians to the addition of enough of their land to the military reservation at Fort Sill to permit" allotment of 160 acres to each Chiricahua upon the post's abandonment. According to Scott, "this abandonment was expected to take place in the near future, although, in fact, no actual date was set." Yet, Scott said, the "promise was there, and the expenditure of a million and a quarter dollars on a new post, afterward," which pushed "forward the abandonment of the reservation into the far distant future, was in effect a violation of that promise so far as men now alive are concerned." Therefore, the "promise was kept to the ear but broken to the hope," because no Congress would even contemplate any "proposition that required the abandonment of a military post just constructed at so high a cost."

Still, Scott was ever the obedient officer. Regardless of his personal feelings, duty required that he make the necessary recommendations. Thus, having privately broached his doubts about the justness of the War Department's actions, Scott proffered preliminary suggestions on how a resolution of the Chiricahua prisoner-of-war difficulty might best be achieved. Because he believed the Indians experienced dissipation, deterioration, and demoralization, Scott suggested that for their own good, despite the vote recently taken, the welfare of those Chiricahuas electing to remain at Fort Sill dictated their removal along with those wanting homes at Mescalero. However, there were a few Chiricahuas wishing to remain in Oklahoma who, having already adopted the white man's road, could be expected to make good use of any lands and homes that might be given them. Perhaps, therefore, a portion of Fort Sill's acreage bordering on the post's eastern perimeter might be allocated to these particular individuals. Were there objections to this proposal, then possibly several allotments of deceased Kiowas and Comanches could be procured at a cost of $2,500 to $3,000 each.[17]

Several days later, General Wood received Scott's final recommendations on the Chiricahua matter. Scott proposed the procurement of legislation that would resettle those Chiricahuas who so desired in New Mexico. Thereafter, they would receive their freedom. Except for those Chiricahuas who were considered "able to make their way among white men," those who wished to remain at Fort Sill would "be permitted to do so . . . under their present status," because the War Department thought their "best chance of survival" was "with the others who have elected to go with the Mescalero Apaches." As for those Chiricahuas who could easily adjust to white society, they might receive allotments either on Fort Sill's northeast quadrant or on the estates of deceased Kiowas and Comanches that would be purchased from their heirs. These particular Chiricahuas would be freed and then fed and clothed by Interior until they harvested their first crops.[18]

Forwarding Scott's recommendation, Secretary of War Henry L. Stimson advised Interior on November 8 that although he wanted to arrange these Indians' affairs so that no injustice would be done, his department had recently established—at considerable expense— the Field Artillery School of Fire and therefore desired to "realize on the value of its plant." Stimson hoped Interior would concur with Scott's suggestions.[19]

On December 15, 1911, Assistant Interior Secretary Carmi A. Thompson approved the first of Scott's recommendations, emphasizing that his approbation rested upon the provision that only those Chiricahuas who so desired be removed to Mescalero. Regarding the second proposition, Thompson insisted that those who desired to remain at Fort Sill be allotted there and released from their prisoner-of-war status.

After all, Thompson said, they were "solemnly promised, on many occasions and by persons whose positions carried with their word weight
of authority," that Fort Sill would be their permanent home. In view of
this, the government's moral obligation was unquestionable. Yet "in
the face of promises made to them, they have seen new preparations
made for the continuance of the military on . . . land" that the Chiricahuas were "led to believe" would "be their future homes." For
"more than two years," Thompson said, the "question of their removal
has been under active consideration." This instilled "in them fear that
they might again be arbitrarily removed and deprived of their houses
and improvements, their horses and stock." Therefore, Thompson explained, Interior's cooperation with Stimson's department hinged on
War's adherence to these guidelines.[20]

Support for Thompson's position came from the Indian Office
and the Board of Indian Commissioners. As the Bureau of Indian Affairs viewed the situation, those Chiricahuas who desired to remain at
Fort Sill "when freed from the jurisdiction of the War Department, as it
is urgently hoped that they will soon be, should be allotted there."[21]
Echoing the Indian Office, the Board of Indian Commissioners believed
plain justice demanded that each Chiricahua prisoner who wished to
remain at Fort Sill "should receive an allotment of not less than eighty
acres." Regarding the 1897 Kiowa and Comanche agreement that enlarged Fort Sill for the Chiricahuas' benefit, "certainly one-half of the
land thus given" was the "least the Government should be willing to
turn over to those Indians who desire to remain." That "only a few Indians are involved is not the chief consideration, which is, rather,
whether the Government can honorably pursue a course less generous
than that suggested."[22]

Yet, in less than six months, this militant position was reversed
entirely. Interior's line of resistance completely crumbled before the incessant onslaughts generated by the War Department's contentions
that military exigencies mandated the removal of all Chiricahuas from
Fort Sill. This change of heart was especially evident in a report drawn
up by George Vaux, a member of the Board of Indian Commissioners,
during the spring of 1912. The report stated that "in view of the consideration due the War Department, which . . . expended large sums in
plans that would be seriously interfered with by insistence on allotment" of the Chiricahuas "within the more fertile portion of the military reservation," the board concluded that those Chiricahuas desiring

relocation to Mescalero should be so removed and suggested that the secretary of the interior "be authorized to purchase for the remaining Indians who desire to stay in Oklahoma so-called dead Kiowa and Comanche allotments" totaling "not less than eighty acres of agricultural land or 160 acres of grazing land for each Indian." This, the board believed, "would do substantial justice to all parties concerned."[23]

13

Military Functionaries Find
a Friend in the House

▼　　▼　　▼

W hen the War Department shifted the battle to the legislature in its struggle against Interior's strategy to allot the Chiricahuas at Fort Sill, military officials found an extremely useful ally in Oklahoma representative Scott Ferris. A pragmatist, Ferris was a master of the politically expedient, and economic exigencies clearly made Chiricahua settlement and allotment at Fort Sill inexpedient. Oklahoma's Fifth Congressional District comprised Ferris's constituency, which included the city of Lawton, his hometown, and neighboring Fort Sill. Lawton depended on Fort Sill for its economic survival. Hence, not only was Chiricahua allotment at Fort Sill politically inadvisable, but it was also financially unthinkable. Although Ferris and fellow Lawtonians were unopposed to the Chiricahuas' release, they would never permit extinction of the town's economic mainstay by allowing Fort Sill's abandonment. Despite the demands of justice, removing this band of Indians in its entirety to Mescalero seemed the appropriate course to pursue to solve this perplexing problem.

Ferris utilized every means at his disposal to block any measure supporting Chiricahua allotment at Fort Sill. A perusal of the *Congressional Record* conjures visions of Ferris the altruist, boldly championing the freeing of a displaced people unjustly treated. But careful examination of the congressman's correspondence with the War Department readily reveals the true purpose beneath his humanitarian stance. This correspondence conclusively demonstrates that Ferris's close working relationship with the military, as well as his staunch support of the War Department's program to retain Fort Sill for military purposes, enabled military officials to force on Interior and its allies a compromise solution to the Chiricahua allotment question.

Ferris's effectiveness as a War Department ally was evident in the way he dealt with the only piece of legislation designed for this purpose—and with subsequent attempts to revitalize such a measure. In February 1910, Oklahoma senator Robert L. Owen introduced a bill providing for the allotment of land to the Chiricahuas.[1] It stipulated that each Indian was to receive at Fort Sill not less than sixty nor more than eighty acres of farming land. Were any of the land so allotted suitable only as grazing land, then such acreage was to be allotted in double quantities. Furthermore, those Chiricahuas desiring homes elsewhere could be provided such by Interior.[2] In effect, this permitted those who so wished to remove to Mescalero.[3]

Support for Owen's measure quickly coalesced. On February 15, Samuel M. Brosius of the Indian Rights Association explained that additions had been made to Fort Sill for the express purpose of releasing and permanently allotting the Chiricahuas at that installation. Yet, those who loved justice would be astounded to learn that for nearly a generation, "under our Constitution and flag over 250 of our native born people have been deprived of their liberty." They neither perpetrated nor were "charged with committing any offense against the United States." Brosius demanded an immediate end to this situation. These Indians had been promised by the government permanent homes and allotments at Fort Sill, an obligation that should be discharged immediately. At this time, the Chiricahuas were to be released "from their bondage under the military and . . . given the rights of free men."[4]

Several days later, Interior Secretary Richard A. Ballinger informed Minnesota senator Moses E. Clapp that the Chiricahuas had been solemnly promised that Fort Sill would be their permanent home. Since then, they had advanced "in civilization far beyond reasonable expectations" and were "fully qualified to receive and care for allotments in severalty." Ballinger not only saw no objection to the bill, but also heartily endorsed its passage.[5] His fellow senators concurred and passed the measure on March 15.[6] Unfortunately for those Chiricahuas wishing to remain in Oklahoma, Owen's allotment bill later stalled in the House, where it eventually failed to pass.

While the Senate prepared to act favorably on this measure, the Oklahoma senator cautiously queried the War Department on March 11 as to whether it supported the permanent allotment at Fort Sill of those Chiricahuas who did not wish to remove to Mescalero.[7] Major General James Franklin Bell, chief of staff, responded that any plan to allot the Chiricahuas at Fort Sill would materially interfere with "a plan of development in which not only the President but Senator Gore and Representative Ferris, as well as the town of Lawton," were most interested. Owen, Bell suggested, should visit Ferris, who would explain why his plan was inadvisable.[8] Owen soon learned that at a cost of $1.25 million, the army had recently constructed a new post housing the Field Artillery School of Fire. He also discovered that this investment naturally led Ferris to use every means at his disposal to defeat the allotment proposal, thus ultimately dooming Owen's measure.[9]

Ferris soon launched obstructionist tactics designed to remove all Chiricahuas from Fort Sill. His solution, introduced on May 2, was to allot each of them either 160 acres of agricultural land or 320 acres of nonirrigable grazing land "anywhere on the public domain of the United States or the District of Alaska."[10] These allotments were to consist of suitable acreage, with special consideration being given to the Indians' "habits, traits, health and general welfare." Furthermore, in order to speedily remove the Chiricahuas from Fort Sill, the measure allocated sufficient moneys to instantly effect this legislation.[11]

To make the measure more palatable to Interior, Ferris later drafted an accompanying piece of legislation authorizing the secretary of the interior to ascertain where a suitable reservation might be procured on which to allot these Indians. Upon the completion of this investigation, the secretary was to report his findings to Congress. Ferris introduced this measure in mid-May.[12] Several months later, while the bill languished in committee, Ferris attempted to expedite matters. On December 21, he explained to Ballinger that he had earlier requested the House Committee on Indian Affairs chairman to refer his bill to Interior for report. Because the desired information had not been received, Ferris wished to know Interior's position on this issue.

On January 7, 1911, Ballinger replied that Interior had not received the bill, but he assured Ferris it would be carefully considered and fully reported on. Still, Owen's bill was greatly preferable to Ferris's alternative.[13] Supporting Interior's position, the Board of Indian Commissioners also recommended the Chiricahuas' release. Those who desired to remain at Fort Sill were to be given individual allotments there.[14]

Ferris now had the information he needed to formulate a new strategy to defeat the Chiricahuas' allotment at Fort Sill and protect the interests of his constituency. Ballinger's remarks revealed that due to Interior's stand on the issue, a stalemate had developed on the allotment question. If left unchecked, Interior's views might possibly gain wider currency among more influential House and Senate members, a chance that Ferris was unwilling to take. He doubtless believed that if this dangerous situation were permitted to develop, congressional scales could well be tipped in favor of allotting the Chiricahuas at Fort Sill. Consequently, Ferris resorted to pressure tactics, liberally employed against Interior and its allies, to prevent this calamity from befalling Lawton and Fort Sill. Thus, in an attempt to salvage what must have seemed a rapidly deteriorating situation, Ferris wasted little time in lining up military support to ensure that Owen's already-stalled bill remained permanently bottled up.

On January 18, 1911, Ferris advised Secretary of War Dickinson of his belief that Ballinger's position was "a blunder on the part of the Interior Department." Any Chiricahua allotment at Fort Sill would "materially retard and interfere with improvements being made there at this time." Dickinson, Ferris urged, should ask Interior to reconsider its position. Ferris also requested a letter on this issue from the War Department, a letter that reinforced his efforts to defeat the bill. Although he had already expressed his opposition to the bill's passage, he was quite willing to appear before the committee again.[15] Dickinson complied with both requests,[16] advising Interior that, excepting the Eastern and Western Additions, his department was "compelled to oppose any attempt to allot land in severalty" to the Chiricahua prisoners at Fort Sill.[17]

The standoff between the War and Interior Departments over the proper legislative course to pursue and the endeavors to be undertaken to effectively solve the Chiricahua prisoner-of-war problem did not go unnoticed by the Chiricahuas.[18] In February 1911, Asa Daklugie, one of the pro-Mescalero partisans who desired "to secure from the Government their freedom," asked Ferris to advise him and the other Chiricahuas choosing this course of action on the status of their relocation petition. Daklugie hoped Ferris would ascertain the facts in this matter and keep him informed.[19] Ferris not only kept Daklugie apprised but also used his entreaties as leverage in his legislative drive to remove all the Chiricahuas to Mescalero.

Unlike Daklugie, Vincent Natalish implored Robert Owen to "please do all you can to help us remain at Fort Sill."[20] Natalish believed that his people had been "kicked about the country long enough. . . . If we fought for what we thought was our own it was wrong." However, "if we fought with the United States Army against our own people," that, too, was wrong. "Shame," Natalish said, "upon a government to treat its faithful scouts like that."

According to Natalish, when the party examining New Mexico returned to Fort Sill, its members called a tribal council to discuss the results of their inquiry. Basing their decision on the investigating committee's findings, council participants concluded that relocation to Mescalero was ill-advised because the reservation's rocky terrain would not offer adequate sustenance. Therefore, they decided that Fort Sill was the "best home for them."[21] Yet, Natalish said, Colonel Scott, in a later attempt to convince the Chiricahuas otherwise, held "an open council" with them, stating the Mescaleros desired the Chiricahuas "to come and live with them."[22] Furthermore, Scott said military officials and Lawton residents did not want them to remain at Fort Sill.[23] Upon hearing this, the older men thoroughly ignored everything related to them by their own people, deciding to press for removal to Mescalero no matter what the cost. But, Natalish explained, the "younger men, who possess more sense and doubted what Scott said, decided to remain at Fort Sill." Were Scott truly concerned "for the best interest of the poor Apache prisoners he would not have resorted to such representations as good hunting and where they could live their Indian life."[24]

According to Natalish's informants, both Ferris and Walter Roe were present at this council. Roe demanded that the Chiricahuas be justly treated. Ferris said "we will do justice to these Apache Indians." Natalish wondered whether Ferris "meant that he would recall his bill" providing for the Chiricahuas' removal from Fort Sill.[25]

Despite entreaties such as Natalish's, Ferris, effectively assisted by Scott and his fellow officers, continued to push for the desired legislation. In November 1911, recommendations intended to resolve these relocation issues, and so constructed as to be in the War Department's best interests, were drawn up by Scott and transmitted to Major General Leonard Wood, chief of staff, who had been involved in the final phase of the last Geronimo campaign during the summer of 1886.[26] During the winter, legislation was to be procured that would remove from Fort Sill those Chiricahuas electing to reside at Mescalero. Those who desired to remain might do so under their current status. Scott's sole exception to these recommendations permitted ten families capable of properly working allotments to be allotted on Fort Sill's northeastern quadrant and subsequently released from their status as prisoners of war.[27]

Voicing his approval of these provisions, Secretary of War Henry L. Stimson advised Interior on November 8 that his department had expended more than $1 million in the construction of buildings at Fort Sill "for the accommodation of a regiment of field artillery and a field artillery school of fire." Therefore, the military was most anxious to arrange the Chiricahuas' affairs so that "while no injustice shall be done them, the War Department may realize on the value of its plant." Stimson hoped for Interior's concurrence in the matter.[28]

Ferris was perhaps even more anxious than Stimson to resolve the problem. Doubtless irritated at the delay in receiving Scott's report, which would enable Ferris to frame the appropriate legislation, the Oklahoma representative queried Wood as to its whereabouts on December 11.[29] Wood advised Ferris of the report's provisions.[30] Despite his previous approval of all of Scott's recommendations, Wood now shifted the War Department's position to comport with Ferris's complete intransigence on the Chiricahua issue. "For many reasons," Wood wrote, he believed that "it would be a good thing to attempt legislation which would permit Colonel Scott's first recommendation to be carried out."[31]

Ferris introduced just such legislation on January 3, 1912.[32] His bill permitted the secretary of war to release those Chiricahuas desiring removal to Mescalero. Interior would then take custody of these Indians. Those who wished to remain at Fort Sill could do so under regulations prescribed by the War Department.[33]

News of Ferris's bill soon reached Walter Roe, who was in Washington carefully monitoring the situation. Roe, in a move that nearly unnerved Ferris, accompanied H. C. Phillips, secretary of the Board of Indian Commissioners, to Wood's office. They desired to know whether Ferris's bill represented the War Department's views concerning the Fort Sill Apaches. Wood emphatically affirmed that it did. Furthermore, he expressed decided "indignation at what he termed the 'meddling' of certain friends of the Indian."[34]

Wood then told Roe that the military's policy was to remove the Chiricahuas to Mescalero as expeditiously as possible. Action would then be taken to "definitely secure the rights of the remaining Indians to individual tracts of land."[35] In this instance, the War Department intended to propose a change in Ferris's bill that provided for those Indians remaining at Fort Sill, an assertion that doubtless caused Ferris no little alarm. Probably to placate Roe, Wood, upon learning the purpose of the missionary's visit, "expressed his . . . belief that the treatment" accorded the Chiricahuas was nothing less than outrageous and thought that the "Government ought to show the Indians every possible consideration consistent with the state of affairs that had been allowed to grow up at Fort Sill." Roe, Wood suggested, should discuss the matter with Ferris and ask him "to send to the War Department for its recommendation an official copy of his bill." Upon its receipt, "a recommendation would be made that allotments be given the Indians who remain."[36]

Roe took up Wood's suggestion and conferred with Ferris, as shown by Wood's response to Ferris's communiqué of January 21. Doubtless in a state of panic over Roe's explanation of Wood's remarks, Ferris must have wondered whether he could rely on continued military support for Chiricahua removal from Fort Sill. Putting Ferris at ease, Wood stated that he "spoke pretty plainly to the Reverend Doctor and intimated" that he "thought they had all better attend to their own business until your bill has been enacted into law." Roe was an "upright, well meaning type of man," Wood believed, and "is very anxious to have as many Indians settle on the reservation as possible, whereas" Wood and Ferris agreed that "no definite action should be taken . . . until the bulk of the Indians have been transferred." Once this was accomplished, "it is probable that a good many of those who now elect to stay at Fort Sill will follow them." According to Wood, Roe apparently feared "too many will follow, and thinks that those who have been advanced to a certain point ought to be kept at Fort Sill." Had Wood "in any way confused the Doctor's mind as to your attitude and mine, or our understanding of this" issue, he would be pleased to clarify matters by discussing this subject further. Wood believed that Roe, "like ourselves, is really interested in the Indians."[37]

Roe not only called on Ferris but also visited both the House committee room, where he discovered the War Department had approved Ferris's bill after all, and Interior, where he learned that "the Indian Office had expressed its disapproval of the Ferris bill and had proposed an amendment providing for the allotment" of those Chiricahuas remaining at Fort Sill.[38] Besides, Commissioner Valentine understood the Chiricahuas had been clearly promised that Fort Sill would be used "in the future to provide permanent homes for them and their children." Thus, the government was "under an unquestionable moral obligation to them in this matter." Valentine believed "that in honor, there is but one course open to us, that is that we keep our promise and allot at Fort Sill" those Chiricahuas who "elect to stay there, notwithstanding the use to which the War Department desires to convert the land."[39] Acting Interior Secretary Samuel Adams concurred with these views.

Nor was this the only opposition to Ferris's bill. Guion Miller, formerly an Interior Department special agent and currently a Court of Claims special commissioner, soon presented a petition to Congress that vehemently protested the propositions proffered by this legislation. Referring to the Eastern and Western Additions procured for the Chiricahuas' benefit, Miller said the reason why allotment had not as yet been made was difficult to fathom. But one thing was indeed certain: such failure could not have resulted from any consideration of the Indians' welfare.

Ferris, Miller charged, introduced his bill under a misleading title. Under its provisions, the Chiricahuas would "be induced to surrender their rights to land at Fort Sill upon the seductive promise of liberty" were they to relocate at Mescalero. Of course, for those who desired to remain at Fort Sill, "the price of refusing to go to Mescalero" was "continued imprisonment." Simply, they were being bribed to give up their rights in equity at this installation. Yet "justice and every humane and charitable consideration" forbade such removal. "Instead of being induced to go, their going should be prohibited."

Miller urged that the Chiricahuas be allotted on the Eastern and Western Additions and released unreservedly. With the "encouragement and stimulus that would be given them by their freedom, and the knowledge that they were permanently located," Miller believed "they would unquestionably make tremendous progress, and the Apache war would thus tardily be brought to a close."[40]

Miller reiterated these views during a February 23, 1912, conference called at the Indian Office to discuss methods by which Ferris's bill might be modified to permit the allotment at Fort Sill of those Chiricahuas who desired to remain in Oklahoma. Besides Miller, the conferees included Roe, Phillips, Edgar B. Meritt, Brosius, and James A. Carroll. As proposed by the Indian Office, amendment of Ferris's bill involved authorizing Interior to allot the Chiricahuas at Fort Sill on lands ceded by the Kiowas and Comanches. Furthermore, it wanted the bill's title changed to reflect the intention of making the legislation an allotment measure. Participants believed this amendment "represented probably all that could possibly be expected from Congress." Thus, they agreed that "it ought to be supported by them."[41]

The conferees would be disappointed. Ferris steadfastly adhered to his commitment that none of the Chiricahuas be allotted at Fort Sill. Exerting increased pressure upon his opponents, in mid-April, Ferris sent Interior a letter he had received from Asa Daklugie, a leader of the pro-removal faction at Fort Sill.[42] Daklugie, who had been at Mescalero for the past eight months, advised Ferris that "my people at Fort Sill want to be free." He expressed support for Ferris's bill and hoped all his fellow tribesmen would soon come to New Mexico.[43] This communication, Ferris said, went "a long ways toward expressing the sentiment of all the Indians if they could be left free from the meddling of outside parties." Regarding those Chiricahuas not wanting to go to New Mexico, Ferris believed it best "to recommend Kiowa and Comanche dead allotments for them." This was the only compromise Ferris was willing to make and then formulate legislation on whereby those Chiricahuas so desiring might remain in Oklahoma released from their status as prisoners of war.[44]

At this point, perhaps sensing that further struggle against the War Department would prove futile, Interior also began to think in terms of compromise. Indeed, in the face of the latest inducements held out by Ferris and Stimson, Interior's resistance to the removal of all Chiricahuas from Fort Sill completely crumbled. It now only remained to formulate the appropriate legislation.

Interior officials carefully studied Ferris's and Stimson's proposals and submitted their recommendations to Representative John H. Stephens, chairman of the House Committee on Indian Affairs. These recommendations followed Ferris's suggestions. Basically, those Chiricahuas wishing to remove to Mescalero could do so; those desiring to remain in Oklahoma were to be provided with deceased Kiowa and Comanche allotments available in the vicinity of Fort Sill. Although Interior Department officials initially estimated that a total expenditure of $301,000 might well be required to implement the entire transaction, they soon learned that Stephens's committee recommended that Congress appropriate only $100,000 for each purpose.[45]

Ferris must have been elated by this victory. Indeed, he advised Phillips that the committee was disposed to accept Interior's concession concerning this matter. Consequently, Ferris requested the Board of Indian Commissioners' support for the measure.[46] On May 16, his bill was reported with the compromise amendment submitted by Interior regarding the purchase of deceased Kiowa and Comanche allotments for those Chiricahuas not removing to New Mexico. Ferris's revised bill immediately released those Chiricahuas going to Mescalero upon their arrival at that reservation. Those who remained at Fort Sill would retain their prisoner-of-war status until Interior procured Kiowa and Comanche dead allotments for them, whereupon they, too, would be released. The allocation for each purpose would be $100,000, for a total appropriation of $200,000.[47] On the same day, the House Committee on Indian Affairs recommended passage of Ferris's amended bill.[48] A month later, the Senate passed identical legislation prepared by Senator Thomas P. Gore.[49] In time, the measures would converge. Ferris exerted what influence he could to have either his, Gore's, or similar legislation enacted as quickly as possible to dispose of the Chiricahua prisoner-of-war problem for good.

However, ensuing developments in the House nearly nullified his endeavors. Indeed, prior to Senate passage of Gore's bill, Ferris suspected that there existed "very little hope of securing independent legislation regarding the Fort Sill Apaches during the present session of Congress."[50] Consequently, during May and June consultations with H. C. Phillips, Ferris expressed his conviction that salvation of these measures' provisions—including a $50,000 increase in the Chiricahua funding allocation to be utilized at Interior's discretion—depended upon inserting them in the Senate's amended version of the fiscal 1913 Indian appropriation bill.[51] Even so, during the course of compromise negotiations between Interior and the War Department, Ferris saw indications that a difficult struggle lay ahead to salvage even this proposal. As he perceived the situation, there were individuals who were "inclined to believe that the legislation gave the Indians less than they were entitled to," while, at the same time, "there would undoubtedly be many who would contend that it gave too much money to few Indians."[52] Regarding the latter group, Ferris's prediction proved all too prescient. Nevertheless, "stating that he believed the support of all parties interested would be necessary to carry through the proposed plan," Ferris requested Phillips's presence during the conference committee hearings on the Indian appropriation bill[53] and urged all concerned to exert every effort to obtain the inclusion therein of a proviso stipulating the amount requested.[54] Ferris advocated such action as a precautionary device in case his and Gore's Chiricahua legislation failed in the House.

Meanwhile, despite his worry that possible disaster awaited both his and Gore's bills, Ferris continued to press for passage of his legislation. When Ferris's bill came up for a vote on August 19, he requested the House's unanimous consent to substitute Gore's measure—which was essentially identical—for his own as a way to outmaneuver his opponents.[55] As predicted, Ferris's foes, opposing the bill on fiscal grounds, were ready. Illinois representative James R. Mann was the chief antagonist. When Ferris submitted his request for the Gore substitution, Mann immediately engaged his colleague in debate.

Ever the fearless watchdog over the treasury, and ultimately the House nemesis of these proposals, Mann asked Ferris if he did not think that Congress was "doing pretty well by these Indians without authorizing Interior to purchase homesteads for them." Despite this well-timed barb, Ferris calmly cited the War Department's needs and the Chiricahuas' pitiful condition as valid reasons for the substitution. Under these circumstances, Ferris, now calling for a $250,000 appropriation, insisted that this was not an unreasonable sum.

At this point, an unmoved and incredulous Mann exclaimed, "Two hundred and fifty thousand dollars!" Though Ferris said the funding could be reduced by $50,000, Mann wondered whether the government would now be compelled to buy a farm for everyone who had committed a criminal offense. At this, Stephens asked whether Mann knew that only thirty of those confined as prisoners of war at Fort Sill were among the original group brought to the post and that the others were born in captivity. Mann tersely replied, "Let them get out and earn their living." Quickly regaining the initiative, Ferris said Congress had a clear duty to provide land for them. Besides, "their unfortunate condition should excite pity rather than wrath." Mann remained obdurate and coldly suggested that these Indians be released "and earn a living or do without." Upon conclusion of Mann's tirade, Ferris reiterated his request for the Gore substitution. Mann interposed his objection and Ferris's bill went off the calendar.[56] Shortly thereafter, Gore's bill came up for consideration. Ferris immediately asked to have the measure "passed over without prejudice."[57]

Ferris was now forced to carry his struggle for the long-sought resolution to the Chiricahua problem to that segment of the legislative arena then considering the merits of the fiscal 1913 Indian appropriation bill. Senators sympathetic to Ferris's Chiricahua release, removal, relocation, and allotment scheme had indeed incorporated in the revised version of what would become Amendment 114 the provisions earlier contained in the now defeated Ferris and Gore legislation. As inserted in the fiscal 1913 Indian appropriation bill, this amendment appropriated—albeit minus the additional $50,000 funding request—the moneys initially deemed necessary to remove from Fort Sill those Chiricahuas electing to go to Mescalero and to allot beyond Fort Sill on deceased Kiowa and Comanche holdings those wishing to remain in Oklahoma. In attempting to maneuver these items safely past the shoals of congressional opposition, Ferris again encountered Mann in heated debate and also battled antagonistic forces of a different stripe.

CHAPTER

14

Senatorial Subterfuge Nearly Scuttles
the Chiricahua Resettlement Scheme

▼　　▼　　▼

*C*oncerning incorporating Chiricahua prisoner-of-war legislation in the fiscal 1913 Indian appropriation bill, Ferris and his Senate allies braced themselves for a formidable struggle. In the House, Mann once again led opposition forces. His antagonism, however, was but a minor obstacle compared with the floor fight that followed in the Senate. This battle was led by Albert Bacon Fall, the newly arrived senior senator from New Mexico, and his western cronies, who labored diligently for this bill's defeat.

On July 3, 1912, Senator Moses E. Clapp proposed Amendment 114, which, as initially formulated, only requested Interior to report on the probable cost of securing homes in Oklahoma and New Mexico for the Chiricahuas.[1] After a series of House and Senate conferences, legislators reached agreement concerning those provisions contained in a newly revised Amendment 114, which included all items found in the defunct Ferris and Gore bills.[2] On August 17, Clapp called his colleagues' attention to this reconstituted amendment, explaining that overwhelming evidence indicated the Chiricahuas should be released and placed on a reservation. When the Senate first considered the Indian appropriation bill, Clapp said that the original version of this amendment was designed to put the matter in conference in order to provide for the Chiricahuas. As earlier devised, the amendment was not broad enough to authorize the conferees to provide for the Indians' release, removal, relocation, and allotment. Consequently, the conferees had gone beyond the strict limits imposed on them because both the military and other sources produced evidence that such provision ought to be made. This was the reason for the amendment's revision.[3]

A debate immediately ensued that waxed hotly over Amendment 114's merits. On August 19, 1912, New Mexico Senator Thomas Benton Catron insisted his constituents did not want the Chiricahuas removed to his state. They were the "worst band of Indians that have . . . existed upon the American continent." They were also the "most warlike, . . . the most desperate, [and] the most bloodthirsty and murdering [band] that ever . . . existed." Catron then launched into a brief but lurid discussion of Apache warfare in the late nineteenth century. Removal of the Chiricahuas to New Mexico would only precipitate a new conflict because Mescalero did not possess enough irrigable agricultural land to keep them occupied. Now that the prisoners successfully supported themselves at Fort Sill, he reasoned, "why not keep them there?"[4]

Kansas senator Charles Curtis sought a way around this impasse, suggesting that the latest version of Amendment 114 undergo yet another revision to eliminate any mention of either New Mexico or Arizona as potential Chiricahua relocation sites. Simply, the new measure would contain language that merely authorized the Chiricahuas' relief and settlement on lands procured for them by the secretary of the interior. This, Curtis believed, would be acceptable to senators from both states. Believing this proposal would permanently settle the Chiricahuas in Oklahoma, Arizona senator Marcus Aurelius Smith seized upon Curtis's idea, replying that it undoubtedly, as Senator Fall "endeavored to call to my attention," was the solution to the problem. Fall, who later attempted to use this understanding for his own ends, said Ferris informed him that Oklahomans would be pleased to have the Chiricahuas among them. Therefore, Fall explained, the only way they could be kept there was to return the report to the conference committee.[5] Hence, despite Clapp's efforts to save Amendment 114 as earlier modified, the Senate rejected the conference report.

On August 20, the House considered Amendment 114. Having warmed to his task by almost single-handedly demolishing nearly every amendment, as contained in the conference report, to the Indian appropriation bill already debated, Mann tackled 114 with great relish. Though he was amenable to defraying the cost of resettling those Chiricahuas who so desired at Mescalero, he saw "no reason why we should buy farms for the Apache Indians whom we discharge from their nominal confinement." Ferris explained that the allotment expenditure was necessary because there no longer existed public lands for such a purpose. Besides, the "Government ought to feel a little duty toward starting" the Chiricahuas off in the same manner as other Indians. Mann snidely retorted that in "looking after his district, as he always ably does," Ferris supported the proposition out of personal interest.[6] Rejecting both Amendment 114 and the original report, the House requested a new conference.

On August 21, the Senate agreed to Clapp's request for a new conference. Clapp appeared optimistic that a resolution to the Chiricahua prisoner problem might be reached after all, for, in a letter Clapp wrote to Stimson on the same day, he declared his belief that by employing a variation of Interior's earlier recommendations, "we will be able to get the matter in such [shape] that you and the Secretary of the Interior can dispose of it."[7] On August 22, the Senate considered and agreed to a new version of Amendment 114 containing Senator Curtis's compromise proposal.[8] The Senate also provided funding in the amount of $200,000, a sum that later proved insufficient.[9] After similar action by the House, the fiscal 1913 Indian appropriation bill became law on August 24, 1912.[10]

Yet, its passage did not end the controversy over Amendment 114. This provision was subject to interpretation because it failed to specifically identify those lands to be selected for the Chiricahuas by Interior. Doubtless the flexibility of the stipulation was intended so that the War and Interior Departments could finally resolve this difficulty as they saw fit. Also, it attached no conditions regarding how the funds appropriated were to be spent.[11] Both War and Interior Department officials interpreted the legislation as giving them authority to remove to Mescalero those Chiricahuas desiring to settle there.

Evidence soon surfaced that Fall had narrowly construed Amendment 114. J. W. Prude, a Tularosa, New Mexico, merchant who conducted a trading business at Mescalero, informed appropriate officials that Fall's contention that the thirty surviving original prisoners, who otherwise would have been relocated there, constituted a danger to the white descendants of their victims was absurd, because no such persons resided in the area. Anyone who talked "such rot" did so "for a cold blooded selfish motive." Fall did not want them removed to Mescalero for obvious reasons. He owned large herds of sheep and a not insignificant tract of land that abutted the reservation. Prude implied that Fall leased grazing land at Mescalero and desired to protect the profits he made by retaining this arrangement.[12]

Equally evident, the War and Interior Departments were absolutely determined to dispose of the Chiricahua prisoner-of-war conundrum as they deemed best. Respecting Amendment 114's requirements, this meant taking the broad view—particularly regarding the clause that stipulated "such rules and regulations as the Secretary of the Interior and the Secretary of War may prescribe." By September 6, Wood had informed Interior Secretary Walter L. Fisher of his readiness to proceed under this provision and desired to know whether Fisher was prepared to act.[13] Meanwhile, Acting Secretary of War Oliver revealed that his department was devising arrangements to implement the recently enacted legislation and developing guidelines for the Chiricahuas' potential removal from Fort Sill to Mescalero.[14] These directives became official War Department policy on September 12.[15]

Such latitudinarian interpretation of Amendment 114 did not escape Fall's notice. On December 20, 1912, he launched a determined stand against the Chiricahuas' removal to Mescalero. Fall expressed certainty that War and Interior's action illustrated a definite lack of understanding of the historical background behind the legislation's passage. Fall had not the "remotest idea that . . . any attempt . . . would be made to force these Indians off upon the Mescaleros in New Mexico and settle them among the people who suffered so much at their hands." Fall assured Stimson and Fisher that the appropriation bill would never have become law were such a move contemplated at that time.

Indeed, as a matter of history regarding his earlier assent to this proviso, Fall said that after the Senate's adjournment, he called a conference at his residence to reach an understanding concerning Chiricahua relocation to Mescalero. Meeting with Ferris and other interested Oklahomans, Fall said the "whole proposition was thoroughly thrashed out and it was finally agreed between us that the bill must go back to conference" and that Ferris, who favored the "proposition to remove the Fort Sill Apaches would agree that a modification of the language should be reported back to the two houses as would provide an appropriation for" their "location at some other point than Mescalero, and provide for their discharge as prisoners of war." Ferris, Fall said, would verify this statement. "It was thoroughly understood that the money should not be used and could not be used under the proposed wording of the appropriation, to convey these Indians to Mescalero." Fall admitted that this might not preclude beyond a technical construction "the use of the two hundred thousand dollars to pay the traveling expenses of these Indians to Mescalero." Still, there was a "distinct understanding."

Furthermore, Fall's seventeen-mile-long ranch at Three Rivers abutted the reservation, and, he claimed, "eighty acres of my patented land" was situated within Mescalero's current confines. These lands were patented prior to the reservation's creation. Of course, Fall had "no personal interest whatsoever in this matter" and insisted he held neither lease nor "grazing permit of any kind or character upon the Mescalero Reserve and never have had." But Fall's stockmen friends in Lincoln, Chaves, and Otero Counties did lease grazing tracts upon the Mescalero Reservation—and Fall reminded Fisher that these arrangements permitted rents higher than those that could be obtained on the forest reserves. He then not so subtly hinted that to permit the Chiricahuas "to come in and share generally in the range privileges" would eliminate the "income which is now of such assistance in rendering the Mescaleros independent and self-sustaining."[16] Despite Fall's threat, the secretaries remained silent and held their counsel.

Meanwhile, Prude again communicated with Fisher and revealed some rather interesting developments. Vehement opposition to the Chiricahuas' relocation had its origins in Roswell and, aided and abetted by Fall, was instigated solely by stockmen strongly determined to protect their leases and their profits on the Mescalero Reservation. Indeed, they promised a "hard fight." Fall may have denied interest in the whole affair, but his son-in-law was preparing to enter the cattle business. To do so, he planned to lease grazing tracts at Mescalero. Roswell stockmen, Prude explained, circulated a petition that hid their real intentions—a ruse that enabled them to procure as many signatures as they needed from unsuspecting citizens. This petition urged not only that the Chiricahuas be kept in Oklahoma but also that all the tillable land on Mescalero be divided among the Indians there, with the remaining lands to be turned into a national park.[17]

At the same time, a new circumstance arose having the potential to adversely affect the agreement reached regarding resettling on deceased Kiowa and Comanche allotments those Chiricahuas wishing to stay in Oklahoma. In this respect, Interior Department officials soon discovered that improved land was obtainable only at an average price of $3,000 per 160 acres, and unimproved land was available at a cost of $2,000 for each 160-acre parcel. Purchase of such acreage was to include improved land for each of the thirty-two heads of families and unimproved land for each of the fifty-six other Indians who chose to remain in this location. Because each of these individuals was to receive 160 acres, a minimal outlay in the amount of $96,000 for the former and $112,000 for the latter would be necessary. Thus, a total expenditure of at least $208,000 was required for land purchases alone, precluding not only the purchase of such necessities as seeds and clothing and the procurement of farm implements and other essential items, but also a provision for the Chiricahuas' general sustenance until such time as those who remained in Oklahoma became self-sustaining. Consequently, a proper effectuation of the proposed plan to relocate those Chiricahuas desiring resettlement at Mescalero was not possible. The $200,000 allocated for both ends by the fiscal 1913 Indian appropriation legislation was insufficient.[18]

Indeed, given the financial limitations forced upon Interior by an allocation of only $200,000 for the fulfillment of both Chiricahua prisoner-of-war objectives, consummation of the Oklahoma land transaction alone—not to mention the financing needed for the temporary provisioning of those Chiricahuas desiring to remain in this location—required funding beyond the $121,500 that was initially budgeted for this purpose. Therefore, additional moneys in the amount of at least $100,000 were needed to complete this task. Because Congress had already begun preparing legislation for the fiscal 1914 Indian appropriation bill, quick action was needed to insert an amendment allocating this amount. H. C. Phillips did not expect unusual opposition to such an amendment in Congress. Besides, he believed, the influence of Ferris, a member of the House Indian Affairs Committee, and the deep interest in removing the Chiricahuas from Fort Sill would greatly facilitate matters.[19]

Despite such optimism, Interior officials were not as sanguine about the amendment's future success. Lest the proposal completely fail at the hands of congressional opposition, they frantically devised methods to thwart attacks against it. On December 26, Acting Commissioner of Indian Affairs Frederic H. Abbott submitted a proposal drawn up by his subordinate and advised Fisher to informally give Ferris the proposed amendment before the House passed the Indian bill.[20]

At the same time, Abbott submitted to Fisher a draft proposal of correspondence to Fall defending Interior's position.[21] Fall was told that at the time of Mescalero's creation, "possible location of Indians other than Mescalero Apaches upon what is known as the Mescalero Apache Reservation was contemplated." This was "clearly shown in the Executive Order" of February 2, 1874, which both established the reservation and set it "apart for the use of the Mescalero Apaches and such other Indians as the Department may see fit to locate thereon." Therefore, the law's provisions definitely permitted the placement of other tribal groups on these lands "at the discretion of the Department controlling them." Furthermore, despite Fall's objections, Congress allowed such discretionary authority "to stand in the Indian Appropriation Bill."

Secretary Fisher then consulted with President Taft on the matter. According to the president's instructions, he prepared a memorandum for the Senate. Defending his department's request for additional funds to fully achieve both Chiricahua prisoner-of-war objectives, Fisher explained that prior to the fiscal 1913 Indian appropriation bill's passage, when the War and Interior Departments mutually arrived at their original compromise agreement permitting resettlement at Mescalero of those Chiricahuas who so desired, both departments concurred with a carefully formulated estimate for both the completion of the removal and the allotment of the Chiricahuas remaining in Oklahoma. Improved and unimproved allotments, seeds, subsistence, and clothing had to be provided for those staying on. Transportation, housing construction, farm machinery, subsistence, and clothing were to be furnished those Chiricahuas removing to Mescalero. On the basis of these original calculations, expenditures in the amount of $221,500 for the former purpose and $79,500 for the latter—a total of $301,000—were deemed essential. Yet instead of obtaining the moneys initially requested, Interior received funding totaling only $200,000 for the Chiricahuas' relief. This sum, given the price differential between improved and unimproved land located in the area surrounding Fort Sill, was at least $8,000 short of the amount required simply to purchase allotments for all Chiricahuas wishing to remain in Oklahoma. Hence, a minimum of $100,000 was needed to properly complete the tasks required to fulfill the Chiricahua projects. Fisher urged swift passage of an appropriation in this amount.[22]

Unfortunately, Interior's amendment failed to reach the House in time for consideration and inclusion in the appropriation bill passed on January 9, 1913.[23] In the Senate, Catron offered an amendment to the fiscal 1914 Indian appropriation bill in which no part of the $200,000 allocated in fiscal 1913 might be used for the Chiricahuas' removal to Mescalero.[24] On January 25, Catron deftly inserted his amendment at the end of Interior's funding request. Robert J. Gamble, chairman of the Senate Committee on Indian Affairs, raised a point of order against it because it was "not recommended by any standing committee of the Senate." Gamble's objection was sustained.[25]

At this point, Fall interposed his objections and asked to be heard on the matter. Despite evidence to the contrary, Fall declared Interior's action in attempting to remove the Chiricahuas to Mescalero illegal. Of course, there was no objection to these Indians' being removed from Fort Sill, just as there was "absolutely no objection to their being discharged as prisoners of war." But, prevaricating on the actual facts of the matter, Fall said New Mexicans strenuously objected "to receiving them back . . . where they . . . and their fathers made the ground run red with the blood of Americans, descendants of whom are yet living around . . . Mescalero."[26] Could not some other place be found to take these Indians? Fall then asked Gamble to withdraw his point of order. The senator complied. Immediately thereafter, Colorado senator Charles S. Thomas raised the same objection as Gamble's, which was also sustained, thus effectively quashing Catron's proposal.[27] On the same day, the Senate passed the fiscal 1914 Indian appropriation bill.[28] Even so, Fall would be heard from again on the Chiricahua prisoner-of-war matter.

After the Senate passed this bill, it immediately went into conference, agreeing to Interior's additional $100,000 Chiricahua funding request. When the conference report reached the Senate for debate on March 3, Fall immediately objected in his usual luridly descriptive manner and waxed eloquent on an altogether unrelated topic. Essentially, out of resentment for the quashing of Catron's amendment, Fall filibustered against the conference report.[29]

Gamble saw through this tactic. On the following day, to discredit Fall's argument, Gamble attempted to outmaneuver him. Concerning Interior's latest request, Gamble truthfully asserted that—Fall's allegations and objections to the contrary—"under the very provisions of the proposed law . . . no part" of the $100,000 appropriation could be used for the Chiricahuas' removal to New Mexico. In fact, "it absolutely prohibits its use for that purpose." Moneys were "appropriated specifically for the purpose of purchasing lands for the Apache Indians in . . . Oklahoma," inasmuch as the amount originally allocated proved insufficient. "Under such conditions it would necessarily be presumed they would remain there." Besides, Gamble said, in limiting this particular provision, conferees sought to meet conditions demanded by New Mexico's senators.

Responding to Fall's recent objections regarding Interior's implementation of the fiscal 1913 Indian appropriation legislation, Gamble, referring to those purportedly strenuous protestations lodged "against these Indians being located at Mescalero," remonstrations supposedly emanating from individuals living adjacent to this reservation, cited a January 22, 1913, letter from Tularosa residents to the War and Interior secretaries endorsing their decision to resettle in New Mexico those Chiricahuas who desired to be so transferred. Consequently, Gamble maintained that in reality—Fall's assertions to the contrary—no local opposition to this move existed. Actually, Gamble averred, Fall resisted Interior's request for an additional Chiricahua prisoner-of-war appropriation because that department, in executing provisions of the fiscal 1913 Indian appropriation legislation, had used the discretionary authority granted by Congress to remove some of the Chiricahuas to New Mexico.[30]

Letter of support or no, Fall renewed his objections and, twisting the record out of context, attempted to convince his colleagues that all of the Chiricahua prisoners were equally as guilty of atrocities as Geronimo and his fellow belligerents during the last Apache campaign. Then, in an especially acerbic fit of sarcasm, Fall wanted to know where Gamble had obtained "his knowledge of the Fort Sill Apaches." Gamble's reference to reports produced by the War and Interior Departments that dramatically illustrated the Chiricahuas' progress on the road to white civilization only engendered further derision. Endeavoring to portray the observations noted in these reports as utter falsehood, Fall deliberately misinterpreted the secretaries' remarks that unless allotted soon, the Chiricahuas' continued progress would be unduly delayed.

Thus, in an attempt to convince fellow senators that Interior's latest appropriation request was nothing but a ruse to remove to Mescalero those Chiricahuas remaining in Oklahoma, Fall insisted that the secretaries' reports falsely depicted former belligerents as Indians who were now "so well civilized and such Christian gentlemen that they deserve in the eyes and in the opinion of the honorable" secretaries "to rank with the white man or above him." In fact, did one lend credence to these reports, the Chiricahuas were "a very much higher grade Indian than . . . the Mescalero." Regarding the acting secretary of war's remarks in particular, Fall snidely presumed that Oliver desired "to send them as missionaries to the Mescaleros to assist in their civilization." Concluding his harangue, Fall speculated—with, of course, all due respect—that the Senate Committee on Indian Affairs and both secretaries "have shown in this bill and in the reports to which" Fall referred "that they are absolutely at sea, to say the least, upon the subject which they are desiring the Senate to legislate."[31]

Despite Gamble's argument, Fall's filibuster temporarily accomplished its purpose. His obduracy on this issue was limitless. Indeed, throughout the early months of 1913, mounting evidence indicated that the efforts exerted by New Mexico's senatorial delegation "against the success of the Apache people" currently residing on the Mescalero

Reservation knew no bounds.[32] There was, for example, the mysterious Senate bill that Ferris promised to keep a tight lid on while it was pending in the House.[33] This piece of legislation, introduced by Fall on May 2, 1912, purported to be "an act to create a Mescalero national park in New Mexico," though actually the bill "was presumably intended to tie up the Mescalero lands so as to prevent sending there any of the Fort Sill Indians." It was "simply one of a number of attempts looking to the same ends."[34]

Yet Fall's persistent obstructionism was to no avail. Legislation to create a national park out of the Mescalero Reservation "at no time stood any considerable chance of passage."[35] That Ferris succeeded in bottling up Fall's bill was evidenced by a vociferous howl of protest from the Roswell Commercial Club. In a telegram to Fall, members—a number of whom leased grazing rights at Mescalero—expressed their outrage over the Chiricahuas' removal there because this effectively closed the "grandest national park in the world for all time"—with the added result that Fall's "glorious fight for New Mexico" was negated.[36] Regarding the failure of the Indian appropriation bill, there would be a next time, for the "temper of the Senate in not yielding on the Apache item" clearly indicated that New Mexico senators Fall and Catron had "no great following and that their argument is not generally recognized as sound."[37]

Opportunity for renewed consideration of Interior's additional Chiricahua funding request presented itself on April 7, 1913, when the fiscal 1914 Indian appropriation bill was again introduced in the House and subsequently passed by that body on April 22. On June 17, it passed the Senate.[38] After a series of conferences, the entire measure became law on June 30, 1913.[39] With this enactment, the purchase of allotments for those Chiricahuas desiring to remain in Oklahoma could proceed. Upon completion of this project, the remaining Chiricahuas held as prisoners of war at Fort Sill would be released and settled on their new holdings.

Yet, passage of the fiscal 1914 Indian appropriation bill did not completely solve Interior's Chiricahua funding difficulties. A problem of paramount importance concerned the efficiency with which the land allotment sales were conducted: the appropriation would revert to the Treasury "unless expended or obligated prior to June 30, 1914."[40] In procuring these allotments for the Chiricahuas, technicalities that had to be rigidly adhered to—for instance, hearings to determine heirs, petitions for sale, verifications of hearing testimony, and approval of sales—consumed far more time than originally anticipated. As if this were not obstacle enough, by the end of December 1913, the Indian Office learned that expenditures for removal and settlement of those Chiricahuas who desired relocation to New Mexico had been underestimated. This created a serious funding problem in terms of providing allotments for each Chiricahua remaining in Oklahoma.[41]

Essentially, this predicament arose from the joint decision by military and Interior officials to undertake the former task first. The fiscal 1913 Indian appropriation legislation had allocated $200,000 for resolution of the Chiricahua problem. Of this, $78,500 was intended to accomplish the first part of the scheme: relocating some of the Chiricahuas to Mescalero. The actual cost for relocation was $132,500. The difference was borrowed from the remainder of the account, which had received an infusion of $100,000 in fiscal 1914. Therefore, $167,500 remained for the purchase of Chiricahua allotments in Oklahoma, an amount $54,000 shy of what would have been available had not the relocation scheme gone over budget.

Although Interior managed to include the item reappropriating moneys not yet expended on Chiricahua allotments in Oklahoma in the original House version of the fiscal 1915 Indian appropriation bill, there was not enough time to include a request for the additional $54,000 necessary to complete this task. Therefore, this item would have to be introduced in the Senate as an amendment. Perusing House debate on reappropriating the Chiricahua prisoner-of-war moneys earlier mandated by the fiscal 1914 Indian appropriation bill, one might well conclude that Interior officials were overly sanguine in expecting Congress to acknowledge the justification for any additional funding request, or extension thereof, pertaining to the Chiricahuas.

This misplaced complacency was shattered by the February 19, 1914, remarks of Minnesota representative Clarence B. Miller, whose attitude on the issue was as icy as the region he called home. Miller called the House's attention "to what Congress had done for a band of Indians that for some reason has aroused a great deal of sympathy in some parts of the United States." Passionately addressing his peers, Miller, misinterpreting the facts of the matter, venomously blasted Interior's request. "We have had it repeatedly stated that Uncle Sam has misused and maltreated the Geronimo band of Indians held" at Fort Sill. Indeed, "a great many crocodile tears have been shed over it." Actually, there never was "a band of Indians within the confines of the United States," nor "on the face of the earth," that had "had so much done for them, as a band or as individuals, as the United States Government has done for" the Chiricahuas.

Ignoring the fact that most of the Chiricahuas originally taken captive did not bear arms and remained on their reservation during the late Apache hostilities, Miller then equated the vast majority of noncombatants with Geronimo's belligerent minority. Rather than "put them within prison walls" or "behind bars, as we place the whites of similar character and conduct, we" established them "out in the air and on the broad prairies of Oklahoma, letting them live in homes of their own on a reservation" of 50,000 acres. Now, Miller said, they were "being presented with farms we are purchasing for them," with "good equipment to start them well launched in life," for which "a total of three hundred thousand dollars" had already been expended from the federal treasury. Of course, Miller neglected to advise his colleagues that had the Chiricahuas been allotted at Fort Sill as originally promised, the total cost would have been but a fraction of that amount. Miller made these statements "in the hope that those . . . who have been preaching sermons on the treatment of the Apache Band of Indians by Uncle Sam"—and importuning congressmen on the matter—would "have the facts with which they may reflect and shape their ideas accordingly."[42] But Miller missed the real point of the matter. Simply, an overwhelming majority of Chiricahua captives were innocent of any crime against the United States, and, as Vincent Natalish stated, in comparison with his own people, the government treated belligerent Indians of other tribal groups far more fairly.

Despite such acrid criticism, Interior's request for reappropriation of the Chiricahua prisoner-of-war moneys passed the House on February 20, 1914.[43] On February 24, the fiscal 1915 Indian appropriation bill, containing both Interior's reappropriation and additional funding requests for the Chiricahuas, came before the Senate Committee on Indian Affairs[44] and was reported on May 15.[45] Senator Robert L. Owen assured the usual allies and supporters of such legislation that he would exert every effort to prevent elimination of these items.[46] Both he and like-minded colleagues succeeded in maneuvering this particular legislation past the treacherous shoals of southwestern senatorial opposition,[47] and this measure became law on August 1, 1914.[48] With success at hand, H. C. Phillips somberly confided to Hugh Scott that although he believed Major Goode would ensure they received a fair start, those Chiricahuas who remained in Oklahoma required "all the encouragement they can get from their friends wherever located," a prediction that in time would sadly prove all too accurate.[49] In any event, plans could now proceed to complete the Chiricahuas' allotment.

CHAPTER

15

Resettlement at Mescalero and Release
From Military Custody

▼   ▼   ▼

*O*n August 24, 1912, the fiscal 1913 Indian appropriation bill was passed, allocating $200,000 for Chiricahua relief, release, and resettlement. On September 5, Interior's Samuel Adams suggested formation of a board of inquiry comprising a representative from the War Department and a counterpart from Interior. This board would formulate plans and regulations to be submitted to the two departmental secretaries for immediate action.[1] Adams informed the War Department on September 16 that he had selected Kiowa Agency superintendent Ernest Stecker, who was already familiar with the Chiricahuas' situation, as its representative.[2] Acting Secretary of War Oliver notified Interior on September 18 that his department had designated Hugh L. Scott. Oliver suggested the meeting take place on October 1 at Fort Sill.[3] Adams concurred with his proposal.[4]

Throughout these proceedings, Scott's views strongly influenced the board's final decisions. The most crucial recommendation—in fact, the ultimate success or failure of War and Interior's efforts to settle the Chiricahua prisoner-of-war matter hinged upon it—involved who among the Chiricahuas desiring to remain in Oklahoma would be permitted to do so. Staunchly convinced of the correctness of his earlier observations, Scott reasserted his belief that only those who had a "good record for sobriety" and were "sufficiently intelligent, industrious, and physically fit to make a living . . . in the environment" into which they would be thrown should be permitted to remain in Oklahoma. Only fourteen Chiricahuas, the board believed, met these qualifications.[5]

The board's findings were not exactly what Interior had envisioned. Indeed, almost immediately after the board concluded its business, the unsung heroine Hendrina Hospers happened upon ominous reports of the board's decision that stirred Interior to wrath once it fully realized the ramifications of the board's proposal. Interior believed the board had exercised authority that it most certainly lacked. On October 4, Hospers, the Reformed Church in America missionary to the Chiricahuas, explained to Walter Roe that Major George Goode, acting for Scott and Stecker before their arrival, prepared a "list of fourteen men, those who do not gamble or drink, can run a farm, or in case of failure of crops can make a living by a trade. Those fourteen he gave the choice to stay or go. All the others had to go." Such action, Hospers believed, was unjust because there were others who, equally able to earn a living, were most anxious to remain.

Subsequently, during a conference with the Chiricahuas on October 1, Lawrence Mithlo demanded to know why he could not remain. Scott "gruffly told him he was worthless" and "not to say a word." Mithlo, who had set his heart on staying, was a good worker and had "been doing right." He was "all broken up over it." Benedict Jozhe asked, "Why did they have to make a bill and take all that trouble to pass it? Colonel Scott was sent here to make plans. Instead, he arrived with plans already prepared and neglected to ask their wishes, only saying, 'You get out, you stay!'"

Explaining that the Chiricahuas were thoroughly convinced that the military was determined to throw them off the post once and for all, Hospers exclaimed, "No wonder they have lost all faith." Benedict, Hospers said, summed up their feelings on the issue by remarking that they "had had a hard time, but . . . never felt so bad as now." Simply, they were not treated well. Hospers therefore wished to know whether there was anything that Roe could do to assist the Chiricahuas in their hour of need.[6]

Upon receiving Hospers's communication, Roe forwarded the substance of it to the Board of Indian Commissioners, adding that not only were the Chiricahuas' inquiries "summarily dismissed," but the manner in which Scott treated them was "exceedingly overbearing." Furthermore, Roe had predicted this result ever since he learned that

Chiricahuas shocking *feterita* (kaffir corn), a sorghum grain raised at Fort Sill
for livestock feed. *Courtesy Fort Sill Museum.*

the "joint committee appointed for the business consists of military
men" whose viewpoint "will almost certainly be unsympathetic." Roe
believed it essential that every Chiricahua head of family and single
adult be allowed to decide freely whether to remain in Oklahoma or remove to Mescalero.

Somewhat stronger in his October 9 statements to Acting Commissioner of Indian Affairs Abbott, Roe said that while he awaited the
"'preliminary plan' for the Apache settlement" that Abbott had promised to send him, he was "reliably informed that a very obnoxious"
scheme was "already being executed at Fort Sill," an arrangement he
deemed totally unacceptable. Roe believed that Abbott was not "personally . . . informed as to the proceeding." Therefore, Roe insisted that
"not only for the sake of the Apaches, but to avoid a public scandal,
one-half of which your department must bear," the Chiricahuas should
be permitted an "absolutely free choice as to going or remaining." Were,
"after the rank injustice of the past, any of them . . . forced to leave land
given for their permanent homes, and sent out to a remote mountainous
reservation," Roe said, "the thinking people of this country," who

would "be kept thoroughly informed as to all the facts, will be aroused to indignation." Roe also intimated that the matter might even reach the law courts.[7]

Roe's railings rocked Interior and led to an immediate investigation of his accusations. At the same time, to stem any new difficulty that might come from Roe's direction and to give Interior the time needed to conduct this inquiry, Abbott defensively explained to Roe on October 12 that Scott and Stecker had "authority merely to formulate the plan and regulations which are to be submitted for the action of the two Departments." Thus, Roe's information was either incorrect or a result of not understanding the purpose for Scott and Stecker's meeting with the Chiricahuas. Of course, Abbott had yet to see their report because it was still under review by the War Department. Although he believed Scott and Stecker to be properly motivated, Abbott requested that Roe provide additional information on this issue because Abbott desired "nothing to take place in connection with this whole transaction" that could "in any way embarrass the final settlement of the case." After all, Abbott knew Roe and "every other good citizen of this country" desired the matter solved in a "spirit of absolute justice and fair dealing" with the Chiricahuas.[8]

Abbott may have believed Roe was misled, but Roe insisted on the veracity of his information and the integrity of his informant. While Interior fended off Roe, Hospers provided her former superior with additional information. James Kaywaykla, Hospers explained, said he wanted to remain in Oklahoma "but had signed to go. Others feel the same way. . . . Scott bluffed them into going" and "told them if they stayed here they could not look for help from the government anymore. . . . Goode told them those who decided to stay could change to the Mescalero group, but those who decided to go could not change to staying here." Hospers said the military wanted all the Chiricahuas removed and were "doing their best to get them to go."[9]

In view of this, Roe, in an October 16 letter, told George Vaux, a Board of Indian Commissioners member, that he was certain that Scott and Stecker's report would verify his earlier observations. Roe believed the War and Interior Department secretaries meant well. He assured Vaux that he believed Interior was "all right," as was, no doubt, the War Department, "in its somewhat arrogant manner." But experience had amply demonstrated that government "officials, especially military, who deal much with Indians, acquire a dictatorial and summary method which often results in great injustice." Roe expressed the view that Scott and Stecker "have stated dogmatically to the Indians how the thing should be carried out, and not that they were simply preparing a report for Washington."[10]

Scott and Stecker's report had a devastating impact when it finally reached Abbott on October 16 inasmuch as Roe's earlier allegations were proved correct. An infuriated Abbott hurriedly telephoned H. C. Phillips and requested his immediate presence so that both might discuss the report's provisions. Having carefully studied the report, they agreed it would be unacceptable to the parties most interested and that its provisions regarding the "number of Indians who were to stay in Oklahoma would be entirely objectionable."[11] Later, Abbott called an extended conference, during which participants strenuously conveyed the conviction that "anything except a free choice" would have a "very injurious effect" on the Chiricahuas.

Concurring with the conferees' views, Abbott said he also planned to recommend that a committee representing War, Interior, and the Board of Indian Commissioners "be directed to ascertain" the Chiricahuas' wishes.[12] Echoing these sentiments to a certain extent, H. C. Phillips, on October 29, forwarded for the Secretary of War's edification a strongly worded memorial that emphatically expressed the Board of Indian Commissioners' views on the matter. Before the War Department endeavored to carry out Scott and Stecker's recommendations, Chiricahua family heads and single adult band members were to be "given another and unrestrained opportunity to decide whether they" wished allotments in Oklahoma or removal to Mescalero. All those who elected Oklahoma—"not merely the five families mentioned in the report"—were to be provided with equipment and allotted land on the former Kiowa and Comanche Reservation.[13]

While directives for such investigations were being formulated in Washington, certain military officials at Fort Sill attempted to hasten the day when all Chiricahuas would be removed from that installation. Resuming fulminations against their presence on "his" military range, Captain Dan T. Moore, commandant of the Field Artillery School of Fire, loomed large as the most prominent of these persons. His activities soon secured the War Department's scrutiny. This department's response not only elucidated what actually transpired at Fort Sill in relation to the Chiricahuas and their projected removal therefrom, but also clearly revealed that, at the very least, any moral basis—not to mention the legal ramifications involved—the military might have claimed for insisting upon the compromise agreement recently concluded by both departments was nonexistent: the military's victory was merely a political triumph.

Knowing full well that the War Department's position on the Chiricahua allotment and removal issues was, to say the very least, extremely tenuous, and consequently wishing to prevent any erosion of the War Department's hard-won gains, Colonel Edwin St. John Greble admonished Moore with the utmost severity. "For God's sake," Greble said, "don't burn up Goode's grass for that herd of Apache cattle; don't fire on windy days." Moore was to "turn out the whole garrison to fight fire if necessary." There was a "chance to get rid of these Indians provided the Indian people can be kept quiet until we get them away from Sill." Were "Goode and the other people down there" to "stir up trouble about the military burning up the cattle's winter feed there will be hell to pay again."[14] Therefore, to protect its flanks in permanently procuring Fort Sill for purely military purposes, the War Department lent its full cooperation to Interior's recommendations that an investigation be launched to ascertain the Chiricahuas' wishes on the removal and allotment issues and that these Indians be given absolute freedom of choice in the matter.

Indeed, had "the Indian people" received a copy of Greble's letter to Moore, or even word of this communiqué, there most definitely would have been "hell to pay again." For the Indian rights activists would have spared no effort in utilizing this document as damning evidence in exposing the military's true motives regarding the Chiricahua removal matter and in demonstrating that the Chiricahuas' legal rights had been violated. This would arouse public opinion—generated by incessant outpourings of moral indignation and righteous wrath—to an unprecedented fever pitch whereby the War Department might well be forced to reconsider its position and renegotiate a compromise solution more favorable to the Chiricahua prisoners of war. Of course, it was not in the War Department's interest to permit such a development.

At a conference called on the afternoon of November 21, 1912, Abbott said the secretary of war accepted Interior's October proposals.[15] To initiate action on the Chiricahuas' resettlement, Abbott outlined a plan whereby those desiring to go to Mescalero would be removed first, while, simultaneously, the process of settling those Chiricahuas who wanted to remain at Fort Sill would begin. A special Indian Agent would be "directed to confer with . . . Stecker regarding suitable lands for allotment, of approximately 160 acres each," for those electing to stay in Oklahoma once released from military custody.[16] They were to "report . . . the estimated cost of procuring . . . such . . . allotments on the former Kiowa and Comanche reservation," each 160-acre allotment "to be worth approximately three thousand dollars."[17] Although the Interior Department originally planned to spend $121,500 for this purpose, Abbott now indicated that, of the $200,000 allocated by Congress in the fiscal 1913 Indian appropriation bill for Chiricahua relief, anywhere from $75,000 to $80,000 would be needed to acquire Kiowa and Comanche allotments. In reality, because the Mescalero project required funding in the amount of $54,000 beyond the $78,500 available, only $67,500—vis-à-vis the fiscal 1913 appropriation—remained for the purchase of such allotments and for provisioning those Chiricahuas electing to stay. If necessary, Congress would be asked for additional funds to complete the land acquisition. Later that afternoon, Abbott met with Scott, who was to be the War Department's representative at the upcoming Fort Sill conference, to thrash out any differences on the stated objectives for the meeting with the Chiricahuas.[18]

Scott opened the proceedings on December 1 by extolling Mescalero's virtues, expressing the belief that resettlement there was the "only salvation for you as a people." Still, he wished them to "feel absolutely free, each one to vote for what you believe to be the best for yourself and family."[19] On December 2, this commission certified the Indians' decisions as freely arrived at, reporting that 176 elected to go to Mescalero and 88 opted to remain in Oklahoma.[20] During this canvass, Eugene Chihuahua, speaking for all concerned, said that "we feel happy today because we think you are going to free us." Naiche was also "glad that the War Department and Interior Department have given us a chance to get a home" and would "set us free."[21]

By January 1, 1913, preparations began in earnest for those Chiricahuas removing to New Mexico. At Mescalero, additional clothing, blankets, tents, heating stoves, and lumber for flooring and tent framing were stockpiled to be made available to the Indians upon their arrival.[22] Transportation also had to be arranged. Preparations for their reception were completed on March 29.[23] During the late afternoon of Wednesday, April 2, 1913, a Rock Island Railway special train bearing 163 soon-to-be-released Chiricahua prisoners of war slowly steamed out of Fort Sill.[24] Those Chiricahuas remaining in Oklahoma would be released as soon as they could be placed upon their allotments.

As the train hurtled westward, its passengers doubtless wondered what the future held in store, especially because the government had thus far broken faith with them. Mildred Imach Cleghorn, one of

Group photograph of the last Chiricahua gathering before the majority of
them departed Fort Sill for the Mescalero Indian Reservation
in New Mexico, April 1913. *Courtesy Fort Sill Museum.*

the Chiricahuas who was born into captivity at Fort Sill and remained
in Oklahoma, explained that many of those bound for Mescalero "hated to leave Fort Sill." Because the Chiricahuas "were not treated as if
they were in jail," there was not so much the satisfaction of receiving
one's freedom as there was the sadness of being denied the homes permanently promised them.[25]

Chief Loco's grandson, Raymond Loco, who was also born into
captivity at Fort Sill and remained in Oklahoma, eloquently stated the
situation. Those who went to Mescalero had "learned to love Fort Sill"
while they were there. Therefore, the "day of separation was a day of
great sorrow. There was weeping and wailing, in part due to a new
found love for their homes, in part due to separation from friends and
relatives." There was no "sense of freedom or big sigh of relief that this
was all over. When they were on the train," the Indians were not only
puzzled but also apprehensive, wondering, "What's going to happen to
us?" Because of the way they had been dealt with by government officials during the recent past, "they did not know" whether the "promise

Group of Chiricahuas lunching beside Chicago, Rock Island, and Pacific Railway cars just prior to their departure for the Mescalero Indian Reservation, April 1913. *Courtesy Fort Sill Museum.*

that was given to them would" be fulfilled. Thus, they asked, "Is this really true? Are we going to find a paradise?" Is there "everything waiting for us over there?" Are "we going to begin a new life like we had in the old days?" They were "not overjoyed, they were not happy; they were disturbed."[26]

Upon their arrival at Mescalero on April 4, Major Goode officially transferred custody to Agent Clarence R. Jefferis, at which time their prisoner-of-war status terminated.[27] The Chiricahuas soon busily engaged themselves in making camp at the agency, where they would remain until construction of their dwellings at White Tail Springs was completed.[28] According to messages received from the Mescalero Agency, there were no reports of "open outbreak of hostilities between the Indians and white settlers" as allegedly "feared by the New Mexican politicians and cattlemen."[29]

Evidence soon surfaced that such fears were absolutely groundless. "From all accounts," Brigadier General Hugh L. Scott said, the "only dissatisfied people over the situation are Senators Fall and Catron." Actually, New Mexico as a whole cared nothing "about the matter one way or another. . . . Far from deluging this country once more in blood as we used to read in the Senatorial screeds last fall," the Chiricahuas, Scott said, were "looking for some baseball club to tread on their coattails when the only blood likely to flow would be that of the umpire."[30]

Thus, in mid-May, the first battle the Chiricahuas engaged in since arriving at Mescalero was a baseball contest held in Cloudcroft with that city's team. According to the sports columnist for the *Weekly Cloudcrofter*, the game was an "easy victory for the Indians, the score standing 22 to 2 in their favor." The columnist then noted that "numerous errors on the part of the Cloudcroft team were responsible for the defeat." Actually, the "Fort Sill boys romped around the diamond and ran scores while some of the Cloudcroft boys were trying to put the ball somewhere—just where was not always plain." Goodwill further manifested itself in that "no one wanted to 'kill the umpire' or scalp anybody," and thus the "game passed off pleasantly." Indeed, one reporter noted that the "visitors expressed themselves as being highly pleased with the courteous treatment shown them while there and no doubt they will be back again."[31]

Their return engagement took place in July. Scott sent notice of it to Washington and observed that such a felicitous outcome directly contradicted Fall's predictions of renewed carnage in Arizona and New

Chiricahua Apache prisoner-of-war baseball team. *Courtesy Fort Sill Museum.*

Mexico.[32] On July 28, 1913, Acting Secretary of War Henry Breckin-ridge transmitted Scott's memorandum to Interior "to complete the record of the movement of the Apache Indians from Fort Sill to . . . Mescalero."[33] Thus, at least for the Chiricahuas who removed there, an era replete with unfulfilled promises, dashed hopes, and shattered expectations drew to a close. Only time would prove whether their removal to New Mexico had launched them on the long-awaited road to happiness, prosperity, and contentment.

Still, there were those who thought that at least some measure of justice had finally accrued to those Chiricahuas removing to Mescalero. Reformed Church in America missionaries, for example, believed that the most important event to occur in 1913 regarding their labors among the Chiricahuas was the "restoration to freedom by the Government of Geronimo's band of Apaches."[34] Echoing this view, the Board of Indian Commissioners deemed this undertaking its most significant work of the year because the endeavor had resulted in formulation of a "fair, just, and equitable plan for the removal of the Fort Sill Apache prisoners of war from their lands" on the military reserve in

Oklahoma to "their new homes . . . in New Mexico." According to the board, this task was "accomplished in a manner highly creditable to the Government, and in a way" that not only "fully provided for the physical needs of the Indians in their new homes," but also offered "in the future a means of proper civilization and development." The board also strongly recommended that, concerning the management of each Chiricahua's personal property, all efforts be exerted to "develop their sense of independence and responsibility," thereby preventing a "backward industrial tendency or a going back from individualistic to tribal customs."[35] Only one task remained before those Chiricahuas staying on in Oklahoma were finally freed: concluding the arrangements for their allotment.

CHAPTER

16

Liberated Into Penury:
A Most Parsimonious Chiricahua
Allotment in Oklahoma

▼   ▼   ▼

*D*espite the Board of Indian Commissioners' views, as expressed in 1913, regarding how Chiricahua personal property at Fort Sill should be treated, the manner in which the Bureau of Indian Affairs initially handled the situation did not bode well for those remaining in Oklahoma. Most worrisome was the government's sale of the Chiricahua cattle herd, profits from which nearly bypassed the Indians' individual accounts. This sale was particularly ill-advised in that it destroyed their primary economic base. Forced into an agricultural lifestyle, most of those Chiricahuas remaining in Oklahoma were unable to sustain themselves beyond a subsistence level due to insufficient tillable acreage, government failure to provide the goodly supply of seed stock initially promised, and the high cost of farm machinery.

The cattle sale was undertaken for two reasons: first, so that those Chiricahuas removing to Mescalero might obtain their share of the proceeds and, second, so "that steps may be taken at the . . . earliest possible date to purchase the necessary supplies, land and equipment, and to remove and settle these Indians in their new homes to be provided . . . in Oklahoma." Preparations for the sale began on January 3, 1913, when Interior Secretary Walter L. Fisher suggested to his

▲ *167* ▲

Chiricahua and white cowboys assembled for the last roundup of
Apache cattle, May 1913. *Courtesy Fort Sill Museum.*

counterpart in the War Department that Major Goode be directed to
execute this transaction.[1] On April 21, Goode sold 5,638 branded head
for $234,540.80.[2] This amounted to slightly more than half the herd,
the remainder being unbranded calves that were uncounted but included in the sale.[3] Each family ticket was to be prorated more than
$1,600. These moneys were to be immediately distributed to each
Chiricahua as personal property "for the purchase of stock, farming
implements," and "furniture to establish the Indians in their new
homes."[4] On April 30, the War Department recommended Interior's
approval of these measures.[5]

   Interior's reply illustrated the Indian Office's lack of understanding that the herd was owned individually, not tribally, as evidenced by
Abbott's desire to follow the arrangements originally proposed: to wit,
that "that part belonging to those remaining in Oklahoma shall be divided pro rata and deposited as individual Indian moneys under" Interior's jurisdiction.[6] Outraged, Goode emphatically stated that he had
"never seen that agreement." Goode knew that General Scott had never
reported the cattle herd and the money derived therefrom as Chiricahua "tribal property." Quite to the contrary, Goode said, "Scott vol-
untarily and frequently" cautioned him "against letting any . . . cattle
money get into the treasury as tribal funds." Sale of the remaining

Chiricahuas engaged in the final roundup of their 10,000-head
cattle herd, 1913. *Courtesy Fort Sill Museum.*

property, such as houses, fences, wagons, and other farm stock, yield-
ed a remaining balance in the general Apache fund of approximately
$20,000. This, Goode said, could appropriately be deemed tribal funds.
Therefore, Goode fully intended to distribute all of the proceeds from
the sale of the cattle as individual moneys.[7] To do otherwise would
"not only be a bitter disappointment to me but a cruel blow" to the
Chiricahuas because "nobody but myself knows what it would mean
to the Indians if" such a "right and just . . . plan . . . should fail now."[8]
Fortunately, Mescalero Agent Jefferis agreed with Goode and convinced the Indian Office to approve his recommendations.[9]

Goode then devoted his energies to securing land allotments for
those Chiricahuas remaining in Oklahoma. This work was accomplished with the cooperation of Ernest Stecker and Special Indian Agent
Charles L. Ellis, who completed the purchase of this acreage, a transaction well under way by late winter 1913. Stecker and Ellis reported
that they examined 125 parcels of allotted Kiowa and Comanche lands.
Notice that sale petitions were ready for execution was sent to Kiowas
and Comanches interested in selling these holdings.[10]

By May, sale petition hearings—a necessity because these allotments were, in some cases, inherited lands, and, in other cases,
lands held by Indians not yet deemed competent—were concluded.
Of the available allotments, 101 quarter-sections were found suitable

Chiricahuas gathering their entire cattle herd for shipment and sale, 1913.
Courtesy Fort Sill Museum.

for agriculture. Yet there were problems. Most of the desirable tracts were encumbered by valuable cotton leases that did not expire until December 31, 1913. Also, these allotments were worth $161,650 ($46,350 below the $208,000 earlier estimated as the minimum sum required for this purpose), an amount that, at the time, exceeded by $94,150 the sum then available—$67,500—for the purchase of such lands. Ellis and Stecker therefore suggested that only eighty acres of agricultural land be allotted each Chiricahua.[11] Then, on June 30, 1913, the fiscal 1914 Indian appropriation bill was passed, allocating an additional $100,000 for purchase of allotments. A sum of $167,500 was now available for completion of this transaction, an amount $5,850 more than the $161,500 quoted by Stecker and Ellis in May as necessary to effect the purchase (although $40,500 less than the original $208,000 computation). Yet, Stecker and Ellis, in an October 1913 communiqué to their superiors, broached a similar recommendation that caused no little difficulty for the Indian Office.[12]

Of particular interest in connection with the $40,500 discrepancy is that, although enactment of the fiscal 1915 Indian appropriation bill provided (along with previous allocations) a total of $354,000 to fund Interior's Chiricahua objectives, reconciliation of the $54,000 Mescalero oversight failed to redound to the benefit of those Chiricahuas remaining in Oklahoma. To wit, the $354,000 sum included

$132,500 for removing those Chiricahuas who so desired to Mescalero, and $221,500 (the amount Interior had originally sought for this purpose) for allotting and provisioning those Chiricahuas who remained in Oklahoma (vis-à-vis the late 1912 estimate, $208,000 would be used to purchase allotments, and $13,500 would be used to buy provisions). Yet, of the additional $54,000 provided by the fiscal 1915 Indian appropriation legislation, no evidence has been uncovered to suggest that any of the $40,500 now available to meet the $208,000 originally intended to purchase allotments (vis-à-vis the $167,500 actually so earmarked in 1913) for those Chiricahuas remaining in Oklahoma was ever utilized for this purpose. This corroborates Mildred Imach Cleghorn's assertion that none of the Chiricahuas who stayed in Oklahoma received 160-acre allotments.

Meanwhile, word of the insidious allotment proposal proffered by Stecker and Ellis leaked out almost before the ink had dried. With righteous indignation, representatives of the Society of American Indians, the Indian Rights Association, and the Lake Mohonk Conference on the Indian howled that injustice was once again being visited upon the Chiricahuas. According to the Society of American Indians, it was "unmistakably true that the amount of land . . . contemplated for each Apache" was "160 acres of improved land for each family head, and 160 acres of unimproved land for single individuals and dependents." Due to the "character of southwest Oklahoma farms and the Indians' special aptitude" for stock raising, justice demanded "they be given lands sufficient to make a living." This was especially imperative because the Chiricahuas stood on the "threshold of freedom with such high hopes for the future."[13] H. C. Phillips, now with the Lake Mohonk Conference on the Indian, informed Samuel M. Brosius on October 27 that he had a similar understanding. Phillips said "it would be most unfortunate at this time to even appear to break faith with any of these Indians." Action of this sort would reopen the whole question, thereby running the danger of renewing "the criticism we worked so hard last winter to overcome."[14]

While Brosius immediately applied the usual pressure,[15] Phillips advised Commissioner of Indian Affairs Cato Sells on November 1 that "in the various estimates submitted to Congress," the record would show the "proposed basis of allotment was 160 acres." Also, Phillips said, "it was the understanding in the Indian Office and among the Indians affected that allotments" of this size would be provided. Phillips hoped the charge leveled by the Society of American Indians had no basis in fact, because the "Fort Sill matter has caused a great deal of bitterness in the past." Previous criticism "was so violent as to upset several tentative plans and to hamper legislation for the settlement of the question." Were the Chiricahuas, "whether for lack of money or because of legal restrictions, offered only eighty acres each," Phillips feared the "old criticism would come back in full force, and whether just or unjust," this "would be most unfortunate when we are on the verge of a final disposition of so vexing a question."[16]

Defusing what could well have been a potentially explosive situation, Sells agreed that an allotment of 160 acres was to be given each Chiricahua remaining in Oklahoma. Regarding the understanding concerning the nature of the improved and unimproved lands that the Chiricahuas were to receive, completion of the allotment project required a greater expenditure than originally anticipated—although Sells believed the expense fully justified. Therefore, Sells assured his critics that the Indian Office had the Chiricahuas' "interests at heart" and proceeded, just as quickly as circumstances permitted, to place "them in suitable home sites."[17]

With this matter now settled, Interior next tried to ward off criticism from the War Department. In late October, Chief of Staff Leonard Wood complained that Fort Sill's commanding officer had reported that the Chiricahuas' resettlement might be delayed indefinitely. Hoping the commissioner would expedite matters, Wood thought it most desirable that they be removed from Fort Sill early in the spring, ostensibly to keep the promises made to them.[18] Actually, Wood's request was a thinly veiled disguise concealing the irritation and impatience exhibited by those officers connected with the Field Artillery School of Fire at having to suffer the Chiricahuas' presence at Fort Sill. Evidence that military officials were overanxious about the situation came from Major Goode, who said he would have "some posters printed 'Damifino' to hand out to the Fifth Field Artillery and Officers of the School of Fire when they" next asked, "When are you going to get these Indians off the reservation?"[19]

Actually, the War Department need not have been so petulant. As the time drew near for the expiration of the leases on those allotments destined for Chiricahua settlement, the Indian Office issued the necessary instructions for completion of the sale. On November 12, 1913, Sells directed Ellis to "procure from the present allottees . . . relinquishment of all their right, title and interest in and to the allotments to be purchased." Also, heads of families and single persons over eighteen years of age "should be given first consideration" in the matter of tract selection.[20] Sells reminded Ellis on December 12 that the regulations governing the Chiricahuas' allotment contemplated the purchase of 160-acre tracts for each Indian, provided such acreage could be procured for the amounts designated.[21]

On January 12, 1914, Stecker and Ellis reported that the Chiricahuas' selection of allotments was well under way.[22] Writing to Scott, Goode said he had "carefully inspected all the allotments" and found them "very good." He also described the Chiricahuas as "well pleased with them and crazy to get settled. I had a hard time bringing them around to a reasonable point of view" because of friends' advice "to hold out for everything in the calendar." Goode was "working the Indians hard, every man, every day," because it was the "only way to keep them from going 'up in the air.'" Then, in a moment of reflection, Goode noted that "we have worked and worried a heap over this business, and it is doubtful if we ever get full credit except from the good Lord."[23] By March 7, 1914, those Chiricahuas remaining at Fort Sill were removed to their new homes[24] and finally released from their ignoble status as prisoners of war.[25]

A few items of business yet remained. A considerable amount of real property had to be converted into cash.[26] In the course of executing these duties, Goode reported that the Chiricahuas had "more land in cultivation and . . . their crops in better condition—due to their intelligent labor—than the average white farmer in their neighborhood."[27] Convinced they were "finally launched," Goode believed that "whether they sink or swim will depend on themselves. Some of them will make it I know."[28]

By June 26, 1914, Goode reported that with the disposal of all the Chiricahuas' common property, he had accomplished those remaining tasks related to the Chiricahuas' former captivity at Fort Sill. According to Goode, the "condition of these Indians at the time they were turned over" to Interior "was in every way excellent." They were "hopeful . . . their new life" would promise them "success and prosperity." Having said this, Goode then explained that the "rendering of this report" terminated his duties as their officer-in-charge.[29] With the submission of Goode's final report, not only did the Office of Apache Prisoners of War close its doors forever, but an era that had witnessed as unprecedented and unconscionable a case of injustice as was ever visited upon a single tribe of American Indians finally came to a close.

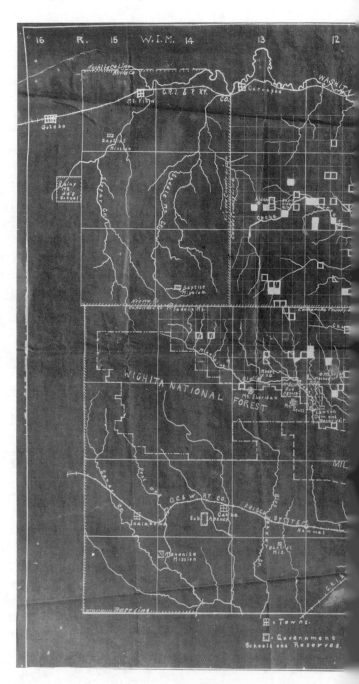

Map showing locations of potential
Chiricahua land allotment sites.

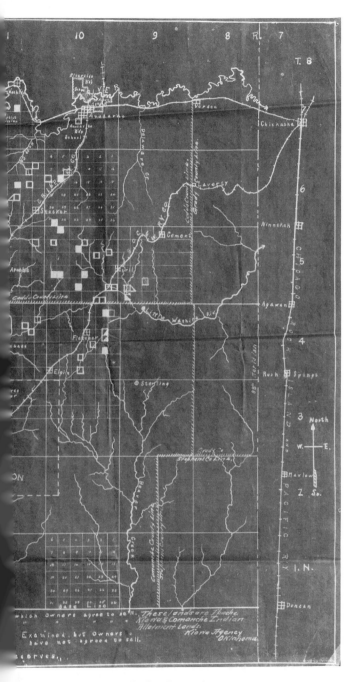

Courtesy Haverford College Library,
Quaker Collection.

Thus, after nearly twenty-seven years of captivity, the Chiricahuas remaining in Oklahoma were relieved of their status as prisoners of war. Yet, for all the efforts to salvage the compromise agreement, this victory seemed almost ephemeral. Concern over the Chiricahuas' ability to withstand onslaughts against their economic, social, and political integrity was especially manifest in Goode's conjecture that "some of them will make it I know." Essentially, the Chiricahuas' survival remained an open question subject to the intensity of debilitating pressures hurled against them. Therefore, although they had been released from captivity, the very real question was whether the Chiricahuas had become a truly free people.

Epilogue
Quest for Freedom:
A Case of Justice Denied

▼   ▼   ▼

As expounded by Chiricahua informants, freedom, as well as justice, entailed more than liberation from an unjust confinement of nearly an entire people held, for reasons of economic, military, and political expediency, for crimes they never committed. Actually, Raymond Loco explained, "as defined by whites," freedom is a concept that Indian people found difficult to express. In earlier times, Loco began, speaking metaphorically, they only knew true freedom "when the buffalo roamed the plains, when the rivers ran clean and when the grass was green and abundant." Today, by contrast, Loco continued, many American Indians, confronted with an alien environment, still lack a number of tools—vocational, technical, and academic skills, for example—needed to make their way unimpeded in the larger society. Under such circumstances, Loco declared, "there yet exists a bond for the Indian." Furthermore, Loco said, only when the dominant society freely provided these tools of assimilation, while at the same time not only sanctioning but also unreservedly endorsing the Native Americans' right to economic inviolability, as well as their right to retain their cultural, social, and political integrity, would American Indians be truly free.[1] Thus, in the Chiricahuas' case, although they were released from military custody, the true degree of their liberation is debatable because the federal government failed, in providing just compensation, to affirm their right to at least some measure of economic stability and to retain intact their political, cultural, and social structures. In this context,

Mildred Imach Cleghorn could therefore truthfully claim that although the Chiricahuas were finally released from their status as prisoners of war, "We were not free!"[2]

While those Chiricahuas who removed to Mescalero managed to retain—with great struggle—a meager measure of their former cultural life, their economic fortunes declined precipitously. Indeed, decades passed before they again experienced anything remotely resembling the degree of prosperity known at Fort Sill. Initially, a number of the "Mescaleros did not take kindly to the newcomers, although at the time it was said they welcomed the ex-prisoners with open arms."[3] After their arrival, the Chiricahuas were "separated from the Mescaleros"[4] and placed twenty miles northeast of the agency in the White Tail district, a narrow eight-mile-long valley more than 7,000 feet in elevation and subject to severe winter cold, heavy snowfalls, late and early frosts, and occasional spring and summer droughts.[5]

In an area that "was not the best place to make a living,"[6] each Chiricahua family was allotted only fifteen acres for agricultural purposes, an amount that even the Indian Agent admitted was inadequate to support the average Indian family.[7] Although the Chiricahuas relied upon their oat crop in order to purchase such items as cornmeal, coffee, sugar, clothing, and necessary utensils,[8] there were years when the harvest was either a total failure,[9] or scanty at best.[10] Little wonder the Chiricahuas' crops were insufficient to provide them with enough foodstuffs for an entire year's subsistence,[11] and even less surprising that, owing to a dearth of employment opportunities, they were barely able to survive.[12] Conditions were so difficult that many of them existed on less food than whites fed their dogs.[13] As if to exacerbate matters, the $16,000 General Apache Fund, supposedly allocated in 1913 to the New Mexico–bound Chiricahuas, had yet to be received by these Indians in 1918.[14] In 1919, Ernest Stecker, formerly of Anadarko and now Indian Agent at Mescalero, reported the Chiricahuas as "very much disheartened." Many of them wished they had remained in Oklahoma. Indeed, even Asa Daklugie, explaining that he and Eugene Chihuahua bore the major responsibility for bringing the Chiricahuas to Mescalero, later said that "at the time we did it we did not have the wisdom to know that we were making a terrible mistake. We thought that we made the right decision."[15]

During late spring 1920, Major General Hugh L. Scott, a former chief of staff, visited Mescalero in his capacity as a member of the Board of Indian Commissioners. According to Scott, the Fort Sill Apaches came

Brigadier General Hugh Lenox Scott. *Courtesy Fort Sill Museum.*

to this agency "full of courage and hope" because the government promised to establish them "in as good an economic condition as when they were at Fort Sill." Interior, the Chiricahuas claimed, had failed to fulfill this pledge. Consequently, Scott said, "they became discouraged and have retrograded since coming under" Interior's jurisdiction.[16]

Raymond Loco said of Scott that "the man who was responsible for" the Chiricahuas' removal to New Mexico saw their "plight and how they were living in poverty." Scott "gathered them together" and said, "I am sorry. I am responsible for your people moving here." If any wished to return to Oklahoma, he said he would be glad to take them back. Several, Loco said, did return. "But the rest felt themselves committed and said they would try to begin life anew at Mescalero."[17]

Life was nearly as difficult for those Chiricahuas who remained in Oklahoma. According to Raymond Loco, they were "dumped into poverty."[18] Although allotted near the general vicinity of Fort Sill, the Chiricahuas nevertheless continued to consider this post their rightful home and believed the land contained thereon "was stolen from them."[19] Although it had promised them a year's subsistence, the government never delivered. Such negligence forced the Chiricahuas to use their cattle money for food instead of purchasing seeds, implements, and livestock.[20] "Our fathers had to ride out looking for jobs" in order to obtain "a few dollars to survive on" until a crop could be made. Times were so difficult, Loco said, that he recalled the day his family dog brought home a live chicken. "The dog must have known that we were hungry."[21]

By 1920, the government had yet to reimburse the Chiricahuas for rations not yet received, a sum totaling $11,500. In addition, thirteen individuals remained to be allotted according to law.[22] Those who had managed to secure allotments were, in the words of Mildred Cleghorn, "land poor" because, in truth, none of her people received 160 acres. Cleghorn, a recent Fort Sill Apache tribal chairperson, said that the "closest they got was 158 acres and the least amount they got was 23. A majority received 80 acres apiece." Even had each Chiricahua remaining in Oklahoma received a full 160-acre allotment, it would not have been sufficiently large to provide adequate sustenance. This was yet another example of Uncle Sam's failure to "follow through" on assurances given to Indians by the government.[23]

Elaborating on this theme, Raymond Loco conjectured that had the Chiricahuas been left at Fort Sill to tend their cattle business, they most likely would have become one of the wealthiest tribes in Oklahoma. "We would have elected a business committee to go back and forth to Washington to make the white man toe the line." But rather than let the Chiricahuas prosper, the government "took that away from us. They destroyed us altogether." Instead of being recognized as a member of the Warm Springs band of Chiricahuas, Loco said, "I'm deceitfully referred to as a Fort Sill Apache now" merely because he was a former prisoner of war.[24]

Furthermore, Loco said, "we were scattered. We were not placed so as to be in a community." Thus, "in the course of time, we lost our heritage, our traditions and customs."[25] Even their language was passing into oblivion.[26] As Loco observed, "We lost everything."[27] Essentially, what Raymond Loco described was nothing less than the virtual extinguishment, over time, of Chiricahua cultural and tribal identity.

What befell the Chiricahuas after liberation from their ignominious status and forced removal from Fort Sill is one of the principal reasons the Chiricahua Apache prisoner-of-war saga is unparalleled in the annals of American Indian–federal government relations. The only exception is the nearly total extermination of the Pequots as a consequence of the 1637 war of annihilation waged against them by Massachusetts Bay Colony authorities under British rule. The survivors, although placed on several small reservations located in Connecticut, were proscribed from being acknowledged as Pequots and experienced complete demoralization. Later, they lost even those lands to white agrarian aggrandizement. When they were subsequently amalgamated with other southern New England Algonquin remnants, their tribal identity was obliterated. Many of them eventually became incorporated into what today is known as the Brothertown Indian Nation of Wisconsin.[28]

Under U.S. Indian policy administered by the Bureau of Indian Affairs, numerous tribal entities suffered rank injustice. However, these experiences, though calamitous, were neither of the same magnitude as those that befell the Pequots nor of the same severity as the Chiricahua prisoner-of-war saga. The Modocs provide an important example. In 1873, at the end of the Modoc War, which was fought to regain territory located in California's Lost River region, only four conspirators were hanged for the murder of peace commissioners (including General Edward R.S. Canby). One hundred fifty-three dissident Modocs were temporarily taken captive and removed to Oklahoma, where a reservation was established for them at Quapaw in 1874.[29]

Like the Modocs, the Santee Sioux of Minnesota were also driven to insurrection. At the end of their 1862 uprising, 303 Santees were scheduled for execution. President Abraham Lincoln commuted the sentence of all but thirty-nine of the condemned men, among whom was Little Crow. These individuals were hanged in Mankato. Their families, as well as those of the men originally slated for the gallows, were taken captive and held for six months at Fort Snelling, where 130 died during the hard winter of 1862–1863. Subsequently, they were released, exiled to the Dakota Territory, and eventually established at the Niobrara Agency in the Nebraska Territory in 1865.[30] Less severely treated, despite a more intense and extensive period of warfare, were the Oglalas under Red Cloud; the worst they suffered was removal from their western Nebraska homes in 1877 for eventual resettlement on the Pine Ridge Agency in South Dakota in 1878.[31] Both Santee and Oglalas were able to remain in their general region and were not removed to an unfamiliar area with a debilitating climate.

Also losing the struggle for their homelands were the Kiowas, Comanches, Arapahos, and Northern and Southern Cheyennes. The 1867 Treaty of Medicine Lodge, however, established reservations for these particular tribes in southwestern Oklahoma, which was, at least, a plains environment.[32] During the course of the Red River War, waged in the early 1870s, seventy captives were taken from all but the Northern Cheyennes and held as prisoners at Fort Marion, Florida, for a period not to exceed five years.[33] In 1883, those Northern Cheyennes remaining in Oklahoma were returned to their general region and settled on the Tongue River Reservation in Montana.[34]

The Nez Percé are a final noteworthy example. After their unsuccessful 1877 flight from military pursuit—an event engendered by murders of white settlers in a desperate attempt to prevent Anglo intrusion into the Nez Percé western Idaho homeland—Chief Joseph and his dissident band were taken captive and incarcerated at Fort Leavenworth, Kansas, for eighteen months. They were subsequently resettled in Oklahoma and released from their status as prisoners of war. Although they suffered a high mortality rate because the climate of the region was unhealthy for them, these Indians managed to obtain some measure of prosperity raising stock. In 1882, the federal government removed twenty-nine widows and orphans to Lapwai, located on their former southeastern Washington and northeastern Oregon reservation. Nez Percé still remaining in Oklahoma were returned to the Northwest in 1885. Chief Joseph and 149 fellow band members were resettled at the Colville Indian Reservation in Washington, and 188 were removed to Lapwai.[35]

It should also be noted that following the ends of the Civil War and World War II, not even Confederate, German, and Japanese prisoners of war were so ill-treated by the U.S. government. All were released from federal prison and concentration camps, paroled, and returned to their former homes.

As compared to the Chiricahuas, all of the aforementioned tribes were belligerent. None were held in captivity for more than five years. They either had new reservations established for them or were returned to reservations in the general region from which they had been originally removed. As Vincent Natalish observed, all received better treatment at the federal government's hands than did the nearly 400 nonbelligerent Chiricahuas so callously removed from their Arizona homes in 1886.

Consequently, consideration of the circumstances that befell the Chiricahuas leads to the inescapable conclusion that Raymond Loco did not overstate the Chiricahuas' cultural and economic devastation after their release from military custody. As Morris Opler noted, the Chiricahuas, while at Fort Sill, continued to exert "pressure for conformity to tribal standards . . . upon families and individuals." Comparing the post–Fort Sill experience of the Chiricahuas who stayed in Oklahoma with that of those who removed to Mescalero, Opler observed that those Chiricahuas remaining in Oklahoma were no more successful— indeed, they were less so—than those who departed for New Mexico in maintaining their tribal identity, even though the latter, ironically enough, were more traditional. Due to difficult economic circumstances, the Oklahoma Chiricahua community, already scattered around the Apache and Fletcher areas, suffered an ever increasing lack of social cohesion.[36] Consequently, as Henrietta Stockel elucidates, many Oklahoma Chiricahuas married outside the tribe and "ceased to observe the traditional rituals and customs."[37] In addition, for all practical purposes, they lost their language, another casualty of the acculturation process. Although Stockel notes that a "core group of descendants" has endeavored "to revitalize their people by teaching traditional ways and practices," an admittedly "arduous and thankless" undertaking,[38] Opler finds "no reason to believe" that the "trend toward dispersion of the Fort Sill Apache and their absorption into the general population of the region" will "be reversed."[39]

Economically, the change was not only drastic, it was total. Prior to their initial reservation experience at San Carlos and Fort Apache, the Chiricahuas "subsisted on the products of hunting, gathering of uncultivated roots and vegetables, and raiding. . . . These Apaches were not agriculturists to any great extent."[40] Upon their removal to Mescalero and settlement on their Oklahoma allotments, they had become acculturated as agriculturists and stock raisers, occupations once basically foreign to them. Ironically, removal from Fort Sill meant these Indians would be unable even to profitably employ these new skills, let alone adequately sustain themselves. Had they been given Fort Sill and allowed to function as a tribal entity, what transpired after their release would not have occurred.

It is an incontrovertible fact that the War Department was morally and legally obligated to transfer ownership of Fort Sill to the Chiricahua Apache prisoners of war for their reservation. Indeed, Hugh L. Scott's acculturation plan envisioned the whole of Fort Sill being given to these Indians in fee simple so that their cattle herd could become their economic mainstay. To this end, the Eastern and Western Additions to Fort Sill, totaling approximately 27,000 acres, were procured from the Kiowa and Comanche Indians in 1897 for the "permanent location of the Apache prisoners of war thereon." Why, then, did Fort Sill not pass into Chiricahua ownership as originally intended?

The key to this puzzle—an understanding of which also requires familiarity with the circumstances surrounding the 1867 Treaty of Medicine Lodge—lies in the phrases "only for military purposes" (as inserted in the February 17, 1897, agreement with the Kiowas and Comanches that procured the Eastern and Western Additions for the Chiricahuas' permanent settlement) and "for exclusive use for military purposes" (as incorporated into the February 26, 1897, presidential executive order that officially attached these parcels to Fort Sill). Years later, these phrases would be liberally interpreted by War Department officials to mean outright ownership of Fort Sill. Although the Medicine Lodge Treaty stipulated that the Kiowas and Comanches had to accept posts already established on their reservation, it did not obviate their rights to lands encompassed by these installations. Also, their consent was needed for additions to these posts. Therefore, the agreements that established the original 1871 post at, and 1897 additions to, Fort Sill required that this land be returned to the Kiowas and Comanches when no longer needed for military purposes or until the United States purchased it outright.

This was the case for two essential reasons. First, as explained in 1901 by Judge Advocate General George B. Davis, Fort Sill was merely a military reservation superimposed on an Indian reservation. During council proceedings convened on February 17, 1897, Hugh L. Scott told Kiowa and Comanche participants that the phrase "only for military purposes" accorded the 1897 additions the same status as the original post officially established in 1871. Scott inserted this language, which was intended to protect the interests of all concerned, including the Chiricahuas, and prevent any possible aggrandizement by white intruders of that portion of the Kiowa and Comanche Reservation upon which Fort Sill was situated. In other words, this phrase was meant to guarantee that only the military would utilize this particular tract of land until such time as it passed into Chiricahua hands by purchase from the Kiowas and Comanches.

Furthermore, within the contextual framework of the 1897 presidential executive order, the term *use* can in no way be construed—contrary to the military's interpretation thereof—to signify ownership. All this language ever conveyed to the military was right of occupancy. It never granted the War Department fee simple to this tract of land. Yet, faced with Fort Sill's potential abandonment, the War Department changed its position by 1903. Military officials therefore deliberately misinterpreted the aforementioned 1897 clauses to mean ownership, thereby meeting new exigencies that demanded Fort Sill's retention for field artillery training. This was especially possible after ratification in 1900 of the 1892 Jerome Agreement. Although ownership of Fort Sill passed to the United States, title had yet to be issued to the Chiricahuas. With the War Department's change of mind, such action did not come to pass.

However, the War Department does not bear complete culpability for the despoliation wreaked upon the Chiricahuas after their forced removal from Fort Sill. In this regard, the Interior Department also merits not inconsiderable opprobrium. Deliberately associating those Chiricahuas not guilty of insurrection with Geronimo and his fellow belligerents, for reasons of political expediency, Interior refused to retake custody of these Indians in 1897 and 1902 as so importuned by the War Department. Had Interior not missed its opportunity in this regard, the Chiricahuas would have had Fort Sill as their permanent home. Furthermore, the cattle herd that was to be their economic mainstay would not have been sold at a loss, thereby casting the Chiricahuas into penury upon their release and thus denying them the prosperity they would otherwise have enjoyed.

There was at least one mitigating factor in the War Department's favor. Although pro–Fort Sill in sentiment, upper-echelon military officials were not anti-Chiricahua. Consistent with the department's interests, they did express a genuine concern for these Indians' welfare. Lower-echelon officers, detailed to such duty, labored diligently on behalf of their Chiricahua charges, attempting to make the best of what later became a hopelessly dismal and irreversible situation.

In this regard, Hugh Lenox Scott emerges as a tragic hero. Scott, the chief architect behind the plan designed to allot the Chiricahuas at Fort Sill, exerted every effort to uphold their best interests. He at least recognized the necessity, as did, interestingly enough, George Purington, of providing the Chiricahua prisoners with communal grazing lands were these people, each of whom owned heads of cattle on an individual basis, to survive economically. This was the only reason for procuring the Eastern and Western Additions to Fort Sill. On this basis, Scott believed a compromise whereby communalistic and individualistic principles would be combined was imperative. Simply, Scott knew that individual holdings of 160 acres or less of southwestern Oklahoma grazing land would never provide the Chiricahuas with an adequate income, making survival difficult in the extreme. Years later, when ordered to preside over the destruction of the Chiricahua civilization plan that he had originally initiated, Scott—undoubtedly feeling helpless—must have experienced a cruel, bitter, and telling blow as he advised his former charges they would have to depart Fort Sill forever.

Yet for all this—with the very definite exception of those Arizonans who would not permit the Chiricahuas' return under any circumstances, and possibly barring Albert Fall, Scott Ferris, and Dan Moore, all of whom had their covert reasons for opposing the most efficacious measures redounding to the Chiricahua prisoners' benefit—there were no hard-core villains lurking in ambuscade about the stage upon which the Chiricahua Apache prisoner-of-war drama unfolded. The great irony of the whole heart-wrenching Chiricahua saga is that the white participants therein were also prisoners; that is to say, they were chained to and victimized by their own and others' attitudes, prejudices, and preconceived ideas about how policies relating to Indian welfare might best be implemented.

Surfeited with the Calvinistic ideology of individual effort, the government at large could never accept such a compromise as Scott's. Interior was shackled by more than just its fear of political repercussions were the Chiricahua prisoners released prior to Geronimo's demise; after all, Interior officials believed, any man—white or Indian—with 160 acres should be able to provide for himself. Even so, Interior's efforts in this direction were stringently hampered by a U.S. Congress that failed to gather all the particulars of the matter.

Consequently, Congress never understood that it dealt with an innocent and displaced people wrongfully removed from and forever denied their former southwestern homeland. Members never fully grasped the real point at issue—namely, justice. Hence, this legislative body did not comprehend why the government should subsidize the Chiricahuas' pursuit of the noble agrarian dream when, like anyone else, these Indians not only could but should labor and sweat to earn the acreage they desired. This argument was ludicrous in the extreme, because the government largely failed to provide its erstwhile charges with the means to do so. Sadly enough, despite the overwhelming evidence that not even a white man could expect a reasonably adequate return on 160 acres of southwestern Oklahoma farmland, the Chiricahuas were expected to make do or do without.

In turn, the views embraced—evidence to the contrary—by those held captive to their concepts not only led to the Chiricahuas' nearly total economic ruin but also heightened what was definitely a tragedy in that expression's truest meaning. As Vincent Natalish cogently observed, tribes that were actually belligerent received better and fairer treatment at the hands of the U.S. government than did the surviving 260 Chiricahuas held captive by political expediency for an unconscionable period of nearly twenty-seven years, twenty of them spent at Fort Sill expecting to receive this installation as their reservation. Yet, when liberated, they were denied both the permanent homes promised them and a viable economic base on which to sustain themselves.

For these reasons alone, the situation confronting the Chiricahua Apache prisoners of war—unlike the treatment, egregiously sordid as it was, accorded other tribal groups throughout the history of American Indian–federal government relations—was unprecedented. Had justice been rendered throughout their quest for freedom, the economic, social, cultural, and political disaster that befell the Chiricahuas after their release from military custody would not have transpired. Rather than being delivered into cultural disintegration and economic destitution, they would truly have been set free.

Notes

▼ ▼ ▼

ABBREVIATIONS

(These abbreviations are used in the Notes only.)

AG = Adjutant General

AGDF = Adjutant General's Document File

AGO = Adjutant General's Office

AICD = Archives and Iconographic Collections Division

ARBIC = *Annual Reports of the Board of Indian Commissioners*

ARCIA = *Annual Reports of the Commissioner of Indian Affairs*

ARSW = *Annual Reports of the Secretary of War*

CAD = Civil Archives Division

CF = Central Files

FAM = U.S. Army Field Artillery and Fort Sill Museum

HD = House Document

HR = House Report

IAR = Indian Archives

LC = Library of Congress

LJFB = Legislative, Judicial, and Fiscal Branch

MAD = Military Archives Division

MD = Manuscripts Division

MHI = U.S. Army Military History Institute

NARA = National Archives and Records Administration

NRB = Natural Resources Branch

OHS = Oklahoma Historical Society

OMB = Old Military Branch

RACC = Records of the U.S. Army Continental Commands

RAGO = Records of the Adjutant General's Office

RBIA = Records of the Bureau of Indian Affairs

RBIC = Records of the Board of Indian Commissioners

RDMO = Records of the Department of the Missouri

RG = Record Group

RHCIA = Records of the House Committee on Indian Affairs

RHR = Records of the House of Representatives

RSI = Records of the Office of the Secretary of the Interior

SD = Senate Document

SED = Senate Executive Document

SI = Secretary of the Interior

SW = Secretary of War

PROLOGUE

1. "Chiricahua" is the general appellation applied to the Apache prisoners of war throughout this work. Several principal bands—Chokonens (true Chiricahuas), Ojo Calientes (Warm Springs), and Mimbreños—constituted the Chiricahua Apache prisoners of war. For an explanation of this nomenclature, see Angie Debo, *Geronimo: The Man, His Time, His Place* (Norman: University of Oklahoma Press, 1976), 12; Morris Edward Opler, "Chiricahua Apache," in William C. Sturtevant, gen. ed., *Handbook of North American Indians,* Vol. 10, *Southwest,* ed. Alfonso Ortiz (Washington, D.C.: Smithsonian Institution Press, 1983), 401 and 417–418; H. Henrietta Stockel, *Women of the Apache Nation: Voices of Truth* (Reno: University of Nevada Press, 1991), 2; and John R. Swanton, *Indian Tribes of North America* (Washington, D.C.: Smithsonian Institution Press, 1974), 328–329. Morris E. Opler, a noted anthropologist who conducted much fieldwork among the surviving remnants of these bands, observed that "language, culture, intermarriage [and] similar social organization . . . point to common tribal association" (personal communication of Morris E. Opler to John Anthony Turcheneske, Jr., June 17, 1977).

2. Elizabeth M. Page, *In Camp and Tepee: An Indian Mission Story* (New York: Fleming H. Revell, 1915), 237.

3. Important accounts that treat the conquest of the Chiricahuas include Samuel M. Barrett, ed., *Geronimo's Story of His Life* (New York: Duffield, 1906); Odie B. Faulk, *The Geronimo Campaign* (New York: Oxford University Press, 1969); Frank C. Lockwood, *The Apache Indians* (New York: Macmillan, 1938); C. L. Sonnichsen, ed., *Geronimo and the End of the Apache Wars* (Lincoln: University of Nebraska Press, 1990); Michael Lynn Tate, "Apache Scouts, Police, and Judges as Agents of Acculturation, 1865–1920" (Ph.D. diss., University of Toledo, 1974); Dan L. Thrapp, *The Conquest of Apacheria* (Norman: University of Oklahoma Press, 1967); and Dan L. Thrapp, *Victorio and the Mimbres Apaches* (Norman: University of Oklahoma Press, 1974). A related work concerning the reaction of Arizona's territorial press to Geronimo's surrender is John Anthony Turcheneske, Jr., "The Arizona Press and Geronimo's Surrender," *Journal of Arizona History* 14 (Summer 1973): 133–148.

CHAPTER 1

1. Faulk, 161.

2. Ibid., 163.

3. The Chiricahua prisoners of war reached Holbrook, Arizona, on September 12 "after a very difficult march through rain and mud" (Oliver O. Howard to AG, September 14, 1886, in Senate, *Letter from the Secretary of War, transmitting, in response to the resolution of February 11, 1887, correspondence with Brigadier General Nelson A. Miles relative to the surrender of Geronimo,* 49th Cong., 2d sess., 1887, SED 117, 15–16).

4. Faulk, 164.

5. Interview with Raymond Loco (hereafter cited as RLI) conducted by John Anthony Turcheneske, Jr. (hereafter cited as JAT), Apache, Oklahoma, November 11, 1976 (the second half of the interview took place on November 12). Raymond Loco was the grandson of Chief Loco of the Warm Springs Apaches.

6. Interview with Mildred Imach Cleghorn (hereafter cited as MICI), conducted by JAT, Apache, Oklahoma, November 11, 1976 (the second half of the interview took place November 12). Concerning this situation, additional details, most graphically described, are contained in H. Henrietta Stockel's splendid medical history of the Chiricahuas, *Survival of the Spirit: Chiricahua Apaches in Captivity* (Reno: University of Nevada Press, 1993), 77–80.

7. RLI.

8. Eve Ball, *Indeh: An Apache Odyssey* (Norman: University of Oklahoma Press, 1988), 133.

9. Faulk, 164.

10. Nelson A. Miles, *Personal Recollections and Observations of General Nelson A. Miles* (Chicago: Warner, 1896), 528. Miles reported that "ten car loads of Apache Indians, with guards, passed Albuquerque at 2:30" a.m. (Howard to AG, SED 117, 74). Related works include Virginia Weisel Johnson, *The Unregimented*

General: A Biography of Nelson A. Miles (Boston: Houghton Mifflin, 1962) and Nelson A. Miles, *Serving the Republic: Memoirs of the Civil and Military Life of Nelson A. Miles* (Freeport, New York: Books for Libraries Press, 1971).

11. See John Anthony Turcheneske, Jr., "Arizonans and the Apache Prisoners of War at Mount Vernon Barracks, Alabama: 'They Do Not Die Fast Enough!,'" *Military History of Texas and the Southwest* 11 (1973): 197–226.

12. Interview with Blossom Haozous (hereafter cited as BHI) conducted by JAT, Apache, Oklahoma, November 11, 1976 (the second half of the interview took place November 12).

13. Mildred Imach Cleghorn, "A Statement," foreword to *The Apache Rock Crumbles: The Captivity of Geronimo's People*, by Woodward B. Skinner (Pensacola, Florida: Skinner Publications, 1987), iv.

14. Lyman Walter Vere Kennon, "The Case of the Chiricahuas," *North American Review* (August 1890): 253.

15. Women's National Indian Association, "The Disposition of the Apaches," *Indian's Friend* (October 1890): 1.

16. Britton Davis, *The Truth About Geronimo* (New Haven, Connecticut: Yale University Press, 1929), 233. Related works include John Gregory Bourke, *On the Border With Crook* (New York: Charles Scribner's Sons, 1891); George Crook, *Resumé of Operations Against the Apache Indians* (Omaha: n.p., 1886); Charles F. Lummis, *General George Crook and the Apache Wars* (Flagstaff, Arizona: Northland Press, 1966); and Martin F. Schmitt, ed., *General George Crook: His Autobiography* (Norman: University of Oklahoma Press, 1960).

17. For the definitive work on the Sierra Madre campaign, see Dan L. Thrapp, *General George Crook and the Sierra Madre Adventure* (Norman: University of Oklahoma Press, 1972). See also John Gregory Bourke, *An Apache Campaign in the Sierra Madre* (New York: Charles Scribner's Sons, 1958).

18. Davis, 145–150. See also Eve Ball, *In the Days of Victorio: Recollections of a Warm Springs Apache* (Tucson: University of Arizona Press, 1970), 176–177. James Kaywaykla, who narrated for Ball the events discussed in this work, was himself a Chiricahua prisoner of war.

19. See Ralph H. Ogle, *Federal Control of the Western Apaches, 1848–1886* (Albuquerque: University of New Mexico Press, 1970). Also extremely useful in this regard is Thrapp's discussion in *Conquest of Apacheria*.

20. See discussion in Davis and Faulk. See also *Testimony of General Nelson A. Miles, February 15, 1890, Removal of the Apache Indian Prisoners: Hearings on the Senate Resolution in regard to the removal of the Chiricahua Apache Indians from Mount Vernon, Alabama, to Fort Sill, Indian Territory* (hereafter cited as *Apache Prisoner Removal Hearings*), House File 51A-F16.5 (hereafter cited as HF51A-F16.5), 5–6, RHCIA, RHR, RG 233, LJFB, CAD, NARA, Washington, D.C.

21. David Michael Goodman, "Apaches as Prisoners of War, 1886–1894" (Ph.D. diss., Texas Christian University, 1969), 1.

22. Ibid., 2.

23. Ibid., 5.

24. Thrapp, *The Conquest of Apacheria*, 345–346.

25. Goodman, 2.

26. Ibid., 5.

27. Ibid., 3.

28. Crook to Philip S. Sheridan, April 1, 1886, in Crook, *Resumé of Operations Against the Apache Indians*, 15–16.

29. Goodman, 3.

30. Ibid., 4.

31. Ibid., 11.

32. Ibid.

33. Several excellent discussions of where these Apaches were to be sent are contained in Joseph C. Porter, *Paper Medicine Man: John Gregory Bourke and His American West* (Norman: University of Oklahoma Press, 1986), 211–224, and Robert Wooster, *Nelson A. Miles and the Twilight of the Frontier Army* (Lincoln: University of Nebraska Press, 1993), 148–153. See also Donald E. Worcester, *The Apaches: Eagles of the Southwest* (Norman: University of Oklahoma Press, 1979), 304–309.

34. Goodman, 11–12.

35. Ibid., 12–13.

36. Ibid., 13–15.

37. Ibid., 15–17.

38. Ibid., 17.

39. Ibid., 18–19.

40. Ibid., 19–20.

41. Richard C. Drum to Commanding General, Division of the Missouri, September 12, 1886, SED 117, 73.

42. Alfred H. Terry to AG, September 15, 1886, SED 117, 74.

43. Goodman, 55.

44. Ibid., 22–23.

45. Ibid., 34.

46. Ibid., 36.

47. Nelson A. Miles to Acting Secretary of War, September 29, 1886, SED 117, 21.

48. Goodman, 39.

49. Drum to President Grover Cleveland, September 7, 1886, SED 117, 8–9.

50. Howard to Drum, October 2, 1886, SED 117, 23.

51. Howard to AG, September 7, 1886, SED 117, 8.

52. Cleveland to Drum, September 7, 1886, SED 117, 4.

53. Miles to Acting Secretary of War, September 1886, SED 117, 21; Miles to Sheridan, September 7, 1886, SED 117, 10.

54. Cleveland to Drum, September 8, 1886, SED 117, 11.

55. Leonard Wood, September 8, 1886, journal entry in Jack C. Lane, ed., *Chasing Geronimo: The Journal of Leonard Wood, May–September 1886* (Albuquerque: University of New Mexico Press, 1970), 112.

56. Miles to AG, February 16, 1887, SED 117, 34.

57. Goodman, 43–44.

58. Miles to AG, November 3, 1886, SED 117, 34.

59. Howard to AG, September 9, 1886, SED 117, 12.

60. Drum to Cleveland, September 10, 1886, SED 117, 13.

61. Drum to David Stanley, September 10, 1886, SED 117, 13.

62. Goodman, 59.

63. Howard to AG, September 17, 1886, SED 117, 16; John C. Kelton to Commanding General, Division of the Pacific, September 18, 1886, SED 117, 16.

64. Drum to Howard, September 24, 1886, SED 117, 17.

65. Howard to Cleveland, September 24, 1886, SED 117, 18.

66. Drum to Miles, September 25, 1886, SED 117, 20.

67. Goodman, 61.

68. Drum to Stanley, September 29, 1886, SED 117, 21; Stanley to Drum, September 30, 1886, SED 117, 22; Stanley to Drum, October 1, 1886, SED 117, 22.

69. Goodman, 62.

70. Ibid., 62–63.

71. William Endicott to Sheridan, October 19, 1886, SED 117, 26.

72. Goodman, 64–65.

73. Ibid., 75.

CHAPTER 2

1. Goodman, 77.

2. Ibid., 77, 83.

3. Herbert Welsh, *The Apache Prisoners in Fort Marion, St. Augustine, Florida* (Philadelphia: Indian Rights Association, 1887), 13-14; Goodman, 76.

4. Goodman, 76.

5. Woodward S. Skinner, *The Apache Rock Crumbles: The Captivity of Geronimo's People* (Pennsacola, Florida: Skinner Publications, 1987), 119-120.

6. Wooster, 173.

7. Goodman, 85-91.

8. Ibid., 91.

9. Ibid., 101-104.

10. Ibid., 104-105.

11. Skinner, 167-168.

12. Ibid.

13. Ibid., 168.

14. Goodman, 105.

15. William Sinclair to Richard C. Drum, April 28, 1887, File 1883 AGO 1066, National Archives Microfilm Publication M689 (hereafter cited as M689), Roll 189, RAGO, RG 94, OMB, MAD, NARA, Washington, D.C.

16. Skinner, 171.

17. Ball, *Indeh*, 139.

18. Stockel, *Survival of the Spirit*, 160. (For a graphically detailed description of how the abysmal conditions at Mount Vernon Barracks adversely affected the Chiricahuas, consult pages 137-184 in their entirety.)

19. Marian Stephens Memoirs, Archives and Manuscripts Division, Sterling Memorial Library, Yale University, New Haven, Connecticut, 74.

20. Goodman, 120-121.

21. Sinclair to Assistant AG (hereafter cited as AAG), June 30, 1887, M689, Roll 189; Sinclair to AAG, July 31, 1887, M689, Roll 190; Sinclair to AAG, August 24, 1887, M689, Roll 190.

22. Goodman, 121.

23. Skinner, 176-177.

24. Goodman, 122, 124-125.

25. Richard Henry Pratt to Endicott, January 21, 1888, M689, Roll 191.

26. Goodman, 130-132.

27. Skinner, 177, 179.

28. Goodman, 129.

29. Skinner, 233, 235–236. For descriptions of Sophie Shepard's experiences as missionary and teacher at Mount Vernon Barracks, see Sophie Shepard, "The Apaches at Mount Vernon," *Lend a Hand* (January 1890): 37–42; Sophie Shepard, "The Apache Captives," *Lend a Hand* (March 1890): 163–166; Sophie Shepard, "The Apaches at Mount Vernon," *Lend a Hand* (May 1890): 333–337.

30. Goodman, 135–137.

31. Skinner, 254–255.

32. Ibid., 255–256.

33. Goodman, 157.

34. Skinner, 260.

35. Goodman, 157.

36. Skinner, 255.

37. Goodman, 157–158.

38. Skinner, 260–261.

39. Goodman, 158, 160.

40. Skinner, 262.

41. Goodman, 160–161.

42. Ibid., 159.

43. Ibid., 161–162.

44. Daniel G. Fowle to Redfield Proctor, September 27, 1889, Governor's Letter Book 74, Daniel G. Fowle Papers, Division of Archives, North Carolina Department of Archives and History, Raleigh, North Carolina. For an extended discussion of Proctor's role in this issue, see Collin G. Calloway, "The Vermont Secretary and the Apache POWs: Redfield Proctor and the Case of the Chiricahuas," *Vermont History* 59 (Summer 1991): 166–179.

45. Goodman, 165.

46. Skinner, 262.

47. Goodman, 165.

48. Porter, 254–255.

49. Stockel, *Survival of the Spirit,* 162. For a discussion of what amounted to both a conflict of personalities and a contest of political clout within the military establishment over whether the Chiricahuas were to be finally located in either North Carolina or Oklahoma, see Porter, 256–262.

50. Skinner, 269–270.

51. Goodman, 175.

52. Skinner, 272–273.

53. Goodman, 177.

54. Skinner, 275, 278–280.

55. Goodman, 177–179.

56. Skinner, 282.

57. Goodman, 179.

58. Apache Prisoners of War Memorandum (hereafter cited as APWM), 4, enclosed with George W. Davis to Joseph H. Outhwaite, December 22, 1894, Records of the House Military Affairs Committee, RHR, RG 233, LJFB, CAD, NARA, Washington, D.C.

59. Goodman, 179.

60. APWM, 4.

61. Goodman, 179.

62. Turcheneske, "Arizonans and the Apache Prisoners of War," 201–202.

63. Goodman, 179.

64. Ibid., 180.

65. W. L. Rynerson, Brewster Cameron, W.H.H. Llewellyn, George Christ, and Miguel Salazar to Henry Laurens Dawes, February 1, 1890, Senate File 51A-F14 (hereafter cited as SF51A-F14), Records of the Senate Committee on Indian Affairs, Records of the U.S. Senate, RG 46, LJFB, CAD, NARA, Washington, D.C.; undated communiqué of A. J. Wormsley et al. to House Indian Affairs Committee Chairman, HF51A-F16.5.

66. F. M. Goodman, William J. Ross, and Samuel Hughes transmitting Society of Arizona Pioneers petition to Senate Indian Affairs Committee chairman, February 8, 1890, SF51A-F14.

67. *Apache Prisoner Removal Hearings.* For additional details relating to this episode, see Turcheneske, "Arizonans and the Apache Prisoners of War," and Goodman, 156–193.

68. Skinner, 283–285, 288–289.

69. Goodman, 184–185.

70. Proctor to Dawes, June 25, 1890, SF51A-F14.

71. Goodman, 185.

72. William Wallace Wotherspoon to Post Adjutant, August 31, 1890, M689, Roll 194.

73. Skinner, 306, 308–309.

74. Goodman, 199.

75. Wotherspoon to Post Adjutant, April 30, 1891, M689, Roll 195.

76. Goodman, 200.

77. Skinner, 320.

78. Goodman, 201–203.

79. Ibid., 207–209.

80. Ibid., 217–219.

CHAPTER 3

1. Skinner, 367–368.

2. APWM, December 18, 1894, passim; Skinner, 379.

3. Skinner, 368.

4. Ibid., 379.

5. APWM, December 18, 1894, 11; Skinner, 380.

6. Ibid.

7. ARSW, 1894, 27.

8. T. P. Cleaves to George W. Davis, May 19, 1894, M689, Roll 197.

9. Davis to Nelson A. Miles, August 15, 1894, M689, Roll 197; *An Act making appropriations for the support of the Army for the fiscal year ending June 30, 1895,* Public Law 169, 1894, 6, in M689, Roll 199.

10. This debate on the army appropriation bill for fiscal 1895 (hereafter cited as AAB) took place in the House of Representatives on July 28, 1894. Davis excerpted this report from the *Congressional Record* of that date. The excerpt is cited from M689, Roll 197; AAB, 9350.

11. AAB, 9355.

12. AAB, 9350.

13. AAB, 9352.

14. AAB, 9355.

15. Ibid.

16. Davis to Miles, August 15, 1894.

17. "Apache Prisoners of War," memorandum prepared by George W. Davis, May 1895, M689, Roll 199.

18. Davis to Miles, August 15, 1894.

19. Miles to George W. Davis, August 23, 1894, M689, Roll 197.

20. Marion P. Maus to Miles, September 1, 1894, M689, Roll 197.

21. Report by Hugh L. Scott of remarks of the Apache prisoners of war made to Captain M. P. Maus concerning their wishes to be removed to some other locality, August 29, 1894, Hugh Lenox Scott Collection (hereafter cited as HLSC), AICD, FAM, Fort Sill, Oklahoma.

22. Maus to Miles, September 1, 1894.

23. Miles to George W. Davis, September 3, 1894, M689, Roll 197. In this wise, Miles's reversal of his 1890 stance on the Chiricahuas' removal helps clarify the reaction subsequently expressed by the Board of Indian Commissioners. "The sudden disposition made by the President and his Cabinet of the Apache prisoners, in removing them from Mount Vernon Barracks to the Fort Sill Military Reservation, was a very great surprise to many, especially as it seems to have been promoted by certain Army officers who protested against it a few years ago" (ARBIC, 1894, 35).

24. Second Endorsement by John M. Schofield, September 7, 1894, of George W. Davis to Daniel S. Lamont, September 6, 1894, M689, Roll 199.

25. Davis to Maus, September 19, 1894, M689, Roll 199.

26. Thomas M. Vincent to the Major General Commanding the Department of the East, September 14, 1894, Document File 2614 (hereafter cited as DF 2614), Letters and Telegrams Received Relating to the Moving of the Apaches to Fort Sill, September 1894, RDMO, RACC, 1821–1920, RG 393, OMB, MAD, NARA, Washington, D.C.

27. Wotherspoon to Richard Henry Pratt, September 18, 1894, Richard Henry Pratt Papers (hereafter cited as RHPP), MD, Beinecke Library, Yale University, New Haven, Connecticut. Wotherspoon was the officer-in-charge for the Chiricahua prisoners during the first several years of their confinement in Alabama.

28. Special Orders No. 204, Department of the East, September 18, 1894, in Folder Designation: Apache Indians (hereafter cited as AI), 1894, Box 46, Hugh Lenox Scott Papers (hereafter cited as HLSP), MD, LC, Washington, D.C.

29. James P. Martin to Commanding Officer, Fort Sill (hereafter cited as COFS), September 20, 1894, Fort Sill History File (hereafter cited as FSHF), AICD, FAM, Fort Sill, Oklahoma.

30. Allyn K. Capron to Post Adjutant, October 2, 1894, M689, Roll 198.

31. Maus to Acting AG, Department of the Missouri (hereafter cited as AAGD-MO), DF 2614.

32. MICI, November 11, 1976. Mrs. Cleghorn, born into captivity four years before the Chiricahuas were released and allotted in Oklahoma, said her mother told this story.

CHAPTER 4

1. Ball, *Indeh*, 160.

2. Charles LeBaron to Hugh L. Scott, October 5, 1894, M689, Roll 198; Fort Sill Post Returns, October 1894, Returns From U.S. Military Posts, 1800–1916, National Archives Microfilm Publication M617, Roll 1175, RAGO, RG 94, OMB, MAD, NARA, Washington, D.C.

3. Ball, *Indeh*, 160.

4. LeBaron to Scott, October 5, 1894.

5. Ball, *Indeh*, 160.

6. Marion P. Maus to George W. Davis, October 30, 1894, M689, Roll 198.

7. Charles C. Ballou to Hugh L. Scott, November 1, 1894, M689, Roll 198.

8. Stockel, *Survival of the Spirit*, 199.

9. Ball, *Indeh*, 160; Ballou to Scott, November 1, 1894.

10. Hugh L. Scott to AAGDMO, November 7, 1894, M689, Roll 198.

11. Hugh L. Scott to AAGDMO, October 11, 1894, M689, Roll 197. This measure appropriated $15,000 "for the purposes of the erection of buildings, purchase of draft animals, stock, necessary farming tools, seeds, household utensils and other articles . . . in addition to the sums herein appropriated" (*An Act making appropriations for the support of the Army for the fiscal year ending June 30, 1895*, Public Law 169, 1894, 6, in M689, Roll 199).

12. Hugh L. Scott to Maus, November 5, 1894, M689, Roll 199.

13. George W. Davis to Nelson A. Miles, October 17, 1894, M689, Roll 198.

14. Scott to AAGDMO, November 7, 1894.

15. Scott to Maus, November 5, 1894.

16. Hugh L. Scott to Miles, November 5, 1894, M689, Roll 199.

17. Miles to George W. Davis, November 5, 1894, M689, Roll 199.

18. Frank D. Baldwin to Miles, November 10, 1894, DF 2614.

19. George D. Ruggles to Quartermaster General, U.S. Army, November 12, 1894, FSHF.

20. Hugh L. Scott to George W. Davis, November 23, 1894, M689, Roll 199.

21. Interestingly enough, Grace Paulding, wife of William Paulding, an officer stationed at Fort Sill, observed that "for some reason the government had taken them out of their accustomed tepees and put them in small poorly ventilated cabins with the result that this small remnant of the once proud Apache nation was slowly dying of tuberculosis" (Grace Paulding Memoirs, January 1895, MHI, Carlisle Barracks, Pennsylvania). With a total viewing area of 768 square inches for each of two windows per dwelling space (two such spaces per housing unit), one could well understand Grace's concern (estimates for one Apache house by Hugh L. Scott [hereafter cited as Estimates], January 1895, Folder Designation: Indian House Specifications [hereafter cited as IHS], 1895, Box 46, HLSP). For details concerning health conditions confronting the Chiricahuas while at Fort Sill, consult Stockel, *Survival of the Spirit*, 192–220, 261–266.

22. Hugh L. Scott to AAGDMO, January 20, 1895, DF 2614.

23. Estimates.

24. Hugh L. Scott to AAGDMO, March 3, 1895, DF 2614.

25. Ballou to Hugh L. Scott, March 2, 1895, DF 2614.

26. Scott to AAGDMO, March 3, 1895.

27. Hugh L. Scott to AG, Department of the Missouri (hereafter cited as AGD-MO), April 3, 1895, DF 2614.

28. Hugh L. Scott to AGDMO, July 3, 1895, DF 2614.

29. Scott to AGDMO, April 3, 1895.

30. Scott to AGDMO, July 3, 1895.

31. Wesley Merritt to AGO, June 18, 1895, M689, Roll 199.

32. First Endorsement by Thomas M. Vincent of Merritt to AGO, June 18, 1895, M689, Roll 199; Ruggles to Commanding General, Department of the Missouri (hereafter cited as CGDMO), June 21, 1895, M689, Roll 199.

33. Hugh L. Scott to AGDMO, August 12, 1895, M689, Roll 199; AGDMO to Hugh L. Scott, August 15, 1895, IHS.

34. Scott to AGDMO, August 12, 1895.

35. AGDMO to Scott, August 15, 1895.

36. Daniel S. Lamont to Secretary of Agriculture, August 26, 1895, M689, Roll 199.

37. Julius S. Morton to SW, August 27, 1895, M689, Roll 199.

38. Albert Dean to Morton, September 9, 1895, M689, Roll 199.

39. Hugh L. Scott to AGDMO, December 3, 1895, M689, Roll 199; Hugh L. Scott to AGDMO, January 2, 1896, M689, Roll 199.

40. Memorandum by George W. Davis on the status of certain Indians at Fort Sill and the general policy to be pursued in their control (hereafter cited as Davis Memorandum), December 23, 1895, M689, Roll 199.

41. Hugh L. Scott to AGDMO, November 25, 1895, M689, Roll 199.

42. Ibid.

43. James D. Glennan to the Surgeon General, U.S. Army, November 1, 1895, James D. Glennan Papers, AICD, FAM.

44. BHI, November 11, 1976.

45. ARSW, 1895, 35.

46. Davis Memorandum.

CHAPTER 5

1. George W. Davis to Hugh L. Scott, January 10, 1896, M689, Roll 200.

2. Charles J. Kappler, ed., *Indian Affairs: Laws and Treaties,* Vol. 2, *Treaties* (Washington: Government Printing Office, 1904), 981.

3. Wilbur S. Nye, *Carbine and Lance: The Story of Old Fort Sill* (Norman: University of Oklahoma Press, 1969), 85.

4. H. R. Clum to C. Delano, September 7, 1871, Report Books, Vol. 21, RBIA, RG 75, NRB, CAD, NARA, Washington, D.C.

5. Fourth Endorsement by President Ulysses S. Grant, October 7, 1871, of John Pope to AGO, August 12, 1871, Original Executive Order File, Records of the Bureau of Land Management, RG 49, NRB, CAD, NARA, Washington, D.C.

6. Francis Paul Prucha, S.J., *The Great Father: The United States Government and the American Indians* (Lincoln: University of Nebraska Press, 1984), 775. For details concerning the actual provisions contained in the June 6, 1900, congressional legislation ratifying the Jerome Agreement, consult Kappler, Vol. 1, *Laws*, 709–713. Also, the Jerome Agreement would become "effective only when ratified by the Congress of the United States" (Kappler, Vol. 1, 711).

7. Kappler, Vol. 1, 709. Thus, as Nye notes, "the Fort Sill Military Reservation . . . was exempted from homesteading, being retained by the War Department" (Nye, 305). The federal government paid the Kiowas and Comanches $2 million for the surplus acreage, which included the land on which Fort Sill was situated (Kappler, Vol. 1, 710). Because of the Jerome Agreement's fraudulent nature, which violated the Medicine Lodge Treaty, Lone Wolf, an important Kiowa personage, attempted to block implementation of the Jerome Agreement by suing Interior Department officials. His suit failed. In its monumental January 5, 1903, decision regarding *Lone Wolf v. Hitchcock*, the U.S. Supreme Court held that Congress possessed plenary powers over Indian affairs. Therefore, Congress could abrogate at will various treaty provisions—in this case, Medicine Lodge Treaty stipulations regarding Indian voting procedures required for any treaty amendments—regardless of whether transactions undertaken to secure treaty changes were fraudulent, and, consequently, treaty violations. The Supreme Court believed that congressional approval of the Jerome Agreement was an example of just such a legal abrogation of treaty conditions originally agreed to (Prucha, 775–776). Finally, according to Hagan, the 1867 Medicine Lodge Treaty placed the Kiowas and Comanches on a reservation of three million acres (William T. Hagan, *United States–Comanche Relations: The Reservation Years* [New Haven, Connecticut: Yale University Press, 1976], 38). Of this acreage, therefore, taking into account the land on which Fort Sill was situated (50,000 acres), as well as that set aside for Kiowa and Comanche allotments (480,000 acres) and for cattle grazing (480,000 acres), more than two million acres of the former Kiowa and Comanche Reservation were deemed surplus and were thus available for homesteading.

8. Daniel S. Lamont to Hoke Smith, January 6, 1896, M689, Roll 200.

9. C. C. Duncan to SI, June 20, 1896, M689, Roll 201.

10. Daniel M. Browning to SI, August 3, 1896, M689, Roll 201.

11. Hoke Smith to SW, August 6, 1896, M689, Roll 201.

12. Hugh L. Scott to George W. Davis, August 17, 1896, AI, 1896, Box 46, HLSP.

13. Kappler, 981.

14. Prucha, 775.

15. Scott to Davis, August 17, 1896.

16. Ibid.

17. Hugh L. Scott to AGDMO, August 1, 1896, AI, 1896, Box 46, HLSP. An interesting anecdote regarding the Chiricahuas' eight hours of daily labor is worthy of mention. Francis E. Leupp, who, in his capacity as agent for the Indian Rights Association, visited Arizona and Fort Sill during the summer of 1897, made the following observations (from notes of a summer tour among the Indians of the Southwest by Francis E. Leupp, 1897 [hereafter cited as FEL 1897], FSHF):

> To travel through Arizona and hear people talk of Geronimo, the Apache archfiend, who, if he sets foot in the Territory, would be hanged for murder without the formality of a trial is impressive. But to pass into Oklahoma and finding the same Geronimo putting in his honest eight hours of daily work as a farmer in the fields, and at intervals donning his uniform as a U.S. Scout and presenting himself with the other scouts for inspection, is still more so.

18. Hugh L. Scott to AGDMO, August 21, 1896, M689, Roll 199; Hugh L. Scott to AGDMO, October 1, 1896, M689, Roll 199.

19. Allyn K. Capron to AGO, December 14, 1896, M689, Roll 199.

20. FEL 1897.

21. Capron to AGO, December 14, 1896.

22. Hugh L. Scott to AGDMO, June 30, 1897, M689, Roll 200.

23. Scott to AGDMO, June 30, 1897.

24. Memorandum for the AG by George W. Davis, December 14, 1896, M689, Roll 200.

25. Hugh L. Scott to Chief of Staff (hereafter cited as COS), November 3, 1911, File Number 53119-09-123 Kiowa (hereafter cited as BIAK), CF, 1907–1939, RBIA, RG 75, NRB, CAD, NARA, Washington, D.C.

26. Scott to AGDMO, June 30, 1897.

27. Scott to COS, November 3, 1911.

28. George D. Ruggles to CGDMO, December 15, 1896, Special File 5782, Kiowa-Apache Prisoners of War, Records of the Kiowa and Comanche Indian Agency (hereafter cited as SF 5782), IAR, OHS, Oklahoma City, Oklahoma.

29. Council proceedings in the matter of enlarging the Fort Sill Military Reservation for the purpose of settling thereon the Apache prisoners of war, February 16 and 17, 1897, Fort Sill Apaches (hereafter cited as FSA), General Correspondence, 1899–1918, RBIC, RBIA, RG 75, NRB, CAD, NARA, Washington, D.C. For an excellent account of the Jerome Agreement—including a thorough discussion

of the reasons for its approval by Congress despite its fraudulent nature—see Hagan, Chapter 9, "Negotiating the Jerome Agreement," 201–215, and Chapter 11, "Ratifying the Jerome Agreement," 250–261.

30. Quanah Parker et al., February 17, 1897, SF 5782. This document is the signed agreement upon which President Grover Cleveland based his executive order procuring the Eastern and Western Additions to Fort Sill.

31. Browning to SI, February 25, 1897, BIAK.

32. David R. Francis to the President of the United States (hereafter cited as PUS), February 26, 1897, BIAK; executive order by Grover Cleveland regarding the Eastern and Western Additions to Fort Sill for the permanent location thereon of the Apache prisoners of war, February 26, 1897, BIAK; General Orders No. 14, AGO, March 15, 1897, FSA.

33. Hugh L. Scott to AGDMO, February 28, 1897, M689, Roll 200.

CHAPTER 6

1. George W. Davis to Hugh L. Scott, August 13, 1897, HLSC.

2. James William Harper, "Hugh Lenox Scott: Soldier Diplomat, 1876–1917" (Ph.D. diss., University of Virginia, 1968), 31–32.

3. FEL 1897.

4. Hugh L. Scott to AGDMO, December 3, 1897, M689, Roll 200.

5. Allyn K. Capron to AGO, February 28, 1898, M689, Roll 200.

6. Ibid.

7. William Paulding Memoirs, MHI, Carlisle Barracks, Pennsylvania.

8. Edwin V. Sumner to AGO, April 19, 1898, M689, Roll 200; Edgar R. Kellogg to Sumner, April 19, 1898, in Sumner to AGO, April 19, 1898.

9. Mattie Atkins Morris interview, Lawton, Oklahoma, February 23, 1938, Indian-Pioneer History Collections (hereafter cited as IPHC), 108:453, IAR, OHS.

10. Grace Paulding Memoirs, MHI, Carlisle Barracks, Pennsylvania.

11. Interview with Reverend Doctor Robert Paul Chaat (hereafter cited as RPCI) conducted by JAT, Medicine Park, Oklahoma, November 10, 1976.

12. BHI, November 11, 1976.

13. RLI, November 11, 1976.

14. RPCI, November 10, 1976.

15. Francis H. Beach to AGO, August 22, 1898, M689, Roll 201; William Paulding Memoirs, MHI, Carlisle Barracks, Pennsylvania.

16. Beach to AGO, August 22, 1898.

17. Richard Henry Harper, "The Missionary Work of the Reformed (Dutch) Church in America," *Chronicles of Oklahoma* 18 (December 1940): 329.

18. RPCI, November 10, 1976.

19. Harper, 329.

20. RPCI, November 10, 1976.

21. Frank Hall Wright to Mrs. Charles Runk, n.d., FSA.

22. RPCI, November 10, 1976.

23. Beach to AGO, August 26, 1898, M689, Roll 201.

24. Wright to Runk.

25. "The Apache Mission at Fort Sill," *The Mission Field* (September 1899): 178. Interestingly enough, Blossom Haozous recalled that a number of the Chiricahua elders initially expressed some resentment toward the missionaries (interview with Blossom Haozous conducted by Pat O'Brien, July 22, 1976, Apache, Oklahoma, Bicentennial Oral History Program Collections, AICD, FAM).

26. Ibid.

27. ARSW, 1899, 40.

28. During January 1900, Hyer requested permission to purchase Hereford bulls to restock the Chiricahuas' herd, which request was granted the next month (Benjamin B. Hyer to AGO, January 18, 1900, M689, Roll 201; John A. Johnston to CGDMO, February 7, 1900, M689, Roll 201).

29. ARSW, 1900, 166.

30. George W. Davis to AGO, April 1, 1900, M689, Roll 201.

CHAPTER 7

1. Farrand B. Sayre to AGDMO, August 26, 1900, Fort Sill Records (hereafter cited as FSR): Letters and Endorsements Sent, 1900–1910, RACC.

2. Sayre to AGO, May 11, 1901, FSR.

3. Seventeenth Endorsement by George B. Davis, September 5, 1901, of Sayre to AGO, May 11, 1901, FSR; Acting Secretary of War (hereafter cited as ASW) to PUS, September 20, 1901, M689, Roll 201.

4. Sayre to AGDMO, June 30, 1902, M689, Roll 202.

5. George L. Scott to AGO, June 29, 1901, FSR.

6. First Endorsement by Henry C. Merriam, July 9, 1901, of Scott to AGO, June 29, 1901, FSR.

7. Seventh Endorsement by George B. Davis, October 8, 1901, of Ethan Allen Hitchcock to SW, July 13, 1901, M689, Roll 202.

8. Elihu Root to SI, October 30, 1901, M689, Roll 202.

9. Root to Speaker of the House of Representatives, January 18, 1902, M689, Roll 202. Sayre also planned in mid-1901 to raise moneys for the Chiricahuas' benefit from a stone quarry concession that he hoped to establish at Fort Sill. These plans came to naught for much the same reasons as the grazing lease proposals. At this time, Davis, for some unknown reason, had not yet learned that Fort Sill now belonged to the United States in fee simple. Thus Davis noted that "it is to be observed that . . . Fort Sill . . . is not strictly a military reservation, but is an Indian reservation, and that the military reservation is superimposed thereon. In fact, it has been added to and enlarged to provide for the settlement of the Apache prisoners of war thereon" (Fourth Endorsement by George B. Davis, August 29, 1901, of Farrand B. Sayre to AGDMO, August 14, 1901, M689, Roll 202). It was at this point (August 1901) that Davis finally learned of Fort Sill's new status. But of singular importance here is that, as explained by Acting Commissioner of Indian Affairs A. C. Tonner, who consistently maintained the Bureau of Indian Affairs' position on this matter, "the object of the extension, as understood by this office at the time, was for the purpose of permanently settling the Apache prisoners of war thereon" (A. C. Tonner to SI, September 12, 1901, M689, Roll 202).

10. House of Representatives, *Lease of Lands on Fort Sill Military Reservation*, 57th Cong., 1st sess., 1902, HD 296, 1–2.

11. Sayre to Hugh L. Scott, September 12, 1902, Folder Designation: Indian Affairs (hereafter cited as IA), January 1902 through December 1905, Box 46, HLSP.

12. Sayre to AGO, November 7, 1901, M689, Roll 202.

13. First Endorsement by George L. Scott, November 8, 1901, of Sayre to AGO, November 7, 1901, M689, Roll 202.

14. Second Endorsement by John C. Bates, November 11, 1901, of Sayre to AGO, November 7, 1901, M689, Roll 202.

15. Fifth Endorsement by Elihu Root, November 25, 1901, of Sayre to AGO, November 7, 1901, M689, Roll 202.

16. William A. Jones to SI, December 6, 1901, M689, Roll 202.

17. Jones to SI, January 4, 1902, M689, Roll 202.

CHAPTER 8

1. Farrand B. Sayre to AGO, July 2, 1902, File Number 445841, AG's Office Document File 1890–1917 (hereafter cited as AGDF), RAGO, RG 94, OMB, MAD, NARA, Washington, D.C.

2. William Stanton to AGDMO, July 9, 1902, FSR. At the beginning of 1904, the War Department attributed to Sayre the recommendation of Stanton that the army's interests required that the Chiricahuas be turned over to Interior and removed elsewhere. At that time, the War Department incorrectly dated the letter written by Stanton as July 9, 1903. There is no such letter by Stanton. Nor does

correspondence written by Sayre dated July 9, 1902—or, for that matter, July 9, 1903—exist in the War Department document files.

3. Fifth Endorsement by William C. Langer, August 15, 1902, of Sayre to AGO, July 2, 1902, AGDF.

4. *Washington Post,* August 16, 1902.

5. Hugh L. Scott to AGO, August 30, 1902, AGDF.

6. Second Endorsement by Nelson A. Miles, August 30, 1902, of Scott to AGO, August 30, 1902, AGDF.

7. Special Orders No. 205, Headquarters, Department of the Missouri, November 6, 1902, AGDF.

8. Proceedings of a Board of Officers convened at Fort Sill, O.T., pursuant to Special Orders No. 205, November 18 and 19, 1902, AGDF.

9. Ninth Endorsement by George B. Davis, February 2, 1903, of Sayre to AGO, July 2, 1902, AGDF.

10. Eleventh Endorsement by William C. Langer, March 31, 1903, of Sayre to AGO, July 2, 1902, AGDF.

11. Elihu Root to SI, April 22, 1903, AGDF.

12. Edward J. McClernand to COFS, January 16, 1903, FSHF.

13. Charles Morton to AGDMO, January 12, 1903, FSR.

14. George Bird Grinnell to SW, November 12, 1903, AGDF.

15. Robert Shaw Oliver to Grinnell, November 19, 1903, AGDF.

16. Memorandum report by Enoch H. Crowder (hereafter cited as Crowder Memorandum), December 9, 1903, AGDF.

17. William A. Jones to SI, February 6, 1904, BIAK.

18. Sayre to AGO, February 17, 1904, AGDF.

19. Fourth Endorsement by Samuel S. Sumner, February 24, 1904, of Hitchcock to SW, February 9, 1904, AGDF.

20. William Wallace Wotherspoon to Richard Henry Pratt, March 3, 1904, RHPP.

21. Pratt to Wotherspoon, March 24, 1904, RHPP.

22. Pratt to William Howard Taft, March 23, 1904, RHPP.

23. Oliver to SI, April 4, 1904, AGDF.

24. Jones to SI, April 14, 1904, AGDF.

25. Henry L. Ripley to AGDMO, August 4, 1904, FSR.

26. Walter L. Finley to Ripley, August 21, 1904, FSHF.

27. Henry P. McCain to Commanding General, Department of Texas, August 26, 1904, FSR.

CHAPTER 9

1. Crowder Memorandum, December 9, 1903, AGDF.

2. Walter L. Finley to COFS, August 29, 1904, FSR.

3. George A. Purington to Military Secretary, Department of Texas (hereafter cited as MSDT), May 22, 1905, AGDF.

4. Jesse M. Lee to Military Secretary's Office (hereafter cited as MSO), June 15, 1905, AGDF.

5. Indeed, as much was indicated in a survey taken at this time by Purington, the results of which are detailed in an undated document titled "Apache Indians who want to stay at Fort Sill, O.T., if given farms and grass for their cattle; want to feel that the land is their very own." This survey is contained in the AGDF records.

6. Purington to MSDT, May 22, 1905.

7. Henry L. Ripley to MSDT, May 23, 1905, FSR.

8. Donald J. Berthong, *The Cheyenne and Arapaho Ordeal: Reservation and Agency Life in the Indian Territory, 1875–1907* (Norman: University of Oklahoma Press, 1976), 27–30, 115–116, 120–123, 125–126, 131–133, 142, 201.

9. Lee to MSO, June 15, 1905, AGDF.

10. Thrapp, *General George Crook and the Sierra Madre Adventure,* 33, 84, 98–101, 128, 145, 163, 169; Robert M. Utley, *Frontier Regulars: The United States Army and the Indian, 1866–1891* (New York: Macmillan, 1973), 370, 376–377, 379.

11. Second Endorsement by Adna R. Chaffee, June 24, 1905, of Lee to MSO, June 15, 1905, AGDF.

12. Walter C. Roe to Charles R. Pool, May 9, 1905, Oklahoma Missions Correspondence File, 1904–1906, Box 624, Papers of the Board of Domestic Missions, Gardner Sage Library, New Brunswick Theological Seminary, New Brunswick, New Jersey.

13. Charles W. Taylor to MSO, April 21, 1906, FSR.

14. *Daily News Republican* (Lawton, Oklahoma), October 30, 1908.

15. General Staff Memorandum Relative to the Proposed Removal of the Apache Indians From Fort Sill, August 10, 1907, 31–32, BIAK.

16. Apache Indians: Chatto, Toclanny, Betzinez, Wratten interview with Secretary of War Taft, n.d., AGDF.

17. List of Apache prisoners of war desiring old homes in Arizona and New Mexico, n.d., AGDF.

18. William Howard Taft to MSO, November 23, 1906, AGDF.

19. Purington to MSO, January 7, 1907, AGDF.

20. First Endorsement by Charles W. Taylor, January 10, 1907, of Purington to MSO, January 7, 1907, AGDF.

21. Purington to MSO, January 10, 1907, AGDF.

22. Taft to COS, February 15, 1907, AGDF.

23. Ernest Stecker to Hugh L. Scott, June 28, 1907, IA, January through December 1907, Box 46, HLSP.

24. Memorandum for the Secretary of War on the disposition of the Apache prisoners of war, dictated by James Franklin Bell to William H. Wright, July 9, 1907, AGDF.

25. William P. Duvall to ASW, July 17, 1907, AGDF.

26. Fred C. Ainsworth to William Loeb, Jr., July 24, 1907, AGDF.

27. William Loeb, Jr., to Fred C. Ainsworth, July 25, 1907, BIAK.

28. First Endorsement by Fred C. Ainsworth, July 27, 1907, of Loeb to Ainsworth, July 25, 1927, BIAK.

29. "At the Apache Mission," *The Mission Field* (February 1908): 382.

30. "Among the Apaches," *The Mission Field* (May 1908): 28.

31. Vincent Natalish to Charles Curtis, March 7, 1908, File Number 5-1, Kiowa-Prisoners-Apaches (hereafter cited as KPA), CF 1907–1936, RSI, RG 48, NRB, CAD, NARA, Washington, D.C.

32. Vincent Natalish to Francis E. Leupp, March 7, 1908, BIAK.

33. Natalish to Curtis, March 7, 1908.

34. Jesse E. Wilson to SW, April 27, 1908, AGDF.

35. Natalish to Theodore Roosevelt, January 7, 1909, IA, January through December 1909, Box 46, HLSP.

CHAPTER 10

1. *Lawton Constitution Democrat,* February 18, 1909.

2. Henry M. Andrews to AGO, February 17, 1909, AGDF.

3. *Daily News Republican,* February 18, 1909.

4. *Lawton Constitution Democrat,* February 18, 1909.

5. *Lawton Constitution,* April 10, 1913.

6. *Tucson Citizen,* February 17, 1909.

7. Ibid., February 18, 1909.

8. Editorial, *Arizona Daily Star,* February 19, 1909.

9. *Tombstone Epitaph,* February 28, 1909.

10. Editorial, *Bisbee Daily Review,* February 20, 1909.

11. *Otero County Advertiser,* February 20, 1909.

12. Reports of the Superintendent in Charge of the Mescalero Indian Agency by James A. Carroll, July 27, 1909, Letters to the Commissioner of Indian Affairs (hereafter cited as LCIA), June 1909 through July 1910, Box 33, Records of the Mescalero Indian Agency (hereafter cited as RMIA), RBIA, RG 75, NARA, Denver National Archives Branch, Denver, Colorado.

13. James A. Carroll to James McLaughlin, June 29, 1909, BIAK.

14. Asa Daklugie to Carroll, May 3, 1909, BIAK; Daklugie to Carroll, May 5, 1909, BIAK.

15. Statement of Mescalero Agency Superintendent James A. Carroll in Minutes of Conference held at the Mescalero Agency, New Mexico, June 26, 1909, by James McLaughlin, United States Indian Inspector, with the Mescalero Apaches with reference to Removal of the Fort Sill Apaches to the Mescalero Reservation (hereafter cited as McLaughlin Conference), BIAK.

16. Carroll to McLaughlin, June 29, 1909.

17. McLaughlin Conference, June 26, 1909.

18. McLaughlin to SI, June 30, 1909, BIAK.

19. Frank Pierce to Robert G. Valentine, July 6, 1909, BIAK.

20. Carroll to Commissioner of Indian Affairs (hereafter cited as CIA), July 28, 1909, LCIA, Box 33, RMIA.

21. Samuel M. Brosius to Indian Rights Association (hereafter cited as IRA), July 26, 1909, BIAK.

22. Herbert Welsh to Valentine, August 4, 1909, BIAK.

23. Valentine to Welsh, August 6, 1909, BIAK.

24. Jesse E. Wilson to SI, August 9, 1909, AGDF.

25. Second Endorsement by Henry L. Ripley, August 16, 1909, of Wilson to SI, August 9, 1909, AGDF.

26. Minutes of a conference held at Fort Sill, Oklahoma, August 22, 1909, by 1st Lieut. Geo. A. Purington, 8th Cav., with the Geronimo Apaches (Apache Indian Prisoners of War) with reference to their removal to the Mescalero Indian Reservation, New Mexico, BIAK.

27. A report by George A. Purington relative to the present condition of the Apache Indians, their progress, resources, and the desire of the majority of the band to join their relatives in New Mexico, August 25, 1909, BIAK.

CHAPTER 11

1. *Lawton Constitution Democrat,* November 25, 1909.

2. Ibid., February 18, 1909.

3. Memorandum by James Franklin Bell to SW: Summary of the case of the Apache prisoners of war and the question of the removal of a part or the whole of these people from their present location on the reservation at Fort Sill, Oklahoma, to New Mexico or Arizona, November 18, 1909, AGDF.

4. Ibid.

5. Memorandum by Robert Shaw Oliver to PUS, December 23, 1909, AGDF.

6. Oliver to SI, December 23, 1909, BIAK.

7. Richard A. Ballinger to SW, December 31, 1909, BIAK.

8. Robert G. Valentine to SI, January 12, 1910, BIAK.

9. Memorandum by Samuel M. Brosius: Fort Sill Apache Prisoners, January 26, 1910, Fort Sill Apache File (hereafter cited as FSAF), General Correspondence, 1899–1918, RBIC.

10. Walter C. Roe to Jacob M. Dickinson, December 7, 1910, AGDF.

11. ARCIA, 1910, 54.

12. George L. Scott to Hugh L. Scott, December 14, 1910, IA, February through December 1910, Box 47, HLSP.

13. Memorandum by George B. Davis: The Apache Prisoners of War at Fort Sill, December 13, 1910, AGDF.

14. Nye, 322–323.

15. Edwin St. John Greble to Dan T. Moore, January 18, 1911, Moore-Greble Correspondence (hereafter cited as MGC), Morris Swett Technical Library, Snow Hall, U.S. Army Field Artillery School, Fort Sill, Oklahoma.

16. Greble to Moore, February 23, 1911, MGC.

17. Moore to Greble, March 16, 1911, MGC.

18. Moore to Greble, March 17, 1911, MGC.

19. Greble to Moore, March 23, 1911, MGC.

20. Arthur Murray to Roe, July 21, 1911, AGDF.

21. Memorandum by Arthur Murray for the SW: The Apache Prisoners of War and the Fort Sill Military Reservation (hereafter cited as Murray SW Memorandum), July 20, 1911, IA, January through December 1911, Box 47, HLSP.

CHAPTER 12

1. Murray SW Memorandum.

2. Memorandum by Arthur Murray for the AGO, July 20, 1911, AGDF.

3. Henry P. McCain to Hugh L. Scott, July 24, 1911, IA, January through December 1911, Box 47, HLSP.

4. Robert G. Valentine to Hugh L. Scott, August 8, 1911, Folder Designation: Apache Reports (hereafter cited as AR), Box 76, HLSP.

5. Ernest Stecker to CIA, September 18, 1911, BIAK.

6. Proceedings of Conference with the Apache Prisoners of War on the Fort Sill Reservation, September 21, 1911, AGDF.

7. Continuation of the Conference with the Apache Indians on the Fort Sill Reservation, September 21, 1911, AGDF.

8. McCain to Hugh L. Scott, September 28, 1911, IA, January through December 1911, Box 47, HLSP.

9. James A. Carroll to CIA, September 30, 1911, LCIA, July 1911 through September 1912, Box 34, RMIA.

10. Jason Betzinez, *I Fought With Geronimo* (New York: Bonanza Books, 1959), 193.

11. Notes of a council held by Col. Hugh L. Scott with the headmen of the Mescalero tribe of Apache Indians, relative to the proposed removal of the Apache Prisoners of War from Fort Sill, Oklahoma, to the Mescalero Apache Reservation, New Mexico, October 8, 1911, BIAK.

12. Hugh L. Scott to Albert K. Smiley, October 11, 1911, Albert K. Smiley Papers (hereafter cited as AKSP), Manuscripts Division, Haverford College Library, Haverford College, Haverford, Pennsylvania.

13. Betzinez, 193.

14. Record of proceedings of conference with Apache Indian Prisoners of War, Fort Sill Military Reservation, after the return of the delegation sent to New Mexico and Arizona to look over the ground, October 16, 1911, AGDF.

15. George W. Goode to Hugh L. Scott, October 17, 1911, AR, Box 76, HLSP.

16. Walter C. Roe to Hugh L. Scott, October 6, 1911, AGDF.

17. Hugh L. Scott to COS, November 3, 1911, AR, Box 76, HLSP.

18. Memorandum for the COS, November 6, 1911, AGDF.

19. Henry L. Stimson to SI, November 8, 1911, KPA.

20. Assistant Secretary of the Interior (hereafter cited as ASI) to SW, December 15, 1911, KPA.

21. ARCIA, 1911, 41.

22. ARBIC, 1911, 7–8.

23. ARBIC, 1912, 11–12.

CHAPTER 13

1. Senate, S. 6152, 61st Cong., 2d sess., *Congressional Record* (hereafter cited as Senate, S. 6152), February 4, 1910, 45, 1479.

2. Senate, *A Bill Providing for the Allotment of Land to the Apache and Other Indians Under the Charge of the War Department, Fort Sill Military Reservation, Oklahoma,* 61st Cong., 2d sess., 1910, S. 6152, 1–2.

3. See also Senate, *Apache Prisoners of War,* 61st Cong., 2d sess., 1910, SD 366.

4. Ibid.

5. Richard A. Ballinger to Moses E. Clapp, February 18, 1910, BIAK.

6. Senate, S. 6152, March 15, 1910, 3186.

7. Robert L. Owen to Jacob M. Dickinson, March 11, 1910, AGDF.

8. James Franklin Bell to Owen, March 14, 1910, AGDF.

9. Walter L. Fisher to Walter C. Roe, June 29, 1911, KPA.

10. House, H.R. 25297, 61st Cong., 2d sess., *Congressional Record* (May 2, 1910), 45, 5695.

11. House, *A Bill providing for the allotment of land to the Apache Indians now under charge of the War Department at Fort Sill, Oklahoma, as prisoners of war,* 61st Cong., 2d sess., 1910, H.R. 25297, 1–2.

12. House, H.R. 26048, 61st Cong., 2d sess., *Congressional Record* (May 18, 1910), 45, 6494.

13. Ballinger to Scott Ferris, n.d., BIAK. Ballinger was responding to Ferris's letter of December 21, 1910.

14. ARBIC, 1911, 7–8.

15. Ferris to SW, January 18, 1911, AGDF.

16. Dickinson to Ferris, January 23, 1911, RHCIA.

17. Dickinson to SI, January 23, 1911, FSAF.

18. As early as March 1910, Reverend W. C. Wauchope of the Reformed Church in America, in referring to the Owen bill, reported that the "Apaches who are now prisoners of war are very much interested over the passage of a bill in Congress providing for their being allotted . . . at Fort Sill" (*Colony Courier* [Colony, Oklahoma], March 3, 1910).

19. Asa Daklugie to Ferris, February 14, 1911, RHCIA.

20. Vincent Natalish to Owen, January 4, 1912, BIAK.

21. Ibid. Furthermore, according to the information he received from the Chiricahua delegation that visited Mescalero, Natalish said they observed it to be "worthless for farming and grazing owing to the rugged mountains," and, therefore, "it was decided that . . . Mescalero . . . was no home for them" (Natalish to Curtis, December 6, 1911, BIAK).

22. Natalish to Owen, January 4, 1912. In addition, arguing against any removal to the West, Natalish explained to Senator Curtis in his letter of December 6, 1911, that the "San Carlos Apaches are unfriendly" toward the Chiricahuas. He

also "learned that the Mescalero Apaches are not as friendly as they pretend. Last year a member of the Fort Sill Apaches who was at Mescalero on an extended visit was killed by the Mescaleros. Another Fort Sill Apache . . . who was released and went to Mescalero with his family to live is not enrolled at the reservation and has not the same privileges as the Mescaleros although" prior to going there, they told him they wanted the Chiricahuas "to come and live with them and be one of them."

23. Natalish to Owen, January 4, 1912. For example: "I hope you will be successful in getting the Indians removed for the best interests of Lawton and Fort Sill. . . . We all want to see them go" (C. Tanghi to Ferris, February 12, 1912, RHCIA).

24. Natalish to Owen, January 4, 1912. According to Natalish, "about three and a half years ago, Scott was sent by President Roosevelt to tell the Apache prisoners that Fort Sill is to be their permanent home about the same time I was informed by the War Dept. that they did not want us to remain there." Hugh L. Scott now told "them that the War Department and the people of Lawton do not want" the Chiricahuas at Fort Sill. "I was astounded to learn the attitude . . . Scott had taken in our case and could not believe it was possible for a man of high standing" to "take advantage of . . . ignorant people. . . . If possible, Scott's Apache report should be laid aside and thoroughly looked into before" being put into effect (Natalish to Curtis, December 6, 1911).

25. Natalish to Owen, January 4, 1912.

26. See Hermann Hagedorn, *Leonard Wood: A Biography* (New York: Krause Reprint, 1969), and Jack C. Lane, ed., *Chasing Geronimo: The Journal of Leonard Wood, May–September 1886* (Albuquerque: University of New Mexico Press, 1970).

27. Memorandum by Hugh L. Scott for COS, November 6, 1911, AGDF.

28. Henry L. Stimson to SI, November 8, 1911, RHCIA.

29. Leonard Wood to Ferris, December 12, 1911, RHCIA.

30. Ibid.

31. Wood to Ferris, December 14, 1911, RHCIA.

32. House, H.R. 16651, 62d Cong., 2d sess., *Congressional Record* (hereafter cited as House, H.R. 16651), January 3, 1912, 48, 633.

33. House, *A Bill Authorizing the Secretary of War to Grant Freedom to Certain of the Apache Prisoners of War Now Being Held at Fort Sill, Oklahoma, and Giving Them Equal Status With Other Restricted Indians,* 62d Cong., 2d sess., 1912, H.R. 16651 (hereafter cited as HB 16651), 1–2.

34. Memorandum: Fort Sill Apaches (hereafter cited as MFSA), January 19, 1912, FSAF.

35. Leonard Wood Diary, January 19, 1912, Leonard Wood Papers, MD, LC.

36. MFSA.

37. Wood to Ferris, January 23, 1912, RHCIA.

38. Memorandum of work with Walter C. Roe . . . with reference to the Fort Sill Apaches, January 20, 1912, FSAF.

39. Valentine to Samuel Adams, February 23, 1912, KPA.

40. Guion Miller: A Protest Against HB 16651, February 21, 1912, BIAK.

41. Memorandum of Conference at Indian Office regarding Ft. Sill Apaches and HB 16651, February 23, 1912, FSAF.

42. Ferris to SI, April 16, 1912, BIAK.

43. Daklugie to Ferris, April 9, 1912, RHCIA.

44. Ferris to SI, April 16, 1912.

45. Adams to John H. Stephens, May 2, 1912, BIAK.

46. Memorandum of telephone call from . . . Scott Ferris, May 6, 1912, FSAF.

47. House, H.R. 16651, May 16, 1912, 6608; HB 16651.

48. House, *Relief of Apache Indians held as Prisoners of War at Fort Sill, Okla.,* 62d Cong., 2d sess., 1912, HR 724, 4.

49. Senate, S. 6776, 62d Cong., 2d sess., *Congressional Record* (June 15, 1912), 48, 8234.

50. Memorandum of visit to Washington of Commissioner Vaux (hereafter cited as Vaux Memorandum), June 11 and 12, 1912, FSAF.

51. Memorandum of call on Scott Ferris (hereafter cited as Ferris Memorandum), May 23, 1912, FSAF; Vaux Memorandum; Memorandum of telephone conversation with . . . Scott Ferris (hereafter cited as Ferris Telephone Memorandum), June 17, 1912, FSAF.

52. Ferris Telephone Memorandum.

53. Ferris Memorandum.

54. Ferris Telephone Memorandum.

55. House, H.R. 16651, August 19, 1912, 11336.

56. Ibid., 11337.

57. House, S. 6776, 62d Cong., 2d sess., *Congressional Record* (August 19, 1912), 48, 11340.

CHAPTER 14

1. Senate, H.R. 20728, 62d Cong., 2d sess., *Congressional Record* (hereafter cited as Senate, H.R. 20728), July 3, 1912, 48, 8604.

2. Senate, *Indian Conference Report,* 62d Cong., 2d sess., 1912, SD 919, 11–12.

3. Senate, H.R. 20728, August 17, 1912, 11151.

4. Ibid., August 19, 1912, 11236.

5. Ibid., 11237.

6. House, H.R. 20728, 62d Cong., 2d sess, *Congressional Record* (hereafter cited as House, H.R. 20728), August 20, 1912, 48, 11422.

7. Moses E. Clapp to Henry L. Stimson, August 21, 1912, AGDF.

8. Senate, H.R. 20728, August 22, 1912, 11562.

9. Senate, *Indian Conference Report*, 62d Cong., 2d sess., 1912, SD 938 (hereafter cited as SD 938), 11.

10. House, H.R. 20728, August 24, 1912, 11853.

11. SD 938, 11.

12. J. W. Prude to Hugh L. Scott, September 1, 1912, AGDF.

13. Leonard Wood to Walter Fisher, September 6, 1912, AGDF.

14. Robert Shaw Oliver to Prude, September 18, 1912, AGDF.

15. Oliver to Fisher, September 18, 1912, AGDF.

16. Albert Bacon Fall to SW and SI, December 20, 1912, BIAK.

17. Prude to Fisher, December 24, 1912, KPA. Fall forwarded these petitions, all identical in form, to Fisher from Roswell and Hagerman, New Mexico, and Colorado City, Texas, and promised that more would be forthcoming (Fall to Fisher, December 27 and 31, 1912, KPA).

18. Fisher to SW, December 31, 1912, BIAK.

19. H. C. Phillips to Hugh L. Scott, December 19, 1912, FSAF. See also House, *Relief of Apache Indians Confined at Fort Sill Military Reservation, Okla.*, 62d Cong., 3d sess., 1913, HD 1249, 1–2; Fisher to SW, December 31, 1912.

20. Frederic H. Abbott to Fisher, December 26, 1912, BIAK.

21. Memorandum for Secretary [of the Interior] by F. H. Abbott, December 30, 1912, KPA. The request for a reappropriation of the original $200,000 allocation is contained in Fisher to SW, December 31, 1912.

22. Fisher to the Senate of the United States, December 31, 1912, BIAK.

23. House, H.R. 26874, 62d Cong., 3d sess., *Congressional Record* (January 9, 1913), 44, 1290.

24. Senate, *Amendment to be proposed by Mr. Catron to the bill (H.R. 26874) making appropriations for the current and contingent expenses of the Bureau of Indian Affairs*, 62d Cong., 3d sess., 1913, H.R. 26874, 1–2.

25. Senate, H.R. 26874, 62d Cong., 3d sess., *Congressional Record* (January 25, 1913), 44, 3908.

26. Ibid., 3908–3909.

27. Ibid., 3909.

28. Ibid., 3910.

29. Ibid., March 3, 1913, 4668–4669.

30. Ibid., March 4, 1913, 4832. Actually, there were those in New Mexico who looked forward to the Chiricahuas' arrival. "No doubt the Fort Sill Indians are coming, as there are supplies by the carload here for them. That's more money for Tularosa and Cloudcroft" (*Weekly Cloudcrofter* [Cloudcroft, New Mexico], February 28, 1913).

31. Ibid., 4832.

32. Hugh L. Scott to Phillips, March 7, 1913, FSAF.

33. Hugh L. Scott to Phillips, February 12, 1913, FSAF. Scott was momentarily fearful that the Chiricahuas might not be moved after all. Upon receiving Ferris's assurances, Scott regained his confidence and later observed that "it now seems as if the whole matter will be settled to the satisfaction of everybody except a few grass leasers in New Mexico."

34. Phillips to Hugh L. Scott, March 15, 1913, FSAF.

35. Ibid.

36. Roswell Commercial Club to Fall, March 22, 1913, HM FA Box 53 (5), Albert Bacon Fall Collection, Manuscripts Division, Henry E. Huntington Library and Art Gallery, San Marino, California. This item is used with permission of the Huntington Library. According to Clarence R. Jefferis, who succeeded James A. Carroll as Mescalero Indian Agent, the proposed removal of the Chiricahuas to this reservation "was, and still is, very warmly opposed by certain interests in this section, the most active of which is the Commercial Club of Roswell. . . . As the Office is aware, there are a number of grazing permits in effect on this reservation." Indeed, the "three permittees having the largest holdings are all from the Roswell section; and, when it is remembered that the settlement of the Fort Sill Indians at Mescalero will necessitate the removal of the permittees' stock from the reservation, the opposition of the Roswell Commercial Club may be readily understood." Of course, "the reason given by the Club for opposing the settlement of the Indians here is that the people of the Southwest desire this reservation to be a National Park." (Clarence R. Jefferis to CIA, February 14, 1913, LCIA, October 1912 through June 1913, Box 34, RMIA.) See also Goode to Phillips, September 21, 1913, AKSP; Phillips to Goode, September 27, 1913, AKSP.

37. Phillips to Hugh L. Scott, March 15, 1913, FSAF. Phillips confirmed Scott's "report that Senator Fall talked the Indian Appropriation Bill to death, doubtless because of the Fort Sill item, although he pretended that he would object to the other items as well."

38. Senate, H.R. 1917, 63d Cong., 1st sess., *Congressional Record* (June 17, 1913), 50, 2042.

39. House, H.R. 1917, 63d Cong., 1st sess., *Congressional Record* (June 30, 1913), 50, 2385.

40. Cato Sells to A. A. Jones, September 30, 1913, KPA.

41. A. A. Jones to SW, December 26, 1913, KPA.

42. House, H.R. 12579, 63d Cong., 2d sess., *Congressional Record* (hereafter cited as House, H.R. 12579), February 19, 1914, 51, 3670.

43. Ibid., February 20, 1914, 3726.

44. Senate, H.R. 12579, 63d Cong., 2d sess., *Congressional Record* (February 24, 1914), 51, 3817.

45. Ibid, May 15, 1914, 8627.

46. Owen to Hugh L. Scott, May 30, 1914, IA, January through December 1914, Box 47, HLSP.

47. Phillips to Hugh L. Scott, July 23, 1914, AKSP.

48. House, H.R. 12579, August 1, 1914, 12879.

49. Phillips to Scott, July 23, 1914.

CHAPTER 15

1. First Assistant Secretary of the Interior to SW, September 5, 1912, KPA.

2. Samuel Adams to SW, September 6, 1912, AGDF.

3. Robert Shaw Oliver to SI, September 18, 1912, AGDF.

4. Adams to SW, September 26, 1912, KPA.

5. Hugh L. Scott and Stecker to AGO, October 5, 1912, AGDF.

6. Hendrina Hospers to Mary Roe, October 4, 1912, FSAF.

7. Memorandum submitted to Board of Indian Commissioners by . . . Walter C. Roe . . . with letter of October 8, 1912, n.d., FSAF; Walter C. Roe to Abbott, October 9, 1912, FSAF.

8. Frederic H. Abbott to Roe, October 12, 1912, FSAF.

9. Hospers to Mary Roe, October 10, 1912, FSAF.

10. Walter C. Roe to George Vaux, October 16, 1912, FSAF.

11. Memorandum of consultation with CIA regarding Fort Sill Apaches, October 16, 1912, FSAF.

12. Memorandum of Conference Concerning the Fort Sill Apaches, October 24, 1912, FSAF. Participants noted that during the course of the annual Lake Mohonk Conference recently concluded, Mary Roe and Jason Betzinez "very feelingly pointed out the characteristics of the Indians and the very injurious effect anything except a free choice would have on them." Furthermore, George Vaux, one of the conferees at Lake Mohonk, concluded, "I think if all good friends of the Indians would interest themselves in these people, and in trying to do what they can toward influencing the method to be adopted in handling the situation, it will be a very great advantage." There were those Chiricahuas who "would like to be allotted in the neighborhood of Fort Sill. . . . I hope . . .

that everyone will take an interest in this band of people, who, strange to say, have been kept prisoners by us [thus far] for a period of twenty-five years. Owing to this fact there" were "only a mere half dozen left who had any part in the Geronimo raid. The rest are women and children, or men who were born, bred, and have grown up at Fort Sill. . . . It is another instance of our Anglo-Saxon cruelty that we should sit still and allow it to go that way." (*Report of the Thirtieth Annual Lake Mohonk Conference of Friends of the Indian and Other Dependent Peoples, October 23, 24, and 25, 1912* [Lake Mohonk, New York: Lake Mohonk Conference of Friends of the Indian and Other Dependent Peoples, 1912], 72–73).

13. H. C. Phillips to SW, October 29, 1912, FSAF.

14. Edwin St. John Greble to Dan T. Moore, November 19, 1912, MGC.

15. Memorandum of Conferences at Indian Office, Regarding Fort Sill Apaches (hereafter cited as FSAC), November 21, 1912, FSAF.

16. Abbott to Charles L. Ellis, November 23, 1912, BIAK.

17. Walter L. Fisher to SW, November 25, 1912, BIAK.

18. FSAC.

19. Proceedings of Meeting of Apache Prisoners of War (hereafter cited as POWP), December 1, 1912, AGDF.

20. Committee Sent to Apache Prisoners of War to SW and SI, December 2, 1912, BIAK.

21. POWP.

22. George W. Goode to AGO, March 7, 1913, AGDF.

23. Franklin K. Lane to SW, March 31, 1913, AGDF.

24. Goode to AGO, April 8, 1913, BIAK; Goode to AGO, April 4, 1913, AGDF. In his April 4 letter, Goode noted that he turned over 187 Chiricahuas to Interior. On April 8, Goode explained that 163 were "actually with me" (Goode to AGO, April 8, 1913). See also ARCIA, 1913, 34, and ARCIA, 1914, 56–57.

25. MICI, November 12, 1976.

26. RLI, November 12, 1976.

27. Goode to AGO, April 4, 1913.

28. *Lawton Constitution,* April 10, 1913.

29. Ibid.

30. Hugh L. Scott to Phillips, June 24, 1913, AKSP.

31. *Weekly Cloudcrofter,* May 22, 1913.

32. Hugh L. Scott to AGO, July 16, 1913, AGDF.

33. Henry Breckinridge to SI, July 28, 1913, AGDF.

34. *Eighty-First Annual Report of the Board of Domestic Missions to the General Synod of the Reformed Church in America* (New York: Reformed Church in America, 1913), 13.

35. ARBIC, 1913, 4, 10–11. For dire details of the conditions actually experienced by the Chiricahuas during their first decade at Mescalero, consult John Anthony Turcheneske, Jr., "Disaster at White Tail: The Fort Sill Apaches' First Ten Years at Mescalero, 1913–1923," *New Mexico Historical Review* 13 (April 1978): 109–132.

CHAPTER 16

1. Walter L. Fisher to SW, January 3, 1913, AGDF.

2. George W. Goode to AGO, June 1, 1913, AGDF.

3. Goode et al.: Apache Prisoner of War Cattle Sale Contract, April 22, 1913, AGDF.

4. Goode to AGO, April 23, 1913, File 41294-1913-225 Mescalero (hereafter cited as BIAM), CF, 1907–1939, RBIA, RG 75, NRB, CAD, NARA, Washington, D.C.

5. Lindley M. Garrison to SW, April 30, 1913, BIAM.

6. Frederic H. Abbott to Edwin St. John Greble, May 5, 1913, BIAM.

7. Goode to Greble, May 21, 1913, AGDF.

8. Goode to Greble, June 19, 1913, AGDF.

9. Clarence R. Jefferis to CIA, May 31, 1913, LCIA, October 1912 through June 1913, Box 34, RMIA; Abbott to Education Division, Bureau of Indian Affairs, June 10, 1913, BIAM.

10. Ernest Stecker and Charles L. Ellis to CIA, January 2, 1913, FSAF.

11. Stecker and Ellis to CIA, May 5, 1913, SF 5782.

12. Matter of allotting Apache prisoners of war . . . upon land to be purchased from . . . Indians of the Kiowa Agency, circa October 1913, SF 5782.

13. Memorandum by Henry Roe Cloud: The Case of the Fort Sill Apaches Again, circa October 1913, FSAF. See also Arthur C. Parker to SW and SI, October 18, 1913, KPA.

14. H. C. Phillips to Samuel M. Brosius, October 27, 1913, AKSP. See also Phillips to Brosius, November 1, 1913, AKSP.

15. Brosius to Phillips, October 29, 1913, AKSP.

16. Phillips to Cato Sells, November 1, 1913, AKSP.

17. Sells to Phillips, December 16, 1913, AKSP; Sells to Vaux, December 9, 1913, AKSP. Phillips replied, "The course pursued by your office and the cooperation of" War and Interior "ought to be appreciated by every friend of these Indians. I sincerely hope the funds available will prove adequate to carry out your plan" (Phillips to Sells, December 20, 1913, AKSP).

18. Leonard Wood to SI, October 31, 1913, AGDF.

19. Goode to Greble, October 25, 1913, AGDF.

20. Sells to Ellis, November 12, 1913, AGDF.

21. Sells to Ellis, December 12, 1913, SF 5782.

22. A. A. Jones to SW, January 22, 1912, AGDF.

23. Goode to Hugh L. Scott, January 23, 1914, IA, January through December 1914, Box 47, HLSP.

24. Goode to War Department, March 7, 1914, SF 5782; Stecker to CIA, March 7, 1914, BIAK; Edgar B. Meritt to Vaux, March 12, 1914, FSAF; Meritt to Greble, March 9, 1914, BIAK.

25. ARCIA, 1914, 56.

26. Goode to AGO, February 26, 1914, BIAK.

27. Goode to AGO, June 13, 1914, AGDF; ARCIA, 1914, 57.

28. Goode to Hugh L. Scott, June 2, 1914, IA, January through December 1914, Box 47, HLSP.

29. Goode to AGO, June 26, 1914, AGDF.

Epilogue

1. RLI, November 12, 1976.

2. MICI, November 12, 1976.

3. ARBIC, 1918, 381.

4. BHI, November 12, 1976.

5. MICI, November 12, 1976; William A. Light to CIA, August 6, 1918, Correspondence, Accounts and Other Records (hereafter cited as CAR), Box 26, RMIA; Stecker to CIA, April 30, 1919, CAR, Box 28, RMIA. Interestingly enough, as early as 1900, Special Indian Agent Walter Luttrell reported that "the amount of flat land was limited, and the supply of water was inadequate to sustain intensive agriculture to the extent that the Indians could become self-sufficient." Luttrell also observed that Mescalero was "ideally suited for grazing and timber production." (Martha L. Henderson, "Settlement Patterns on the Mescalero Apache Indian Reservation Since 1883," *Geographical Review* 80 [July 1990]: 229.)

6. MICI, November 12, 1976.

7. Clarence R. Jefferis to CIA, August 28, 1914, LCIA, February 1914–September 1914, Box 35, RMIA. Furthermore, Jefferis said that "it is a certainty that the Fort Sills will derive a comparatively small revenue from their crops."

8. Asa Daklugie, Duncan Bolatshu, and Eugene Chihuahua (hereafter cited as DBC) to Sells, August 1, 1918, IA, March 1918 through April 1919, Box 48, HLSP.

9. DBC to Light, August 1, 1918, CAR, Box 26, RMIA.

10. DBC to Sells, August 1, 1918.

11. Light to CIA, August 24, 1918, CAR, Box 27, RMIA.

12. DBC to CIA, April 15, 1918, CAR, Box 27, RMIA.

13. DBC to Sells, August 1, 1918.

14. DBC to Hugh L. Scott, April 20, 1918, IA, March 1918 through April 1919, Box 48, HLSP.

15. Ernest Stecker to Hugh L. Scott, July 8, 1919, IA, May through December 1919, Box 49, HLSP; Ball, *Indeh*, 311. Raymond Loco said some of them wanted to come back almost immediately after their arrival (RLI, November 12, 1976). Blossom Haozous heard that "a lot of them regretted going there" because conditions at Mescalero were different from what the Chiricahuas had been led to expect (BHI, November 12, 1976). Also, Daklugie said they "had no alternative except that of staying in Oklahoma and becoming farmers. No Apache really wanted to farm; but those who did" were "better off than the ones who came to this reservation. Why? Because," Daklugie said, "those at Fort Sill became dependent on themselves by the farming experience, and they seem to have been strengthened. While it" was "true that we were in captivity in Oklahoma, it was an entirely different type of supervision." Indeed, Daklugie insisted, the "Apaches will tell you that they did better under military control than under civilian administration. The officers at Fort Sill had wisely left both the management and decisions largely up to the chiefs or headmen, each of whom had a village. Their primary functions were to maintain order and standards." But it was "different . . . at Mescalero, even though it is perhaps the richest in natural resources in the United States." (Ball, *Indeh*, 311–312.)

16. ARBIC, 1920, 142.

17. RLI, November 12, 1976.

18. Ibid.

19. MICI, November 12, 1976.

20. Ibid.; RLI, November 12, 1976; BHI, November 12, 1976.

21. RLI, November 12, 1976.

22. Jason Betzinez, James Kaywaykla, and Talbot Gooday to Those Who Believe in a Square Deal for the Indians, December 31, 1920, HLSC.

23. MICI, November 12, 1976; Stockel, *Women of the Apache Nation*, 125.

24. RLI, November 12, 1976.

25. Ibid.

26. BHI, November 12, 1976.

27. RLI, November 12, 1976.

28. Francis Jennings, *The Invasion of America: Indians, Colonialism, and the Cant of Conquest* (Chapel Hill: University of North Carolina Press, 1975), 202–228, 257–260; Bert Salwen, "Indians of Southern New England and Long Island: Early Period," in William C. Sturtevant, gen. ed., *Handbook of North American Indians*, Vol. 15, *Northeast*, ed. Bruce G. Trigger (Washington, D.C.: Smithsonian Institution Press, 1978), 172–173; Laura E. Conkey, Ethel Boissevain, and Ives Goddard, "Indians of Southern New England and Long Island: Late Period," in William C. Sturtevant, gen. ed., *Handbook of North American Indians* (Washington, D.C.: Smithsonian Institution Press, 1978), Vol. 15, *Northeast*, ed. Bruce G. Trigger, 182–183; Arrell Morgan Gibson, *The American Indian: Prehistory to the Present* (Lexington, Massachusetts: D. C. Heath, 1980), 188–189, 197.

29. Muriel H. Wright, *A Guide to the Indian Tribes of Oklahoma* (Norman: University of Oklahoma Press, 1951), 184–185; Keith A. Murray, *The Modocs and Their War* (Norman: University of Oklahoma Press, 1959), 241–317.

30. Roy W. Meyer, *History of the Santee Sioux: United States Indian Policy on Trial* (Lincoln: University of Nebraska Press, 1967), 109–174.

31. James C. Olson, *Red Cloud and the Sioux Problem* (Lincoln: University of Nebraska Press, 1965), 247–263.

32. Wright, 80–82, 126, 173–174. For additional discussions, see thorough accounts in Donald J. Berthong, *The Southern Cheyennes* (Norman: University of Oklahoma Press, 1963); George Bird Grinnell, *The Fighting Cheyennes* (Norman: University of Oklahoma Press, 1955); Mildred P. Mayhall, *The Kiowas* (Norman: University of Oklahoma Press, 1962); Virginia Cole Trenholm, *The Arapahoes: Our People* (Norman: University of Oklahoma Press, 1970); and Ernest Wallace and E. Adamson Hoebel, *The Comanches: Lords of the South Plains* (Norman: University of Oklahoma Press, 1952).

33. Wright, 80–82, 173–174; Mayhall, 253–254; Grinnell, 326; Berthong, 403.

34. Wright, 80–82; Grinnell, 398–427.

35. Francis Haines, *The Nez Percés: Tribesmen of the Columbia Plateau* (Norman: University of Oklahoma Press, 1955), 330–337.

36. Opler, "Chiricahua Apache," 409–410.

37. Stockel, *Women of the Apache Nation*, 139. Stockel notes that some traditional sacred ceremonies have been revived but that the "younger generations lead busy lives and, with rare exceptions, pay little attention to their historical heritage." Simply, the "American mainstream has beckoned, and its benefits are so seductive" that Chiricahuas residing in both Oklahoma and New Mexico find difficulty in resisting its inducements. (Stockel, *Survival of the Spirit*, 272.)

38. Stockel, *Survival of the Spirit*, 272.

39. Opler, "Chiricahua Apache," 410. Mildred Cleghorn, though, does not share this pessimistic outlook. According to Stockel, she is convinced that a Chiricahua cultural revival is possible. Even so, one of her principal concerns in this

regard is the diminishing use of the Chiricahua language, which illustrates the extent to which assimilation has adversely affected Chiricahua culture. Cleghorn said that "she spoke only Apache when she was little because her mother and father spoke it at home. And because the words aren't heard in her part of the country anymore, 'I know in my mind what I want to say. But when I say it, it doesn't come out that way.'" Cleghorn explained that she had "forgotten the use of the tongue and how to catch the word in my throat. Even on tape, when I hear it, one almost has to know, or remember, a little bit about the word to get the distinction." (Stockel, *Women of the Apache Nation,* 139, 142.)

40. Docket Numbers 30-A and 48-A, June 28, 1968, 19, *Indian Claims Commission,* 222–325. For further discussion, see Morris Edward Opler, *An Apache Life-Way* (Chicago: University of Chicago Press, 1941).

Bibliography

▼   ▼   ▼

PRIMARY SOURCES

Archival Materials

National Archives and National Archives Branches

Records Relating to the Board of Indian Commissioners

Fort Sill Apache File. Records of the Board of Indian Commissioners. Records of the Bureau of Indian Affairs, Record Group 75, Natural Resources Branch, Civil Archives Division, National Archives and Records Administration, Washington, D.C.

Records Relating to the Bureau of Indian Affairs

File Number 53119-09-123 Kiowa. Central Files, 1907–1939. Records of the Bureau of Indian Affairs, Record Group 75, Natural Resources Branch, Civil Archives Division, National Archives and Records Administration, Washington, D.C.

File Number 41294-1913-225 Mescalero. Central Files, 1907–1939. Records of the Bureau of Indian Affairs, Record Group 75, Natural Resources Branch, Civil Archives Division, National Archives and Records Administration, Washington, D.C.

Records of the Mescalero Indian Agency. Records of the Bureau of Indian Affairs, Record Group 75, National Archives and Records Administration, Denver National Archives Branch, Denver, Colorado.

Report Books, 1871. Records of the Bureau of Indian Affairs, Record Group 75, Natural Resources Branch, Civil Archives Division, National Archives and Records Administration, Washington, D.C.

Records Relating to the Bureau of Land Management

Original Executive Order File. Records of the Bureau of Land Management, Record Group 49, Natural Resources Branch, Civil Archives Division, National Archives and Records Administration, Washington, D.C.

Records Relating to the House of Representatives

Records of the House Committee on Indian Affairs. Records of the House of Representatives, Record Group 233, Legislative, Judicial, Fiscal Branch, Civil Archives Division, National Archives and Records Administration, Washington, D.C.

Records Relating to the Secretary of the Interior

File Number 5-1, Kiowa-Prisoners-Apache. Central Files, 1907–1936. Records of the Office of the Secretary of the Interior, Record Group 48, Natural Resources Branch, Civil Archives Division, National Archives and Records Administration, Washington, D.C.

Records Relating to the U.S. Army

Adjutant General's Document File, 1890–1917, File Number 445841. Records of the Adjutant General's Office, Record Group 94, Old Military Branch, Military Archives Division, National Archives and Records Administration, Washington, D.C.

Document File 2614. Letters and Telegrams Received Relating to the Moving of the Apaches to Fort Sill, September 1894. Records of the Department of the Missouri. Records of the U.S. Army Continental Commands, 1821–1920, Record Group 393, Old Military Branch, Military Archives Division, National Archives and Records Administration, Washington, D.C.

File 1883 AGO 1066, National Archives Microfilm Publication M689, Rolls 197–202. Records of the Adjutant General's Office, Record Group 94, Old Military Branch, Military Archives Division, National Archives and Records Administration, Washington, D.C.

Fort Sill Post Returns. Returns From U.S. Military Posts, National Archives Microfilm Publication M617, Roll 1175. Records of the Adjutant General's Office, Record Group 94, Old Military Branch, Military Archives Division, National Archives and Records Administration, Washington, D.C.

Fort Sill Records: Letters and Endorsements Sent, 1900–1910. Records of the U.S. Army Continental Commands, 1821–1920, Record Group 393, Old Military Branch, Military Archives Division, National Archives and Records Administration, Washington, D.C.

Records Relating to the U.S. Senate

Records of the Senate Committee on Indian Affairs. Records of the U.S. Senate, Record Group 46, Legislative, Judicial, Fiscal Branch, Civil Archives Division, National Archives and Records Administration, Washington, D.C.

State Archival Repositories

Special File 5782, Kiowa-Apache Prisoners of War. Records of the Kiowa and Comanche Indian Agency, Indian Archives, Oklahoma Historical Society, Oklahoma City, Oklahoma.

Manuscript Collections

Albert Bacon Fall Collection. Manuscripts Division, Henry E. Huntington Library and Art Gallery, San Marino, California.

Fort Sill History File. Archives and Iconographic Collections Division, U.S. Army Field Artillery and Fort Sill Museum, Fort Sill, Oklahoma.

Daniel G. Fowle Papers. Division of Archives, North Carolina Department of Archives and History, Raleigh, North Carolina.

James D. Glennan Papers. Archives and Iconographic Collections Division, U.S. Army Field Artillery and Fort Sill Museum, Fort Sill, Oklahoma.

Indian-Pioneer History Collections. Indian Archives, Oklahoma Historical Society, Oklahoma City, Oklahoma.

Moore-Greble Correspondence. Morris Swett Technical Library, Snow Hall, U.S. Army Field Artillery School, Fort Sill, Oklahoma.

Oklahoma Missions Correspondence File, 1904–1906. Papers of the Board of Domestic Missions [Reformed Church in America]. Gardner Sage Library, New Brunswick Theological Seminary, New Brunswick, New Jersey.

Grace Paulding Memoirs. Archives, U.S. Army Military History Institute, Carlisle Barracks, Pennsylvania.

William Paulding Memoirs. Archives, U.S. Army Military History Institute, Carlisle Barracks, Pennsylvania.

Richard Henry Pratt Papers. Manuscripts Division, Beinecke Library, Yale University, New Haven, Connecticut.

Hugh Lenox Scott Collection. Archives and Iconographic Collections Division, U.S. Army Field Artillery and Fort Sill Museum, Fort Sill, Oklahoma.

Hugh Lenox Scott Papers. Manuscripts Division, Library of Congress, Washington, D.C.

Albert K. Smiley Papers. Manuscripts Division, Haverford College Library, Haverford College, Haverford, Pennsylvania.

Marian Stephens Memoirs. Archives and Manuscripts Division, Sterling Memorial Library, Yale University, New Haven, Connecticut.

Leonard Wood Diary. Leonard Wood Papers. Manuscripts Division, Library of Congress, Washington, D.C.

Interviews

Chaat, Reverend Doctor Robert Paul. Interview conducted by John Anthony Turcheneske, Jr., November 10, 1976, Medicine Park, Oklahoma.

Cleghorn, Mildred Imach. Interview conducted by John Anthony Turcheneske, Jr., November 11 and 12, 1976, Apache, Oklahoma.

Haozous, Blossom. Interview conducted by Pat O'Brien, July 22, 1976, Apache, Oklahoma. Bicentennial Oral History Program Collections. Archives and Iconographic Collections Division, U.S. Army Field Artillery and Fort Sill Museum, Fort Sill, Oklahoma.

Haozous, Blossom. Interview conducted by John Anthony Turcheneske, Jr., November 11 and 12, 1976, Apache, Oklahoma.

Loco, Raymond. Interview conducted by John Anthony Turcheneske, Jr., November 11 and 12, 1976, Apache, Oklahoma.

Government Documents

Annual Reports

U.S. Department of the Interior. Board of Indian Commissioners. *Annual Reports of the Board of Indian Commissioners,* 1894–1920.

U.S. Department of the Interior. Office of Indian Affairs. *Annual Reports of the Commissioner of Indian Affairs,* 1910–1914.

U.S. Department of War. Office of the Secretary of War. *Annual Reports of the Secretary of War,* 1894–1900.

General Congressional Documents

Congressional Record, 1910–1915.

U.S. Congress. House. *A Bill Authorizing the Secretary of War to Grant Freedom to Certain of the Apache Prisoners of War Now Being Held at Fort Sill, Oklahoma, and Giving Them Equal Status With Other Restricted Indians.* 62d Cong., 2d sess., 1912. H.R. 16651.

U.S. Congress. House. *A Bill Providing for the Allotment of Land to the Apache Indians Now Under the Charge of the War Department at Fort Sill, Oklahoma, as Prisoners of War.* 61st Cong., 2d sess., 1910. H.R. 25297.

U.S. Congress. Senate. *A Bill Providing for the Allotment of Land to the Apache and Other Indians Under the Charge of the War Department, Fort Sill Military Reservation, Oklahoma.* 61st Cong., 2d sess., 1910. S. 6152.

U.S. Congress. Senate. *Amendment to Be Proposed by Mr. Catron to the Bill (H.R. 26874) Making Appropriations for the Current and Contingent Expenses of the Bureau of Indian Affairs.* 62d Cong., 3d sess., 1913. H.R. 26874.

House Documents

U.S. Congress. House. *Relief of Apache Indians Confined at Fort Sill Military Reservation, Oklahoma.* 62d Cong., 3d sess., 1913. H. Doc. 1249.

U.S. Congress. House. *Relief of Apache Indians Held as Prisoners of War at Fort Sill, Oklahoma.* 62d Cong., 2d sess., 1912. H. Rept. 724.

Senate Documents

U.S. Congress. Senate. *Allotment of Land to Apache Indians.* 61st Cong., 2d sess., 1910. S. Rept. 379.

U.S. Congress. Senate. *Apache Prisoners of War.* 61st Cong., 2d sess., 1910. S. Doc. 366.

U.S. Congress. Senate. *Indian Conference Report.* 62d Cong., 2d sess., 1912. S. Doc. 919.

U.S. Congress. Senate. *Indian Conference Report.* 62d Cong., 2d sess., 1912. S. Doc 938.

U.S. Congress. Senate. *Letter From the Secretary of War, Transmitting, in Response to the Resolution of February 11, 1887, Correspondence With General Miles Relative to the Surrender of Geronimo.* 49th Cong., 2d sess., 1887. S. Ex. Doc. 117.

Treaties, Federal Statutes, and Compensation Decisions

Kappler, Charles J., ed. *Indian Affairs: Laws and Treaties.* Vol. 1, *Laws,* and Vol. 2, *Treaties.* Washington, D.C.: Government Printing Office, 1904.

U.S. Indian Claims Commission. Vol. 19. Docket Numbers 30-A and 48-A. June 28, 1968.

Church and Philanthropic Organization Reports and Proceedings

Eighty-First Annual Report of the Board of Domestic Missions to the General Synod of the Reformed Church in America. New York: Reformed Church in America, 1913.

Report of the Thirtieth Annual Lake Mohonk Conference of Friends of the Indian and Other Dependent Peoples, October 23, 24, and 25, 1912. Lake Mohonk, New York: Lake Mohonk Conference of Friends of the Indian and Other Dependent Peoples, 1912.

Contemporary Newspapers and Magazines

Arizona Daily Star (Tucson, Arizona), 1909.

Bisbee Daily Review (Bisbee, Arizona), 1909.

Colony Courier (Colony, Oklahoma), 1910–1912.

Daily News Republican (Lawton, Oklahoma), 1908–1912.

Lawton Constitution (Lawton, Oklahoma), 1913.

Lawton Constitution Democrat (Lawton, Oklahoma), 1909–1912.

The Mission Field (New York City, New York), 1899–1922.

Otero County Advertiser (Alamogordo, New Mexico), 1909–1913.

Tombstone Epitaph (Tombstone, Arizona), 1909.

Tucson Citizen (Tucson, Arizona), 1909.

Washington Post (Washington, D.C.), 1902.

Weekly Cloudcrofter (Cloudcroft, New Mexico), 1913.

Contemporary Books

Ball, Eve. *In the Days of Victorio: Recollections of a Warm Springs Apache.* Tucson: University of Arizona Press, 1970.

———. *Indeh: An Apache Odyssey.* Norman: University of Oklahoma Press, 1988.

Barrett, Samuel M., ed. *Geronimo's Story of His Life.* New York: Duffield, 1906.

Betzinez, Jason. *I Fought With Geronimo.* New York: Bonanza Books, 1959.

Bourke, John Gregory. *An Apache Campaign in the Sierra Madre.* New York: Charles Scribner's Sons, 1958.

———. *On the Border With Crook.* New York: Charles Scribner's Sons, 1891.

Crook, George. *Resumé of Operations Against the Apache Indians.* Omaha, Nebraska: n.p., 1886.

Davis, Britton. *The Truth About Geronimo.* New Haven, Connecticut: Yale University Press, 1929.

Lane, Jack C., ed. *Chasing Geronimo: The Journal of Leonard Wood, May–September 1886.* Albuquerque: University of New Mexico Press, 1970.

Lummis, Charles F. *General George Crook and the Apache Wars.* Flagstaff, Arizona: Northland Press, 1966.

Miles, Nelson A. *Personal Recollections and Observations of General Nelson A. Miles.* Chicago: Warner, 1896.

———. *Serving the Republic: Memoirs of the Civil and Military Life of Nelson A. Miles.* Freeport, New York: Books for Libraries Press, 1971.

Page, Elizabeth M. *In Camp and Tepee: An Indian Mission Story.* New York: Fleming H. Revell, 1915.

Schmitt, Martin F., ed. *General George Crook: His Autobiography.* Norman: University of Oklahoma Press, 1960.

Skinner, Woodward S. *The Apache Rock Crumbles: The Captivity of Geronimo's People.* Pennsacola, Florida: Skinner Publications, 1987.

Sonnichsen, C. L., ed. *Geronimo and the End of the Apache Wars.* Lincoln: University of Nebraska Press, 1990.

Welsh, Herbert. *The Apache Prisoners in Fort Marion, St. Augustine, Florida.* Philadelphia: Indian Rights Association, 1887.

Contemporary Articles

Kennon, Lyman Walter Vere. "The Case of the Chiricahuas." *North American Review* (August 1890): 251–253.

Shepard, Sophie. "The Apaches at Mount Vernon." *Lend a Hand* (January 1890): 37–42.

———. "The Apaches at Mount Vernon." *Lend a Hand* (May 1890): 333–337.

———. "The Apache Captives." *Lend a Hand* (March 1890): 163–166.

Women's National Indian Association. "The Disposition of the Apaches." *Indian's Friend* (October 1890): 1.

SECONDARY SOURCES

Books

Berthong, Donald J. *The Cheyenne and Arapaho Ordeal: Reservation and Agency Life in the Indian Territory, 1875–1907.* Norman: University of Oklahoma Press, 1976.

———. *The Southern Cheyennes.* Norman: University of Oklahoma Press, 1963.

Cleghorn, Mildred Imach. "A Statement." Foreword to *The Apache Rock Crumbles: The Captivity of Geronimo's People,* by Woodward S. Skinner. Pensacola, Florida: Skinner Publications, 1987.

Conkey, Laura E., Ethel Boissevain, and Ives Goddard. "Indians of Southern New England and Long Island: Late Period." In *Handbook of North American Indians,* gen. ed. William C. Sturtevant. Vol. 15, *Northeast,* ed. Bruce G. Trigger, 177–189. Washington, D.C.: Smithsonian Institution Press, 1978.

Debo, Angie. *Geronimo: The Man, His Time, His Place.* Norman: University of Oklahoma Press, 1976.

Faulk, Odie B. *The Geronimo Campaign.* New York: Oxford University Press, 1969.

Gibson, Arrell Morgan. *The American Indian: Prehistory to the Present.* Lexington, Massachusetts: D. C. Heath, 1980.

Grinnell, George Bird. *The Fighting Cheyennes.* Norman: University of Oklahoma Press, 1955.

Hagan, William T. *United States–Comanche Relations: The Reservation Years.* New Haven, Connecticut: Yale University Press, 1976.

Hagedorn, Hermann. *Leonard Wood: A Biography.* New York: Kraus Reprint, 1969.

Haines, Francis. *The Nez Percés: Tribesmen of the Columbia Plateau.* Norman: University of Oklahoma Press, 1955.

Jennings, Francis. *The Invasion of America: Indians, Colonialism, and the Cant of Conquest.* Chapel Hill: University of North Carolina Press, 1975.

Johnson, Virginia Weisel. *The Unregimented General: A Biography of Nelson A. Miles.* Boston: Houghton, 1962.

Lockwood, Frank C. *The Apache Indians.* New York: Macmillan, 1938.

Mayhall, Mildred P. *The Kiowas.* Norman: University of Oklahoma Press, 1962.

Meyer, Roy W. *History of the Santee Sioux: United States Indian Policy on Trial.* Lincoln: University of Nebraska Press, 1967.

Murray, Keith A. *The Modocs and Their War.* Norman: University of Oklahoma Press, 1959.

Nye, Wilbur S. *Carbine and Lance: The Story of Old Fort Sill.* Norman: University of Oklahoma Press, 1969.

Ogle, Ralph H. *Federal Control of the Western Apaches, 1848–1886.* Albuquerque: University of New Mexico Press, 1970.

Olson, James C. *Red Cloud and the Sioux Problem.* Lincoln: University of Nebraska Press, 1965.

Opler, Morris Edward. *An Apache Life-Way.* Chicago: University of Chicago Press, 1941.

———. "Chiricahua Apache." In *Handbook of North American Indians,* gen. ed. William C. Sturtevant. Vol. 10, *Southwest,* ed. Alfonso Ortiz, 401–418. Washington, D.C.: Smithsonian Institution Press, 1983.

Porter, Joseph C. *Paper Medicine Man: John Gregory Bourke and His American West.* Norman: University of Oklahoma Press, 1986.

Prucha, Francis Paul, S.J. *The Great Father: The United States Government and the American Indians.* Lincoln: University of Nebraska Press, 1984.

Salwen, Bert. "Indians of Southern New England and Long Island: Early Period." In *Handbook of North American Indians,* gen. ed. William C. Sturtevant. Vol. 15, *Northeast,* ed. Bruce G. Trigger, 160–176. Washington, D.C.: Smithsonian Institution Press, 1978.

Stockel, H. Henrietta. *Survival of the Spirit: Chiricahua Apaches in Captivity.* Reno: University of Nevada Press, 1993.

———. *Women of the Apache Nation: Voices of Truth.* Reno: University of Nevada Press, 1991.

Swanton, John R. *Indian Tribes of North America.* Washington, D.C.: Smithsonian Institution Press, 1974.

Thrapp, Dan L. *The Conquest of Apacheria.* Norman: University of Oklahoma Press, 1967.

———. *General George Crook and the Sierra Madre Adventure.* Norman: University of Oklahoma Press, 1972.

———. *Victorio and the Mimbres Apaches.* Norman: University of Oklahoma Press, 1974.

Trenholm, Virginia Cole. *The Arapahoes: Our People.* Norman: University of Oklahoma Press, 1970.

Utley, Robert M. *Frontier Regulars: The United States Army and the Indian, 1866–1891.* New York: Macmillan, 1973.

Wallace, Ernest, and E. Adamson Hoebel. *The Comanches: Lords of the South Plains.* Norman: University of Oklahoma Press, 1952.

Wooster, Robert. *Nelson A. Miles and the Twilight of the Frontier Army.* Lincoln: University of Nebraska Press, 1993.

Worcester, Donald E. *The Apaches: Eagles of the Southwest.* Norman: University of Oklahoma Press, 1979.

Wright, Muriel H. *A Guide to the Indian Tribes of Oklahoma.* Norman: University of Oklahoma Press, 1951.

Articles

Calloway, Collin G. "The Vermont Secretary and the Apache POWs: Redfield Proctor and the Case of the Chiricahuas." *Vermont History* 59 (Summer 1991): 166–179.

Harper, Richard Henry. "The Missionary Work of the Reformed (Dutch) Church in America." *Chronicles of Oklahoma* 18 (September 1940): 252–265; (December 1940): 328–347; 19 (June 1941): 170–179.

Henderson, Martha L. "Settlement Patterns on the Mescalero Apache Reservation Since 1883." *Geographical Review* 80 (July 1990): 226–238.

Turcheneske, John Anthony, Jr. "The Arizona Press and Geronimo's Surrender." *Journal of Arizona History* 14 (Summer 1973): 133–148.

———. "Arizonans and the Apache Prisoners of War at Mount Vernon Barracks, Alabama: 'They Do Not Die Fast Enough!'" *Military History of Texas and the Southwest* 11 (1973): 197–226.

———. "Disaster at White Tail: The Fort Sill Apaches' First Ten Years at Mescalero, 1913–1923." *New Mexico Historical Review* 13 (April 1978): 109–132.

Dissertations

Goodman, David Michael. "Apaches as Prisoners of War, 1886–1894." Ph.D. diss., Texas Christian University, 1969.

Harper, James William. "Hugh Lenox Scott: Soldier Diplomat, 1876–1917." Ph.D. diss., University of Virginia, 1968.

Tate, Michael Lynn. "Apache Scouts, Police, and Judges as Agents of Acculturation, 1865–1920." Ph.D. diss., University of Toledo, 1974.

Additional Sources

▼   ▼   ▼

PRIMARY SOURCES

Government Documents

House Documents

U.S. Congress. House. *Relief of Apache Indians Held as Prisoners of War at Fort Sill, Oklahoma.* 62d Cong., 2d sess., 1912. H. Rept. 917.

Senate Documents

U.S. Congress. Senate. *Appropriation for Bureau of Indian Affairs.* 62d Cong., 3d sess., 1913. S. Doc. 1128.

U.S. Congress. Senate. *Estimate of Appropriation for Inclusion in the Indian Appropriation Bill.* 62d Cong., 2d sess., 1912. S. Doc. 695.

Treaties, Federal Statutes, and Compensation Decisions

U.S. *Statutes at Large.* Vol. 15. "Treaty With the Kiowas and Comanches." October 21, 1867.

Contemporary Articles

"Apache Prisoners in Fort Marion." *Lend a Hand* (June 1887): 324–327.

"The Apache Prisoners of War." *The Outlook* (May 25, 1912): 142.

Bourke, John Gregory. "General Crook in the Indian Country." *Century Magazine* (March 1891): 643–660.

Clum, John P. "Apache Misrule: A Bungling Agent Sets the Military Arm in Motion." *New Mexico Historical Review* 5 (April 1930): 138–153, and (July 1930): 221–239.

———. "The Apaches." *New Mexico Historical Review* 9 (April 1929): 107–127.

——. "Geronimo." *New Mexico Historical Review* 3 (January 1928): 1–40; (April 1928): 121–144; and (July 1928): 217–264.

——. "Victorio, Chief of the Warm Springs Apaches." *Arizona Historical Review* 2 (January 1930): 74–90.

Crook, George. "The Apache Problem." *Journal of the Military Service Institute* 7 (October 1886): 257–269.

Davis, O. K. "Our Prisoners of War." *The North American Review* (March 1912): 356–367.

Jozhe, Benedict. "A Brief History of the Fort Sill Apache Tribe." *Chronicles of Oklahoma* 39 (Winter 1961–1962): 427–432.

Miles, Nelson A. "On the Trail of Geronimo." *Cosmopolitan Magazine* (July 1911): 249–262.

"Prisoners of War for Thirty Years." *The Outlook* (November 1911): 555.

Roe, Walter C. "Another Apache Atrocity." *The Southern Workman* (April 1912): 209–218.

SECONDARY SOURCES

Books

Basso, Keith H., ed. *Western Apache Raiding and Warfare: From the Notes of Grenville Goodwin*. Tucson: University of Arizona Press, 1971.

Clum, Woodworth. *Apache Agent: The Story of John P. Clum*. Boston: Houghton Mifflin, 1936.

Ellis, Richard N. *General John Pope and U.S. Indian Policy*. Albuquerque: University of New Mexico Press, 1970.

Thrapp, Dan L. *Juh: An Incredible Indian*. El Paso: Texas Western Press, 1973.

Wellman, Paul I. *Death in the Desert: The Fifty Years' War for the Great Southwest*. New York: Macmillan, 1935.

Articles

Ball, Eve. "The Apache Scouts: A Chiricahua Appraisal." *Arizona and the West* 7 (Winter 1965): 315–328.

East, Omega G. "Apache Indians in Fort Marion, 1886–1887." *El Escribano* 6 (January 1969): 11–27; (April 1969): 3–23; (July 1969): 4–23; and (October 1969): 20–38.

East, Omega G., and Albert C. Manucy. "Arizona Apaches as 'Guests' in Florida." *Florida Historical Quarterly* 30 (January 1952): 294–300.

Ellis, Richard N. "Copper-Skinned Soldiers: The Apache Scouts." *Great Plains Journal* 5 (Spring 1966): 51–67.

Harte, John Bret. "Conflict at San Carlos: The Military-Civilian Struggle for Control, 1882–1885." *Arizona and the West* 15 (Spring 1973): 22–44.

King, James T. "George Crook: Indian Fighter and Humanitarian." *Arizona and the West* 9 (Winter 1967): 333–386.

Opler, Morris Edward. "A Chiricahua Apache's Account of the Geronimo Campaign of 1886." *New Mexico Historical Review* 13 (October 1938): 360–386.

Turcheneske, John Anthony, Jr. "Captain John Gregory Bourke: Soldier and Ethnologist on the Apache Frontier, 1882–1886." *The Cochise Quarterly* 5 (Spring 1975): 3–17.

———. "'It Is Right That They Should Set Us Free': The Role of the War and Interior Departments in the Release of the Apache Prisoners of War, 1909–1913." *Red River Valley Historical Review* 4 (Summer 1979): 4–32.

———. "The United States Congress and the Release of the Apache Prisoners of War at Fort Sill." *Chronicles of Oklahoma* 54 (Summer 1976): 199–226.

Worcester, Donald E. "The Apaches in the History of the Southwest." *New Mexico Historical Review* 50 (January 1975): 25–44.

Dissertations

Mason, Joyce Evelyn. "The Use of Indian Scouts in the Apache Wars, 1870–1886." Ph.D. diss., Indiana University, 1970.

Index

▼   ▼   ▼

▲ *239* ▲

Gooday, Talbot, 122, *123*, 124, 125
Goode, George W., 122, 125, 154, 164, 168–169
Gore, Thomas P., 140–141
Grazing land, 60. *See also* Cattle
Greble, Edwin St. John. *See* St. John Greble, John
Grinnell, George Bird, 85

Haozous, Blossom Wrattan, 49, *51*
Harrison, Benjamin, 21, 25, 26
Harvesting, *57*, 58, 93, 157. *See also* Agriculture
Hay bailing, *57*, 58, *93*
Holbrook, Ariz., 2
Hospers, Hendrina, 101, *102*, 156–158
Housing, 20, 29; Fort Sill, 44–47, *46*, 49, 58
Howard, Guy, 25, 27–28, 31–32
Howard, Oliver Otis, 12–13, 40
Hughes, Robert Patterson, 21
Hyer, Benjamin B., 72

Illness, 15; cattle, 48, 68
Indian appropriation bills: 1913, 143–145, 153, 155, 161; 1914, 149–150, 152; 1915, 153, 154, 170
Indian Rights Association, 16, 117, 171; Mount Vernon Barracks, 21–22; North Carolina site, 23, 27–30
Interior Department, 4–5, 82–85, 103, 107–112

Jackson, Richard A., 21
Jefferis, Clarence R., 164, 169
Jerome Agreement, 54, 56, 60–61, 78, 86, 117, 185, 202(n 7)
Jones, William A., 78, 86–87, 89
Joseph, Chief, 182
Jozhe, Benedict, 122, 156

Kaffir corn. *See* Corn
Kayatennae, village, *59*
Kayihtah, 12
Kaywaykla, James, 111–112, *112*, 122, 158
Kellogg, Edgar R., 70
Kellogg, William, 25
Kelton, John C., 23

Kennon, Lyman Walter Vere, 4, 25–26
Kingsbury, Henry P., 92
Kiowa and Comanche Reservation, 54–55, 73–74; settlement, 76. *See also* Jerome Agreement

Lake Mohonk Conference of Friends of the Indian, 19, 29–30, 171, 218–219(n 12)
Lamar, Lucius Quintus Cincinnatus, 8–9
Lamont, Daniel, 30, 54–55
Land allotment, 61, *65*, 73–79, 160–161, 167–176, *174–175;* Ferris' bill, 133–134; Owen's bill, 132–133
Land prices, 147–148
Langdon, Loomis, 11
Lee, Jesse M., 92, 93–95
Leupp, Francis E., 67, 102, 108
Lincoln, Abraham, 181
Little Crow, 181
Loco, Raymond, 21, 70, 162–164, 177, 179–181
Luttrell, Walter, 221(n 5)

Magoosh, 109–110
Mann, James R., 141–142, 144–145
Martine, 12
Massachusetts Indian Association, 16, 21, 29
Maus, Marion, 6–7
McLaughlin, James, 108–110
Medicine Lodge Treaty, 54, 56, 202 (n 7)
Meritt, Edgar B., 138
Merriam, Henry C., 76
Merritt, Wesley, 61–62
Mescalero Agency, 108–111, 124, 135; resettlement, 155–166, *163–164*, 178–180, 213–214(nn 21, 22), 222(n15); War Department directive, 146
Mescalero Apaches, 213–214(n22)
Miles, Nelson Appleton, 2, 5–14, 33, 83; Senate Resolution 42, 27
Military: participation by Chiricahuas, 29, 68–69; reservations, 34, 53–66. *See also* War Department